KENNY NOYE

by Wensley Clarkson

BLAKE

Published by Blake Publishing Ltd,
3 Bramber Court, 2 Bramber Road, London W14 9PB,
England

First published in paperback in Great Britain 2002

ISBN 1 85782 407 5

British Library Cataloguing-in-Publication Data:
A catalogue record for this book is available
from the British Library.

Typeset by t2

Printed in Great Britain by
Bookmarque Ltd, Croydon, Surrey

3 5 7 9 10 8 6 4 2

Papers used by Blake Publishing are natural, recyclable
productsmade from wood grown in sustainable forests. The
manufacturing processes conform to the environmental
reguoltions of the country of origin.

To Spain ...
the last frontier

Author's Note

Many of the characters described here would not have made it into this book if it had not been for my numerous sources who, naturally, would rather you did not know their identity.

So to all the 'faces' I've met over the past three years and the policemen who've given me a helping hand, I say, 'Thank you.'

Without their help, this book would not have been possible.

Some of the dialogue used in this book was constructed from available documents, some was drawn from courtroom testimony, and some was reconstituted from the memory of participants.

Glossary

Backhander	Bribe
Bird	Prison sentence
Blag	Robbery
Brief	Solicitor
Bungs	Bribes
Clink	Prison
Coke	Cocaine
Cozzers	Police
Cronies	Associates
DCI	Detective Chief Inspector
DCS	Detective Chief Superintendent
DEA	Drug Enforcement Agency
DI	Detective Inspector
DS	Detective Superintendent
E	Ecstasy
Faces	Top criminals
Fence	Criminal who sells stolen goods
Finger	Accuse
Fitted up	Framed
Frummers	Orthodox Jews
Grass up	Tell police about another criminal
Manor	Area where a criminal operates
Met	Metropolitan Police
NCIS	National Criminal Intelligence Service
Nicked	Arrested
Old lag	Long-term prisoner
Pavement artist	Robber

Puff	Cannabis
Scam	Deception
Screws	Prison officers
Shooter	Gun
Snitch	Informant
Stitch up	Set up
Stretch	Stay in prison
Team	Gang of robbers

'I hope you all die of cancer.'

**— Kenny Noye's response to the Old Bailey jury when he
was found guilty of his role in handling the Brink's-Mat
gold in 1986**

*'During my career, I made a point of mixing with criminals. It is
essential that you do so. You cannot expect them to give
information about crimes if you ostracise them except when you
want information from them.'*

**— Former Scotland Yard Flying Squad Commander
Ken Drury**

'No. We won't leave it, we will get that sorted out right now.'

**— Kenny Noye's response to a question by the
prosecutor at his Old Bailey trial for the murder of
Stephen Cameron in April 2000**

Prologue

The beige 3-litre Vectra headed off slowly behind the shining new dark blue Mitsubishi Shogun as it began twisting and turning down the hill from the big villa up on the cliff overlooking the tiny hamlet of Atlanterra. Two other vehicles — a Golf GTI and an Astra — joined the convoy from different positions as the Shogun hit the straight road out of Atlanterra through the village of Zahara de los Atunes and towards the town of Barbate seven miles north. The Shogun eventually drove straight through Barbate and headed on to a narrow road that ran through a forest towards the small, beachside community of Los Canos de Meca.

Minutes later the Shogun driver picked up an attractive brunette woman from her rented beachside house and the couple headed once again back towards Barbate at high speed. Behind them, their shadows had decided that because the road was so quiet and the area so sparsely populated, they would use only the 3-litre Vectra to follow their subject. The two other cars moved separately back to Barbate to await instructions.

Then disaster struck as the Shogun sped through the isolated forest road from Los Canos to Barbate.

'We lost him at the second curve,' one of the pursuers later explained. 'He just disappeared. There was a crossroads up ahead and he could have gone in any of three directions.' For the next half an hour no one caught even a glimpse of that dark blue Shogun. Perhaps their subject had been tipped off about the surveillance operation? He was certainly someone with a lot of friends in high places. Maybe he had slipped through their grasp once again.

As the minutes ticked towards eleven, it was decided that the three cars should float around Barbate in the hope of spotting that distinctive Shogun with Belgian plates parked up in the busy town. They just prayed he was eating dinner somewhere.

At just after 11pm, the driver of the Vectra spotted the Shogun parked near the town's best known fish restaurant. Minutes later all three of the pursuing cars met in an adjoining street. The occupants bought some litre bottles of beer from a nearby bar and three of them got back in the Astra and double parked it virtually in front of the restaurant. Then they began playing Prodigy's 'Firestarter' at full blast on the car stereo.

Three of the men then tumbled out of the car and manoeuvred themselves near enough to their subject's table to establish that he was definitely their man. He was just ordering a bottle of Rioja and a seafood salad. More officers then linked up from the other cars nearby and they began weaving in a group back up the pavement towards the restaurant.

Then four of the 'drunks' surrounded their subject's table. The man and his female companion tried to ignore them in the hope they would go away. The last thing they wanted was some aggravation with a bunch of drunken hooligans.

Just then one of the 'drunks' dropped his bottle of beer on the floor and leapt on the man. There was a smash of a glass on the table. The man got his subject in a painful headlock and fell to the ground with him. Two other men then piled in and locked on to each of the subject's arms which were yanked up behind his back while a fourth man handcuffed him.

Astonished customers looked on as the four burly men literally picked their subject up off the floor and carried him to the back of the Astra. The man's female companion got up and immediately walked off into the darkness.

As two of the men got in the front of the Astra, the man they had grabbed shouted, 'Why am I being detained? I wanna see a lawyer and I wanna see a doctor.'

Britain's most wanted man, Kenneth Noye, had finally been apprehended...

1: A Den of Thieves

Across the Thames from the City of London lies the borough that was for centuries effectively the second largest city in England — the Borough of the South Works of London Bridge, or Southwark. Borough High Street runs directly from London Bridge.

In 1197 two 'tycoons' swapped a pair of manors from their real estate portfolios. The Archbishop of Canterbury accepted Lambeth, on the Thames bank about a mile west of the Borough, in exchange for Dartford in Kent. He decided to use it as his town house instead of adding it to his investments, and Southwark innkeepers profited from the increase in travel between Canterbury and London.

Along the Bankside of the river between east Lambeth and Southwark, the Bishops of Rochester and Winchester bought properties, which their successors leased out. In Henry VIII's reign Rochester's cook, Richard Ross, poisoned the soup at a banquet and became the sole victim of Henry's new penalty for poisoners. He was boiled alive.

Meanwhile Winchester's properties became notorious as brothels. The carnival atmosphere of the Bankside was further enhanced by a bear-baiting ring, theatres and the first of the south bank pleasure gardens. All these attractions also encouraged the criminals of the day to head into the crowds to pickpocket and scavenge off the rich visitors. Then they headed back to their homes in the dreadful slum areas around Mint Street ('the Mint') and south of Union Street ('Alsatia').

Eastwards, numerous leatherworks centred on the district of Bermondsey. The drawback to tanning, however, was the obnoxious odour that drifted across the entire area. As a result, Bermondsey developed atrocious slums and by the 1840s Jacob's Island was the worst area of urban deprivation in London. It was from these south bank slums that the great 19th century cholera epidemics sprang.

With the arrival of the railways, Waterloo station dominated east Lambeth to such a degree that it dragged the residential neighbourhood down even further, and the riverside became a dismal region of filthy, rundown warehouses. Squalid Bermondsey became the epicentre of violence and ill-health among the poor and deprived, caused primarily by dreadful overcrowding.

The most appalling 19th century infanticide took place in the Old King's Head Tavern, in Greenbank, Tooley Street, just west of where London Bridge Station stands today.

In 1843, shy brush salesman Edward Dwyer, whose propensity for violence had already resulted in one heavy jail sentence, was putting in a hard day's drinking at the tavern.

By nine in the evening, his wife and mother-in-law came in and started abusing him for being drunk in front of his friends. They slapped him, and left him to look after his three-month-old baby. He left the child on the street outside until his drinking friends persuaded him to fetch it in.

Increasingly inebriated, Dwyer began making bizarre drunken remarks to his pals.

'Blood on a brick,' he said, 'would look very funny. Blood on the wall would look very queer. If a bullock's head was beat against the wall there would be plenty of blood on it.'

Then before anybody could stop him, Dwyer picked up the baby by its thigh and smashed its head on the bar counter over and over again.

Bermondsey never shook off the stench of real poverty until more than a hundred years later when the combined efforts of Hitler's bombing raids and the economic realities of life in post-war Britain effectively flattened much of the Thameside slums.

After the War, the descendants of those disease-ridden ghetto victims finally turned their backs on the cobbled streets and were encouraged to start afresh in the suburbs that were gradually sprouting up in the cleaner air and green fields beyond south east London.

And that is where our story begins...

* * *

Kenneth James Noye was born in Bexleyheath, Kent, on 24 May 1947. He was soon known as 'Kenny' to everyone in the Noye household.

Without smog, concrete jungles of housing developments or shocking extremes of wealth and poverty, Bexleyheath was supposed to represent the acceptable new face of south east London, with many of the area's appealing features but few of its bad habits.

Pipped by Bromley in the race to become *the* prestigious suburb, Bexleyheath was for a long time thought of as an insignificant location between central London and the Garden of England, Kent. However, by the time Kenny Noye was born just after the end of World War II, it had assumed a comfortable mantle all of its own.

Built on a clumsy curving hill, Bexleyheath was not exactly scenic, but compared with the mean streets of Bermondsey it was sheer luxury. It also possessed some traditional reminders of London life — a fine range of pubs, chippies and pie and eel shops, plus an evocative and nowadays well-tended history.

Basking in relatively clear air away from the smoke-ridden industrial docklands of Bermondsey and Rotherhithe, the image of Bexleyheath as healthy, lower middle class and conservative was very true to a large extent. However, many found it strange to swap those rundown rows of terraced houses in the docklands for the characterless square bungalows that were the essential ingredient of residential streets such as Jenton Avenue, Bexleyheath, where the Noyes resided.

However, for the first few years of his life, Kenny Noye probably could not have wished for a better place to grow up.

Noye's father Jim had become a fully trained communications engineer when he served his country with the navy during World War II. It had been a lot different from his pre-war days as a junior docker in Bermondsey.

After the war, Jim Noye turned his newly found skills to great use by becoming a telecommunications expert at the GPO. His wife Edith was a strong, blunt-speaking lady who took young Kenny under her wing from an early age. She worked three nights a week as manageress of the nearby Crayford Dog Track.

The Noyes were proud of the fact that they both worked. Supporting the family was paramount. There was never any question of scrounging off the State — that certainly wasn't the Noye way.

Kenny Noye was in many ways the apple of his mother's eye for his entire childhood. But he was also quite a handful. At just three years old, he broke his nose falling out of a tree in a neighbour's garden while pinching apples. It left him with a disfigured nose, which many would later comment gave the clear impression he'd once been a prize fighter.

In fact, little Kenny didn't even realise his nose had been broken in the fall until three weeks later when he was taken to hospital complaining of a 'pain in the nose'.

When Kenny was five years old he went into a shop with his mother, slipped behind the counter when no one was looking, opened the cash till and started helping himself to money.

A shop assistant went to the cash register to ring up a sale and noticed the till open. Little Kenny was caught only when his mother saw a ten bob note (50 pence) sticking out of the top of his wellington boots as they were about to leave the shop.

His cousin Michael remembers: 'Those wellington boots were crammed with dosh (money). It was typical Kenny. He couldn't keep his hands out of things.'

Michael and Kenny's parents spent a number of holidays

together at Kent coastal resorts such as Margate and Whitstable during those early years of Kenny Noye's life.

One time Kenny and Michael, then both aged six, were playing near a well in the grounds of a pub. Their fathers — who were brothers — warned the young boys not to play by the edge of the well.

'It was typical of Kenny. We were told not to go near the well, but he persuaded me to balance on the edge of it and we both fell in,' explained Michael.

The two boys miraculously avoided serious injury, but had to be rescued by firemen who lowered a ladder to the bottom of the well. They were both given a 'right slapping' by their respective fathers for disobeying them.

By all accounts Kenny Noye was a charming, troublesome child. These days he might even have been described as hyperactive.

'He got away with a lot of things because he was very cheeky,' adds Michael. 'But he couldn't keep out of trouble for a minute. A right handful.'

Kenny was in the habit of clambering all over neighbours' cars parked in the short driveways to the bungalows that lined Jenton Avenue, Bexleyheath.

Kenny's fascination with cars was fuelled by the fact that his dad could not afford one in those days. With war rationing and low wages they were still considered a very special luxury. That made cars an object of great curiosity — and envy.

Once Kenny was caught inside a neighbour's car pretending to drive it. He was impersonating the noises of the car, as he tried to change gear.

Kenny's obsession with cars would grow into a much more serious habit by the time he reached his teens.

Inside number eight Jenton Avenue, Kenny was regularly disciplined by his father, but this had little effect on curbing his energetic behaviour.

Young Kenny Noye was already boasting about what he would do when he grew up. 'Earn lots of money,' he insisted to anyone who would listen.

Kenny's parents were faintly amused by the young boy's pledges about the future.

One family friend never forgot the day he was at the Noye's home and Kenny's father turned around and said proudly: 'Kenny's going to make a success of his life. He's going to be very rich, I know it.'

Another of Kenny Noye's favourite pastimes in Jenton Avenue was knocking on people's doors and then running away before they answered.

'He loved getting away with it. His eyes would light up with the excitement,' recalled one family member.

There was a sweet shop at the end of Jenton Avenue, which Kenny and his friends loitered around most afternoons. Frequently they would steal empty bottles of Tizer by slipping through the side gate where all the empties were stored. Then Kenny and his friends would walk brazenly into the front of the shop and claim the penny back per bottle and buy sweets with it.

Kenny Noye's alertness to all around him, his perceptiveness, even at that young age, was noticed by many of his contemporaries. And, very occasionally, those powers of observation were put to good use.

When Kenny was eight years old he and his cousin Graham visited a local public swimming baths. Graham — six at the time — lost his footing and fell in, knocking himself on the edge of the crowded pool in the process.

Kenny responded immediately by diving straight in and pulling his young cousin to the edge of the pool.

No one realised what had happened except for Graham who many years later explained: 'Kenny saved my life that day and we used to joke about it afterwards because he was always saying I owed him a favour. But you know what? He never told another soul about what happened. He was a bit embarrassed by it all and he made me promise not to tell anyone either. It was as if he didn't think he really deserved any praise for saving my life.'

As Kenny Noye developed into a talkative, intelligent — and somewhat spoilt — child, so his parents became increasingly busy at their respective jobs trying to make ends meet and support their growing family. Every time Kenny got caught stealing apples from a neighbour's tree or causing mischief in Jenton Avenue his father read him the riot act but it made little impression.

By this time Kenny was attending the nearby Brampton Primary School. Also at the school was his next door neighbour in Jenton Avenue, Janet John. Even at that young age she recalled that Kenny left a lasting impression.

'He was very much Jack-the-lad and if anything you'd feel a bit wary of him, you know, of getting too close to him. You'd also feel you wouldn't want to get on the wrong side of him.'

By the time Kenny reached twelve, he was a striking-looking boy, five foot in height with a well-defined face, strong eyebrows and deep, dark narrow brown eyes.

When he enrolled at Bexley Secondary Modern School, he possessed a determined streak that made him appear much brighter than many of his classmates. He also had a biting wit and a photographic memory that surprised many of his friends and teachers.

'He never forgot anyone's name and he recognised people's faces before they even had a chance to introduce themselves,' said one childhood friend.

Some of the boys in his class were jealous of his good looks and Kenny was sometimes bullied in the school playground between classes. However, he rapidly learned to defend himself and the bigger, older boys soon left him alone. Like so many things in his life, Kenny would one day exploit those experiences to his own advantage.

Back at home, Kenny's mother Edith kept the family's modest three bedroom bungalow in Jenton Avenue spotlessly clean and was always clearing up after everyone.

'If a crumb was spilt on the lounge carpet she'd appear with a dust pan and brush within seconds. It did make it a little tense for visitors,' explained one family member.

Young Kenny always remembered to give his mother birthday cards and gifts and Mother's Day cards. Their closeness was noticeable to many of their relatives.

'She'd always slip him a few bob whenever she could afford it,' one relative later mentioned. 'He really was her favourite.'

Kenny also developed what was to become a virtually lifelong obsession with clothes. Even in his early teens, he somehow managed to afford to buy an average of one new shirt every month. And he constantly changed the style of his dark, thick hair. He had a paper round and occasionally handled stolen bicycle parts. He even boasted to one friend that he'd earn more money then some of the dads of his schoolmates by the time he was 15. Then he began supplementing his income with a sideline that was to make him one of the most feared pupils in school.

Those earlier encounters with bullies had encouraged him to launch his own protection racket. Money, as usual, was the primary motivation. The racket centred around taking dinner money off first-formers.

'He would wait outside Graham Road for the little kids and demand money from them with his gang. Then he would beat them up anyway. They were too afraid to sneak on him,' said one former classmate.

Noye wasn't exactly the stereotype of a bully, but he certainly had some of the characteristics — he didn't know how to show his real feelings and he was self-confident and spoilt by his mother.

Once a teacher overheard Kenny demanding protection money from a younger boy. He was called into headmaster Clifford Lester's office. The Head slammed his fists on the desk in front of Kenny and told him to turn his pockets out. He did as he was told. Out came a referee's whistle and half the contents of the school tuck shop.

'And the rest, boy,' ordered his headmaster.

Kenny then removed almost five pounds in loose change — ample evidence of his protection racket.

As a matter of rule the police were not called in, but Kenny was disciplined with a cane.

This time his mother and father were summoned by the

headmaster and told that if their son didn't change his habits he was heading for some serious trouble.

The atmosphere at Bexley Secondary Modern was very work-orientated, with Headmaster Lester doggedly trying to ensure his all-boys school produced good exam results. The majority of pupils were expected to take their 'O' Levels and then start work. In the early 1960s jobs were a lot easier to find and in Kenny Noye's world university was completely out of the question.

The main sport at Bexley was football, although there was an extremely successful hockey team. But Kenny Noye did not particularly like team sports. He preferred boxing and often trained at a local gym.

As schoolfriend Paul Upward later recalled: 'Kenny's mind wasn't really on team games. He didn't like losing and told me he'd rather be out earning a crust.'

However, Noye continued to face regular bouts of corporal punishment. Once he was ordered to report to the Headmaster's office after swearing at a teacher. He was beaten with a cane on the hand five times.

However, none of the boys were ever expelled for bad behaviour. As physics master Denis Sale explained: 'There was nowhere else to send them after our school. We really were the end of the road, so to speak.'

Kenny's school friend Paul Upward never forgot the day Noye decided secretly to record a teacher and then play it back during the same lesson, much to the amusement of his classmates. He was immediately sent to the Headmaster for a caning.

Also at school, Kenny graduated from occasionally handling stolen bike parts to a bicycle stealing gang. He specialised in stripping down bikes and making entirely new models out of them. Making money was already his main priority.

* * *

Kenny Noye's relationship with his father sometimes led to a strained atmosphere in the house, which encouraged Noye's self-destructive personality to emerge.

As a child, he did not receive the sensory stimulation he required from his family and increasingly found it difficult to establish a boundary between himself and the world beyond his caring mother and sister Hilary (three years younger than Kenny). He was becoming an all-encompassing individual, seeing things from his own perspective and no one else's.

Other family members noticed how fearless he was becoming and how he would try to manipulate situations to suit himself and no one else. He also seemed incapable of appreciating when he hurt other people's feelings. He felt little remorse and certainly no sympathy for his victim.

Beneath the bubbling, chatty exterior was an inner sadness caused because he found it difficult to take part in any childlike preoccupations. Childhood was supposed to be a pleasurable experience in which the developing individual learned how to be happy and derive happiness from as many situations as possible. But Noye's few childhood friends soon concluded that he was not capable of enjoying things in the normal sense of the word.

However, Noye's development had its own twisted logic, steeped in terror of some unpleasant memories and fears that were permanently stored in his mind.

Also young Kenny Noye tried to convince himself that he would never struggle financially in the way his father had done. He vowed to marry only when he was wealthy. Kenny Noye had no intention of repeating history.

✵ ✵ ✵

When Noye was 13 he and his cousin Michael went by train to Northampton to see a girl whom Kenny had met a few weeks earlier during a summer holiday on the Kent coast.

Michael Noye takes up the story: 'We hopped on this train without paying our fares and ended up in Northampton. We never paid to go anywhere if we could help it.'

But the girl Noye wanted to see wasn't at home, so he and

his cousin wandered around Northampton. Within an hour Kenny persuaded his cousin to scale a wall and break into a shoe factory after they'd spotted an open window. The Noye cousins stole seven pairs of shoes and even managed to hide them when a policeman stopped them just after they'd left the premises.

At 14, Kenny Noye sold programmes twice a week at the greyhound track where his mum was the manageress. It was a hotbed of local villains and Kenny — observant and perceptive as ever — soon worked out the real winners and losers.

Often he'd slide into the bar and sit in a corner listening to the 'dodgy deals' going down. He was fascinated by these tough, edgy characters in their sheepskin coats who seemed to have endless bundles of £5 notes in their pockets. These twisted values intruded upon young Noye's life with increasing frequency and made him fairly confused about morals.

He was also developing a terrible temper. If he didn't get what he wanted he often became violent.

Sometimes, noted his relatives, it was a hair trigger reaction provoked by the smallest incident. Instead of taking a deep breath and walking away from potentially difficult situations, Noye would head straight into them.

One childhood friend recalled: 'Once we were queuing for a bus together and this bloke shoved in front of us. Kenny went bloody bananas and shoved this geezer up against the side of the bus and started hammering him. I had to pull him off in the end and the other bloke was not a pretty sight.'

Noye's friends noted that he never seemed willing to curb his temper. He felt so convinced of his own abilities that he wouldn't compromise in any way.

He believed he could get away with anything and most of the time he did precisely that.

2: The Freeloading Mod

In the gritty dockland areas of south east London where Noye's parents had grown up, petty thieves were still stealing tea chests off lorries and selling every commodity they could lay their hands on. Sometimes truck drivers were even kidnapped while their loads were stolen, but usually no one was harmed. Everything was fair game — cigarettes, spirits and clothing. Often railway containers were raided at night and their contents would end up on local street markets the following day.

The docklands were still a breeding ground for criminals, even if some of them had moved with their families out to suburbs such as Bexleyheath. Stealing was a way of life, proved by the fact that many of the husbands and fathers of families in places like Bexleyheath spent much of their time back at their old familiar haunts near the Old Kent Road.

As former Kray twins' henchman Freddie Foreman explained years later: 'You went out and you took chances and did all the villainy and put your life on the line, your liberty on the line, but there would be a nucleus of people around you who'd make sure you survived.'

That was the way it was.

One of Kenny Noye's friends at the time was a pint-sized child who had been known to the local police since the age of ten when he stole wallets and belongings from tourist coaches parked on Constitution Hill, in central London. They parked there every day because it was near Buckingham

Palace. Naturally, no one took much notice of a little boy dressed in shorts and a school cap.

Kenny was impressed when the boy told him he could make £10 or £15 in just one day by selling everything to a fence.

Being a 'fence' seemed to Noye a much more profitable — and safer — way of making money out of crime. Fences were well organised and respected 'businessmen' in the community. Everyone — even the youngest children — noticed the aura surrounding them.

As Freddie Foreman explains: 'They got great respect because of their mannerisms and their obviously affluent lifestyle. They always looked smart. They knew how to dress well. They'd have a little business going, they'd drive a decent car and they'd spend their money wisely.'

As dock workers on both sides of the Thames lost their jobs, they had to find ways of replacing the high wages (and bungs) they'd been earning over the years.

The only high earnings that still existed were as printers in London's Fleet Street where all the national newspapers were published. It was a lucrative trade often passed down through families. But print jobs were rare, so it was no surprise that, as teenagers grew up in the late 1950s and early 1960s, the fast-emerging heroes were the pavement artists — armed bank robbers — who'd scoop a few thousand pounds on a couple of 'jobs'. True, they sometimes got caught by police, stood trial at the Old Bailey and went down for a long stretch. But at least they lived in style.

Noye and his friends and family frequently got angry about the long sentences given to such criminals who were regarded in many ways as modern day Robin Hoods.

* * *

In the 1950s bank raids were usually carried out in the dead of night, with a master safecracker pitting his wits against whatever security arrangements happened to be in operation at the time.

However, as lock design and other security improved, tackling a safe was becoming an increasingly difficult task. Even the use of gelignite was no longer a sound bet — a device had been developed that, if triggered by the force of an explosion, simply threw extra bolts across the safe door.

Criminals introduced oxyacetylene torches to get around this problem, but these proved to be slow and cumbersome and, on occasion, would actually reduce the contents of a safe to charred paper before the door could even be forced open.

The armed robbery scene developed as wages increased and firms had to hire companies to transport their cash to factories and offices on wage day, Fridays.

There were no security companies in those days. More often than not two or three trusted workers in a company would be given a few extra bob to pick up the cash from a nearby bank, armed with a cosh if they were lucky.

Inevitably some workers began informing their friends of this transportation of relatively large sums of money and robberies became commonplace.

As one pavement artist from those days explained: 'It was easy pickings because these "guards" were just ordinary workers and they didn't want to get bashed up or put up a fight to protect the firm's money.'

At that time most wages were carried in canvas cricket bags that would be snatched in seconds, thrown into a waiting car and driven around the corner to a quiet cul-de-sac, usually near a railway path/bridge, where a changeover car would be waiting on the other side. Often the takings would be re-invested into honest businesses.

'The objective was to get enough money to retire and then go into a straight business,' explained someone who should know. 'Then you could put your kids through good schools, buy your own home and get a decent motor car, even manage a holiday abroad.'

Robbers then began to turn to 'across-the-counter' bank raids. Old-style attacks on bank safes didn't require any confrontation on the part of the robbers, but going into a bank in broad daylight did, so it was essential for the robbers to be able to guarantee control. Early in the 1960s firearms began to appear with alarming regularity.

By then banks began installing screens to protect their cashiers. The risk in such raids was higher, the rewards were generally lower, so once again those intent on armed robbery looked for new methods.

Cash in transit seemed the answer. Britain might have been fast becoming a cashless society due to the increased use of cheque books and credit cards, but the consumer society still needed ready money and plenty of it.

As a result, during the 1960s specialised security firms emerged to take on the responsibility of transferring money, with armoured vans replacing vulnerable clerks carrying briefcases. It was these vans and their guards that became the focus of robbers' attentions.

By the start of the 1960s south-east London firms were dominating such crimes around the capital. Wealthy criminals would finance robberies, but they would never dream of telling the experts how to do their jobs. These were professionals.

But as the money grew so too did the risks.

Post Office vans became a good target because they had just one driver and he usually didn't even know what he was carrying. The robbers would have a snitch inside the main Post Office who would be able to tell when there was a lot of cash on board such vans.

The reward for a career as a robber — besides the cash — was underworld fame. Picking up the evening paper and seeing a banner headline POST OFFICE VAN HIJACK and knowing that most people inside that criminal community would immediately be able to tell who'd carried out the job.

In this environment prison became the natural breeding ground for bigger and bigger robberies, as criminals linked up with new partners inside.

'The clink was where you met different people and heard

different stories and you learned your trade, so to speak. Prison's like a breeding ground. It's like going to university or going to college,' explained one old 'face'.

It was only a matter of time before Kenny Noye would graduate.

* * *

By the age of 14, Kenny Noye was operating a successful stolen bicycle racket, charging younger children protection money at school, doing an early morning paper-round and selling programmes at the greyhound track where his mum worked.

However, Noye lived in a community where the relationship between the police and petty criminals remained a civilised one. Often they would meet each other in the local pub and exchange pleasantries, even though they might have been arrested the previous week.

At fifteen, Kenny Noye got himself a Saturday job in the men's department of Harrods in Knightsbridge, West London. Although the pay wasn't that good, Noye got a large discount on all his clothes and began dressing even more smartly. Working in such a wealthy area of London was a real eye opener to young Kenny Noye. He was fascinated by all the rich and famous people who came into Harrods. He watched their wallets closely and the type of clothes they bought.

Noye never told any of his friends back in Bexleyheath about his new Saturday job because he was a bit embarrassed about working in such a high-class store.

On Sundays Noye also went up to the Strand in central London and sold newspapers. Those papers were supplied to him and an older partner at knockdown prices from the print works of the nearby Fleet Street newspapers. They had all 'fallen off the back of a lorry'.

That year Noye got five 'O' Levels at school and enrolled at the London College of Printing, in Elephant and Castle to

17

study commercial art. The college course led to a much sought-after apprenticeship as a printer. Noye got in through a distant cousin.

Once Noye's apprenticeship was completed he worked nights at a print and advertising works called Swaines, near Fleet Street. But it wasn't at one of the big newspapers and the pay was not enough for Noye, so he took a daytime job driving a tipper-truck on a building site.

Nothing could stop him from feeding his obsession for clothes. He walked into a branch of the men's outfitters, Burton's, wearing an old pair of jeans and a tatty shirt, put on a new suit in the changing-room and ran out of the shop at high speed. One of the shop assistants gave chase but Noye escaped.

'Kenny was that sort of guy. Always prepared to take the risks we didn't think worth taking,' explained childhood friend Michael Phillips. 'I think he got quite a kick out of it.'

Some of Kenny's friends at this time took drugs, such as purple hearts, but Noye refused to touch them. Others even sold them but he showed no interest in such a sideline. It was unknown territory and he didn't even appreciate the product.

Around this time Noye began dating a pretty blonde local girl called Linda. They went out together to numerous local youth clubs. She was the first of many.

Old friend Paul Upward explained: 'He had lots of girlfriends. He was a very smooth operator. He never tried hard, but they used to flock around him in clubs.'

Cousin Michael's brother Graham had first-hand experience of Kenny Noye's romantic instincts when Graham introduced him to his own girlfriend.

Noye immediately pulled Graham aside at a family party and said: 'Cor blimey Gra, I'd like to give her one.'

Graham's girlfriend overheard the remark and stormed off in a huff. Shortly afterwards Graham Noye married her. As Graham Noye explained years later with a grin: 'The wife's never forgiven Kenny for that little episode.'

Sometimes Noye and close friend Paul Upward would go

to a club called The Inferno in Welling, Kent, which was located in an old British Legion hall. It served only coca-cola and played records, but was a convenient location for bored teenagers escaping their parents.

Kenny — already working in Harrods by this time — turned up one night at The Inferno wearing a new jacket that must have cost him at least £20 — which was a small fortune in those days. But he still insisted on bunking into The Inferno and ripped his jacket getting over the fence behind the club.

At the Scala dance hall in nearby Dartford it was the same story. Noye was renowned as someone who would do anything to avoid paying an entry fee. In those days Noye dressed as a mod with a smart short haircut. He wore hush puppies and black suits when he could afford them.

The mods were the scooter boys from the neat south London suburbs whose arch enemies were the rockers — greasy motorbike fanatics who wore tatty leathers and had long hair.

The Mods and Rockers became the two opposing youth groups who emerged in the late 1950s/early 1960s. There were frequent clashes between the gangs at weekends when they descended on south coast seaside resorts.

In the early to mid-1960s, being a Mod was a serious business. Kenny Noye's favourite bands were The Who and The Spencer Davis Group. He eventually graduated to The Small Faces. And — always one to take advantage of any opportunity — he began supplying cheap scooters, which were in incredible demand at the time.

Noye's old friend Michael Phillips recalled: 'Kenny and a friend drove over to my house one day on a pair of scooters. Kenny sold me one of them and then drove off on the back of his mate's. I'd paid him the money but I never managed to get that scooter going. It was typical.'

Noye had his own Vespa scooter for travelling down to the coast with dozens of his other mod friends, but he usually kept away from the clashes with the Rockers despite his short temper. He preferred to wander off on his own and shoplift a few shirts from local clothes stores.

Back in Bexleyheath the police were starting to take an active interest in Kenny Noye. One day he was stopped by a beat officer in the area where he lived because he didn't have any tax on his scooter. 'Kenny got really angry at this copper. He was very lippy and we had to hold him back otherwise he'd have been nicked,' explained a friend.

Noye and his cronies called the police 'the cozzers'. They were the enemy and never to be trusted. He didn't agree with all that friendly stuff in the pub, which his elders went in for.

Around this time Michael Phillips got the clear impression from Noye that he was not happy at home. Noye never invited any of his friends to his house and whenever anyone knocked on the front door they were never asked in.

It seemed Noye was not a happy teenager, but he found it difficult to confide in any of his friends.

However, that attitude manifested itself in a complete and utter disregard for rules and regulations. It was almost a contempt for society. Noye didn't like people getting better scooters than him, owning flashier suits or having prettier girlfriends. It really grated with him that he didn't have as much money as the wealthiest people in what was then a very class-riddled society. He made up for it by avoiding paying for most things if he could. Noye worried about his small home and how his father struggled to support the family. He was determined to make sure that he became a very wealthy individual by whatever means possible.

Kenny's best friend at the time was Dave Bishop, a tough, streetwise teenager with very similar taste in women, as both men would eventually find out to their cost. They socialised and did some business together. Bishop and Noye both pledged that money was their driving force and they would do just about anything to attain real wealth.

Anything.

3: Earning Respect

By the age of 18, Kenny Noye was earning enough money to make his first material dream come true. He bought himself a bright yellow Ford Cortina Mark 1 and still kept a scooter for regular weekend outings with local Mods.

Noye never fully explained to his friends where and how he earned his money once he left school.

'He said he was a builder, but I never saw any evidence of this,' says friend Paul Upward today. 'We just didn't ask.'

By this time, Noye was five feet eight inches tall, fairly muscular and looked older than his age. On his evenings off he began visiting some of the legendary clubs and bars in and around the Old Kent Road, in the heart of south-east London.

Noye liked to blend into the background in such establishments and he observed some of the most infamous criminals of the mid-1960s. Noye was intrigued by these flashy characters in their big cars and mohair suits. Whenever he got talking to anyone, he'd invent stories about himself — embellishing his position in life. He wanted to make himself more interesting to potential criminal partners.

Noye also began distancing himself from his family because he did not want to involve them in his activities.

However, his criminal instincts did sometimes let him down.

In 1966 Noye, aged 19, and his cousin Michael went up to Old Street in the centre of London to look at a scooter that was for sale, or so they would later claim.

Cousin Michael takes up the story:

'Kenny said the scooter was in this yard, but it seemed to be locked up so I gave him a hand to bunk over the wall. He then stood on some pallets and helped me over the wall as well. Then we climbed down a fire escape into the yard, but the scooter wasn't there. Kenny said the bloke must have sold it before we got there. We began wandering around the building and suddenly we found ourselves surrounded by the Old Bill.'

Both youths were arrested for trespassing and were locked up overnight at Old Street police station. But Kenny Noye's attitude towards the police nearly got him into even more trouble.

'Kenny was a bit lippy and they took his blankets away in the cells that night. He didn't like the Old Bill,' explained Michael Noye.

The two youths got off with a conditional discharge, although the police were convinced they had intended to break in and steal the contents of that factory.

Today Michael Noye refuses to be drawn on any of the other criminal activities he and Kenny were involved in at that time.

'None of it harmed anyone. A bit of thieving and a bit of this and that,' is all Michael Noye will say.

But the relationship between the two cousins began fading after Kenny's protective mother Edith called Michael Noye's mother to complain: 'Your Michael's always getting Kenny into trouble.'

Then Michael Noye's mother turned to her son one day and said: 'Stay away from Kenny. He's bad news.'

* * *

Kenny Noye spent a lot of time tinkering with the engine of his beloved Ford Cortina, which was parked outside the family home in Bexleyheath. He even attached flashy hubcaps and luminous flaps behind each wheel arch, not to mention sticky go-fast stripes on each side of the bodywork.

As Kenny Noye's circle of acquaintances grew so did their criminal habits. One of his friends had left school, got himself a job in a meat warehouse and immediately became involved in smuggling out carcasses of beef on lorries. He was just fifteen at the time.

Noye stayed at home in Jenton Avenue because he didn't want to end up in a crummy bedsit. He wouldn't leave until he'd saved enough to buy his first home. Noye's criminal activities were apparent to all around him. South-east London had always been a law unto itself. Why should things change just because the family had moved out to the suburbs?

* * *

South-east London was the home of many of the nation's armed robbers.

The criminal influence could be traced back to a subculture of which Kenny Noye knew a great deal.

Even the Great Train Robbery in 1963 played a part in this process because most of the robbers came from south-east London. The heroic status those criminals achieved in the eyes of many was nowhere more evident than on the streets where they grew up. Armed robbery had already taken on a romantic hue all of its own, but now it was positively glamorous.

Crime had always been a way out of the doldrums for the masses of unemployed, many of whom had been part-time villains anyway. But armed robbery was paying the biggest returns.

In south-east London the status of such criminals put them on a par with film stars in the local community.

When an armed police officer shot dead two gun-toting robbers and wounded a third as they tried to snatch £250,000 from a security van, extra police had to be drafted in to the area to prevent a riot.

Women shouted abuse at police officers from the

balconies of their flats, children taunted them in the street, and seven people at a pub frequented by robbers were arrested on charges ranging from threatening behaviour to assault.

In fact, by the mid-1960s many pubs in south-east London had become places where guns could be obtained relatively easily. And those pubs tended to be no-go areas for the police.

Sixty per cent of all armed robberies in Britain at that time took place in London, and about three-quarters of those that occurred elsewhere were committed by Londoners.

* * *

Kenny Noye had hung around enough villains to know that if he was going to infiltrate the upper echelons of the south-east London underworld he'd have to enjoy a lot of warm pints of bitter in the company of some hard characters. It was the traditional route to take.

As one of those very same criminal 'faces' Freddie Foreman later explained: 'You meet a certain person and you get a rapport with them, you like them and the best way to know that they're OK is through the belly of that man. You get drunk with them. You have a night out and then you see the way they perform and handle themselves. If he doesn't get soppy and start running off at the mouth and get insulting to women or in company and he can conduct himself with or without a drink, then you know he's a good guy.'

Kenny Noye believed that once you got to that stage you simply didn't cross such people. You got involved with them because they were trustworthy. You knew they wouldn't turn you over. You had their trust and they had yours. These were the kind of values that appealed to Kenny Noye — or so it seemed.

Kenny Noye's first really significant criminal operation centred around a stolen car ring. He was responsible for supplying stolen spare parts that had been stripped off the vehicles after they'd been seized. For almost a year, Noye became a well-known local supplier of cheap car parts in south-east London and Kent.

However, someone inside their 'team' informed on Noye and the rest of the gang to the police. Noye was arrested and ended up in court accused of handling stolen vehicles.

The magistrate decided that he'd make an example of Noye and his co-conspirators, and he ended up with a one-year stretch in a Borstal near Shaftesbury in Wiltshire. At that jail for young offenders, Noye soon got to know the faces that mattered. They were the smarter, non-violent criminal youngsters that Noye knew instinctively he would come across once he got out again.

Noye looked on his stay in that Borstal as part of his criminal education. He picked up a lot of useful information, gathering names and numbers, which he noted down in a black phone book.

Noye listened to what the other young villains had to say, determined to learn from their mistakes as well as his own. He wanted to run his own 'businesses' in the future. That way, he believed, he would never again be on the wrong end of a prison sentence.

* * *

When losing one's virginity, said Queen Victoria, one must close one's eyes and think of England. Attaching a little more lyricism to the act, the great romantics from Cervantes to Byron saw virgins as roses and their deflowering a poem to passions that would saddle lions.

Kenny Noye had already tasted plenty of passion by the time he reached his late teens. However his first real experience of romance came when he met blonde legal secretary Brenda Tremain as he walked into a lawyer's office in London's Lincoln's Inn Fields, home to many of the nation's barristers.

He'd only just been released from Borstal but was already in more trouble for shoplifting and assaulting a policeman.

Petite, neatly dressed Brenda Tremain lived with her family in Bridge Road, Slade Green in Kent and Noye got talking to her while he was waiting to see a barrister.

Noye eventually escaped with a fine for the shoplifting and assault on a policeman. But, more importantly, he'd found himself a prospective wife.

Brenda, daughter of an ultrasonic engineer and computer worker impressed Noye with her blonde good looks and forthright personality. She attended her local school, Howbury Grange.

As one old friend explained: 'Brenda was a strong woman from the start and Kenny likes them like that. He wants them to stand up to him... to a degree at least.'

On their first date Kenny Noye told Brenda he intended to make enough money to buy a plot of land on which to build a dream home. She was impressed.

Brenda had absolutely no doubt Noye would eventually provide the perfect home and family that he promised her. He'd lost his printing job and bought himself a second-hand lorry and was doing some freelance haulage for various companies in south-east London and Kent.

Kenny Noye soon discovered there were some unexpected advantages to courting Brenda Tremain.

Most Sundays the Tremains would enjoy a drink in their local pub, The Harrow, which was run by a close family friend. It was there that Kenny Noye found himself a new drinking partner, Micky Lawson, who owned a used car showroom at a Shell petrol station opposite the Tremain home.

Lawson, a smartly dressed, wise-cracking character with the definite gift of the gab dabbled in all sorts of businesses besides second-hand cars. Soon he was introducing Noye to some very interesting faces in south-east London pubs like The Frog and Nightgown, The Connoisseur, The Prince of Wales and The Beehive in Peckham. Noye began socialising with even more of the hardest gangsters in London, many of whom had carried out numerous robberies. However, Kenny Noye had no intention of going across the pavement, as robbery was known in those days. He'd already decided that fencing the proceeds was a much safer bet.

Back in those days only a brave and foolish man would try to muscle in on criminals such as south-east London's most feared family, the Richardsons.

In the 1960s, the Richardsons' manor was a hugely profitable empire stretching from south London scrap yards and West End drinking clubs to gold mines in South Africa. Their leader Charlie Richardson was known as the hardest man in south London. But when Richardson was imprisoned after a judge called him 'a disgrace to society' ambitious young criminals like Kenny Noye noticed the gap in the south east London underworld.

As one senior police officer from that manor explained: 'The whole place opened up. People with strong personalities like Kenny Noye decided to move in.' As these new 'faces' began feeling their way into the Richardson territory all sorts of new criminal enterprises started springing up.

Around this time Noye became acquainted with Billy Hayward, one of the most feared gangsters in south-east London. He'd already secured a place in gangland folklore by engaging in a nightclub battle with the Richardson gang over who should control local protection rackets. One of Hayward's men, Dickie Hart, was shot dead in the clash that became known as 'the Battle of Mr Smith's Club' and effectively destroyed the Richardsons' criminal empire. It also made Hayward a legendary figure.

Billy Hayward re-iterated to Kenny Noye that the clever criminals were the ones who handled the stolen goods and money rather than committed the crimes themselves. They'd then invest in small businesses such as minicab companies, launderettes and sometimes even the stockmarket. The stupid villains spent it in clubs and pubs and on the dogs or at the horses.

Noye was already mapping out his own criminal career, but there remained one problem — his continually worsening temper. He got embroiled in an argument in a

Peckham pub with another man who knocked his drink over by accident and then refused to buy Noye a new one. The two men swore at each other, then two friends of the other man began taunting Noye.

Noye walked out of the pub to boos and hisses from the men who presumed he was walking away from the confrontation. Nothing could have been further from the truth.

Noye went straight to his car, opened the boot and grabbed a double-barrelled shotgun he kept 'for emergencies'.

Seconds later Noye burst into the bar of the pub with his fully loaded weapon. The bar went silent.

Noye aimed the double barrelled shotgun at the three men who'd been taunting him.

'You want some of this?'

The three men said nothing.

Another beat of silence followed.

Noye's finger stroked the trigger. The men remained frozen at the bar. No one else dared mutter a word.

Noye's finger began squeezing the trigger.

Then he slowly and deliberately panned the barrel up to the ceiling and fired.

The shot hit a point just above the three men, showering plaster and dust over them. But still they didn't move.

Kenny Noye turned and walked out of the pub. He'd just sent a message to certain people: Kenny Noye was someone to be respected.

However the downside of 'being respected' was that the police began taking a more active interest in Kenny Noye. His record didn't help nor did his attitude towards certain officers. He already had a running feud with one policeman in Bexleyheath who was forever trying to arrest him for a variety of petty offences. At one stage Noye joked to a friend at the time: 'That fucker is driving me crazy. I wish I had a thousand quid to spare. I'd put a hit on him.'

However, Noye's new criminal associates warned him that if he wanted to get on with all his activities he needed to have some policemen on his side. Noye took this advice on board and began putting the feelers out to see whether he could get some useful policemen on his side. Kenny Noye believed that everybody had a price.

He was already making large sums of money as a fence handling other people's stolen goods. The contraband that had begun as car parts had now progressed to occasional lorry loads of whisky and cigarettes. This was followed by watches and jewellery. Noye even tried to win a few policemen over by tipping them off on certain stolen shipments he'd heard about, so they'd leave him to his own devices.

As his business rapidly expanded, Noye opened his own haulage company from a battered caravan behind a garage in a relatively remote Kent village called West Kingsdown.

It was the perfect location for the sort of activities Kenny Noye wanted few people to know about.

4: The Bermuda Triangle

West Kingsdown is a quiet, unprepossessing village about 25 miles from London in the Kent countryside. It once straddled the main thoroughfare between London and the port of Folkestone, but, since the arrival of a nearby motorway, its nearest claim to fame has been its close proximity to the Brands Hatch motor-racing circuit.

Two hundred years ago highway robberies were a regular drawback as horse-drawn coaches passed through en route to Dover and Folkestone. In those days the area consisted of no more than half a dozen cottages and undesirables would hide out in the surrounding countryside before pouncing on the carriages as they passed through.

The community didn't begin to develop properly until servicemen from World War I were rewarded for their bravery by being given a couple of acres each of local land. Even then the population remained sparse.

It was not until the end of World War II that the number of residents started to rise significantly. Many speculative property developers began building houses until the population grew to about 5,000 by the early 1970s when Kenny Noye arrived in the village.

The countryside had been pronounced a green belt area of outstanding natural beauty, but some of the modern box-shaped properties that appeared on the horizon did little to enhance that.

Many people were attracted to West Kingsdown because it was slightly off the beaten track, despite its close proximity to

London. These new residents presumed that West Kingsdown was a crime-free zone.

However, there had actually been two killings in recent years — both domestic crimes involving unhappy couples. The first was when an elderly man beat his wife to death after a row. He then walked calmly to a neighbour's house and advised them to call the police. A few years later another unhappy husband ended the life of his wife in similar circumstances.

By the early 1970s West Kingsdown was becoming a magnet for relatively wealthy people from south-east London. The village was so spread out that they could go about their business without other people observing their every move.

The only police presence in the village was one local bobby. Noye's haulage company, run from a tatty caravan in West Kingsdown, went from strength to strength as did his courtship with Brenda Tremain.

Eventually Kenny Noye and his fiancée Brenda found their dream plot of land in Hever Avenue, West Kingsdown. Kenny Noye immediately hired a team of builders to construct a bungalow and the couple married. Brenda proudly told one friend at the time that West Kingsdown was a place 'where the children could grow up without roaming the streets and sniffing glue.'

Noye's haulage fleet rapidly grew to more than a dozen lorries and his work as a fence of the proceeds of crimes continued uninterrupted.

Even when Noye had a brush with the police soon after he moved to West Kingsdown, he managed to wriggle out of trouble by giving them some information. Noye told two Kent officers that he believed one of his lorries had been hired out to a gang who were carrying a stolen haul of cigarettes and whisky from the continent. He revealed to the police the exact details of the lorry, knowing full well that in fact it was carrying double the amount he had told them. Then Noye arranged for half of the shipment to be unloaded before the police stopped the truck. That left him with half of that load to sell off through various contacts while police believed they had got everything.

'It was a clever scam and there wasn't much we could do about it because it was only after Noye told us about the illicit loads that we could get to them,' explained one Kent detective.

Back in West Kingsdown, Noye's neighbours were becoming irritated by the huge articulated lorries parked in the street near his home in Hever Avenue.

Eventually Noye was reprimanded by the parish council. He didn't kick up a fuss because he didn't want to attract any attention to his activities.

Noye knew that in the long term he needed a much bigger plot of land where he could build his own house and outbuildings, so that he could load and unload his lorries without interference from anyone.

Not long after this, Noye claimed a reward of several thousand pounds by tipping police off about a lorryload of merchandise, stolen from Liverpool docks, that thieves were trying to sell on to him.

He was becoming a useful contact for a number of senior detectives in the Kent police. He'd made a point of nurturing them and not Scotland Yard because his friends in south-east London had advised him that the Metropolitan Police would 'stitch him up'.

Despite the move into the Kent countryside, Noye continued frequenting the pubs and clubs around the Old Kent Road. By now he favoured the open shirt, hairy chest medallion look and had a twinkle in his eye whenever a pretty girl appeared on the scene.

With the Richardsons gone there were about half a dozen firms sprouting up in the area, all planning the sort of crimes that would provide a fence like Kenny Noye with a sizeable income.

* * *

Kenny and Brenda were eventually married at her local

church, St. Augustine's, Slade Green, in August 1970. Brenda's two younger sisters and Noye's sister Hilary were bridesmaids.

* * *

Kenny Noye travelled to the USA in 1971. He used a falsified passport to enter the country after being warned he would never get in because of his criminal record.

In Miami, Noye looked up two men whose names he'd been given by his own criminal friends back in south-east London. The two businessmen described themselves as property speculators. Noye soon discovered they had a very profitable sideline in drug dealing as well. They were members of the local Mafia.

Noye didn't invest any money in drugs because of the stigma attached to drug dealing in Britain. At that time it was considered by many to be 'dirty money'.

However, when his new American friends urged Noye to buy into property in Florida because it was extremely cheap, he asked them to contact him if any good deals came up.

* * *

In 1972 Brenda gave birth to a baby son, Kevin. Two years later she had another boy called Brett. Noye was delighted to have a family and was determined to provide them with the sort of lifestyle he had not had as a child. He was also on the constant lookout for new business opportunities.

He diversified by setting up a series of building companies and made a number of lucrative property deals, including one that netted him £300,000. He invested that money in a mobile homes business in Florida with the help of his new Mafia friends. They asked him to look after some of their investments in Britain, so if either of them tried to cheat the other they'd all have a lot to lose.

One of Kenny Noye's proudest boasts at this time was that he'd supplied much of the equipment used to help build the vast Thames Barrier near Charlton, where the river bordered on Noye's beloved south-east London. Nobody knew if his claim was true, but Noye found it highly amusing that his stolen equipment was being hired out for public money.

Not so amusing was his reputation among other criminals in south-east London and Kent.

One of his associates became so convinced that Noye had informed on him to the police that he and two henchmen turned up at Noye's house when he was away. A terrified Brenda hid herself and the children in a bedroom while the men wandered around the garden looking inside to see whether anyone was in. On his return, Noye promised Brenda they'd move out as soon as he could find a safer, bigger, more private place to live. Meanwhile the Noyes bought two Rottweiler guard dogs as an added security precaution. They were called Sam and Cleo.

When Noye heard that a bungalow on 20 acres of prime land just outside West Kingsdown was up for sale, he slapped down £50,000 cash for the deal and got it before the house even went officially on the market.

The fact that the dilapidated bungalow was a 1930s-built eyesore with three small bedrooms didn't bother Noye. Within weeks of buying the property there was a fire that completely gutted the house.

Noye immediately claimed on his house insurance policy and applied to build a huge mock-Tudor mansion in place of the bungalow.

There was no shortage of equipment for the building work, as Noye was shipping stolen equipment, such as earth movers, to wealthy customers in the Middle East at the time.

Noye then built Hollywood Cottage. It had ten bedrooms, an indoor swimming pool, jacuzzi, huge snooker room and extensive security precautions, including a fully alarmed interior and security cameras at the massive wrought-iron gates at the end of a long driveway. 'Cottage' seemed a wholly inappropriate description.

During excavation Kenny Noye discovered a number of underground concrete bunkers in the garden. The grounds had been used during World War II as part of the wartime headquarters of the Special Operations Executive, the organisation set up in 1940 to assist resistance groups in Nazi-occupied Europe.

Despite all his new-found wealth, Kenny Noye remained the ultimate freeloader. A row of street lights he had installed on the long driveway to his house were secretly tapped into the main electricity supply at the nearby public road, School Lane. Noye even stole the power for his indoor swimming pool heater from another mains supply on the same road.

Kenny Noye kept a fairly low profile after moving into his new, more isolated West Kingsdown home. He occasionally turned up with Brenda and the boys to village fêtes but rarely mixed with people outside his own tightly knit circle.

At this time Noye was describing himself as a 'property developer' to anyone who asked his profession.

When his old childhood friend Janet John babysat Kevin and Brett at Hollywood Cottage one night, she was taken aback when Brenda Noye proudly announced that the fully fitted kitchen had cost £17,000 to build. 'It was worth almost more than our entire house,' recalls Janet John today.

However, the welcome given by Brenda Noye to visitors to Hollywood Cottage was altogether very different from her Jack-the-lad husband. Explained Janet John: 'She was very stand-offish and a bit snooty towards us. She acted as if she was above us all.'

However, beneath her hard exterior, Brenda Noye was a highly superstitious person. She even persuaded Noye to pay thousands of pounds extra to have a Gemini star sign hand-painted on the bottom of their swimming pool.

Inside Hollywood Cottage there was a distinct lack of furniture, apart from very ornate hand-sewn thickly lined curtains that were specially designed to keep out all light. Most of the walls were bare.

'It was very unlived in. It was almost as if Brenda was extremely proud of owning such a huge house but she didn't want to mess it up with any furnishings,' said one visitor.

Each bathroom had twin marble sinks, but everything was

very plain and unimaginative. The dining room had a massive table, but again no pictures on the walls.

In fact Brenda Noye — just like her husband's mother — was completely allergic to any clutter in the house.

'She would rush into the kitchen with the empty cup the moment you'd finished your coffee,' added one visitor.

Despite his reclusive habits, Kenny Noye did sometimes help local causes. He even made a hefty donation to the village Gang Show and other local charities. Noye also allowed the local scouts to use the indoor pool at Hollywood Cottage for swimming practice at least once a week during the winter. However, they were the only strangers ever welcomed on the premises and the Noyes insisted that all the children be taken back to the village scout hut before they were picked up by their parents.

One time Noye turned up at a children's football match in his black pick-up truck with one of his beloved Rottweilers perched threateningly on the flatbed. One of the parents was so concerned that the dog might run on to the pitch and attack the children that she complained to Noye.

'He's a pussycat,' Noye told the woman. 'It's me you gotta worry about.' As she later recalled: 'He just couldn't resist flirting with me and I have to admit that there was something very attractive about him.'

At one stage Noye even kept two pet lion cubs in a pen next to Hollywood Cottage. His two sons Kevin and Brett proudly informed all their friends that he got the beasts 'because he loves animals'.

When Noye got into yet another row in a pub, he told a rowdy drinker: 'If you don't shut it, I'll feed you to me lions.' But the lions didn't last long at Hollywood Cottage because Brenda Noye felt they were a danger to the children.

In West Kingsdown, local gossip about Noye was fuelled after he was charged with illegally bringing a gun into Britain from Florida. Some residents presumed he was a gun runner.

'Whatever he did it earned him a lot of money,' said neighbour Pat Bosley. 'There was always a little bit of the unknown about him. You never quite knew what was going through his head.'

Noye frequently clashed with neighbours over the boundaries of his estate. And he gave out very clear vibes.

Neighbour Kenneth Maw said: 'His features suggested he might have once been a prize fighter, but it was clear that he had a very active mind that was working away. His eyes were always alive, darting around. There was obviously a lot going on upstairs. He was very quick with his responses and his repartee was quite good. He had a good sense of humour. Er, sharp is the word I would use to describe him.'

In the late 1970s and early 1980s at least three family members plus six associates of Noye's moved into West Kingsdown and the surrounding area.

Kent police eventually nicknamed that part of Kent 'The Bermuda Triangle'. Explained one ex-detective: 'Once things went in there they disappeared. It was a like a bit of the wild west in the middle of Kent.'

Others put it more bluntly.

'You couldn't drive through the place without alerting certain locals. Some of them were a highly dodgy bunch,' said another police officer.

As resident Pat Bosley pointed out: 'West Kingsdown seemed to be gaining a reputation as being a place with easy access from south London. It had become quite an attractive place for people perhaps carrying out activities that were not quite on the right side of the law.'

The police had no doubts why the area was so popular. 'The major criminals, particularly from south-east London, were starting to live in these big houses in the country. They'd got a bit wise to the fact that they could be easily observed in their houses in London,' one detective pointed out.

West Kingsdown was the perfect base for someone like Kenny Noye.

5: '9999'

Kenny Noye wanted to build on his fortune, not sit back and rest on his laurels. In the mid-1970s he sold his haulage firm for an alleged £500,000 profit and began looking for a major investment.

Noye got talking to his cousin Graham, who worked as a clerk at the Bank of England. Noye pumped him for information about gold Krugerrands and the gold market in general over family Sunday lunches in West Kingsdown. He also wanted to know more about the workings of the Bank of England.

'Anyone would think you wanted to rob the place,' Graham joked with his cousin on one occasion. Kenny Noye winked and smiled. It wasn't quite what he had in mind.

A few months later, Graham Noye sold his cousin a number of Bank of England gold coins. It was Noye's first real taste of dealing in gold.

Kenny Noye continued to study the market closely and regularly interrogated Graham Noye. He was interested in everything — how tax was paid on profits and all other relevant aspect of gold trading.

Noye soon began bringing large quantities of gold Krugerrands into Britain. At that time they were not liable to VAT. Their gold content was taxable, however, so the coins were melted down and sold with a 15% mark-up.

Being a fence was all very well, but Kenny Noye was putting bigger and bolder plans into action.

* * *

'**Gold:** *Precious yellow non-rusting malleable ductile metallic element of high specific gravity, used as a fundamental monetary medium.*' The Concise Oxford English Dictionary doesn't quite capture the magic of the metal, nor its ability to fascinate and corrupt. For 6,000 years it has been hewn from veins of quartz and pyrites and panned from rivers and streams. Today those nations lucky enough to count it as a major resource — South Africa, Russia, Canada, the USA, Brazil and Australia — mine the precious commodity with relentless efficiency. Even in countries where the amounts to be found do not warrant a highly technical approach, gold fever is just as strong.

Only in this century has it been put to uses other than coinage and jewellery. These days it is an essential ingredient in dentistry and the hi-tech industries, providing high electrical conductivity in printed circles and improving the tonal image of photographic film.

However, such is its rarity that, even now, 90% of all gold produced, estimated to amount to some 2,000 million ounces, can still be accounted for — 45% lies in central banks, such as the Bank of England and the German Bundesbank, where it is kept as a guarantee of economic stability for the governments in question. The Old Lady of Threadneedle Street, for instance, never lets her reserves drop below 500,000 kilogrammes. Another 25% of the world's gold is in private hands — those of either powerful international conglomerates or hugely wealthy individuals — while the remaining 20% is used in jewellery, religious artefacts and dentistry.

Even the 10% that is missing has not vanished without trace. Much of it is stuck in a time warp, entombed on the ocean's floor in sunken galleons and more modern ships, victims of either the elements or marine warfare, where it waits to be rediscovered.

* * *

Yet, even with all these odds stacked against him, Kenny Noye became addicted to the gold market. He educated himself about everything there was to know about it. The precious metal had become a favourite commodity with which to swindle the British government out of value-added tax (VAT), a 15% premium levied on a variety of goods, including gold, when they were sold. Paid at the time by the buyer to the person selling the gold, it should then have been returned to HM Customs and Excise.

However, Noye soon discovered that a variety of scams could easily be operated to deprive the taxman of his share. One was to smuggle gold into the country, then sell it to a reputable dealer. The 15% VAT would then be pocketed by the smugglers.

Another scam was to draw up documents showing that the gold had been exported immediately after its arrival in Britain, which meant it was not liable for VAT. The honest trader, meanwhile, would still have to pay the 15% VAT to the 'company' selling him the metal. That 'company', usually based in short-let office accommodation, would fold within a matter of months without making any VAT returns.

Although similar scams could have been worked on other goods that were subject to VAT, gold was particularly suitable because its high value meant large returns with a minimum of delay. It also had an official price, fixed twice daily by the London gold market, so the smugglers did not have to worry about commercial competitors undercutting their prices, and it was compact and easy to transport.

In the late 1970s VAT frauds in general had one further major attraction — the maximum penalty for indulging in the racket was just two years' imprisonment. Small wonder then, that VAT fraud involving gold had grown increasingly popular among well-organised, more professional criminals like Kenny Noye.

However, there were problems with handling gold. Noye soon discovered that the true origin of ingots of gold had to be disguised and that meant removing identification

41

numbers and assay marks. Many ingots carried their own individually designed hallmarks to signify their purity and, in some cases, a serial number. Absolutely pure gold does not exist — some contamination is always present, however expertly the metal has been refined. Bars with the number 9999 meant that they were 99.99% pure, the highest level to which the metal can be refined, while 999 bars, known in the trade as ten-tola bars (a tola being an ancient Indian unit of weight) were only marginally less perfect.

In order to pull off any scam involving gold, as well as removing the identifying marks, any villains or receivers had to disguise the purity of the bars. Failure to do so would create a risk that legitimate traders would quickly become suspicious that the quantities they were being asked to buy were either smuggled gold or stolen bullion. That meant Noye needed specialised smelting equipment, the sort sold by only a handful of shops in Britain, most of them in the Hatton Garden area of central London, internationally renowned as a centre for the jewellery trade. Such shops were on their guard against suspicious customers ordering smelters, so Noye had to tread carefully.

Besides his increasing interest in gold, Kenny Noye was also constantly trying to improve his contacts in all relevant areas. As a successful fence with his finger in many pies he remained of interest to the local Kent police. And he was, in turn, always looking for new ways of cultivating his own police contacts.

When Noye was given an 18-month suspended sentence for illegally importing that gun that he'd purchased in the States, it brought him into contact with more senior Kent officers. Noye got on particularly well with one young detective and suggested they could 'help each other' over certain matters. As far as the young officer was concerned Kenny Noye was a busy criminal who could be a very useful police informant. But he would not allow Noye to call the shots. Noye was unsure whether he could trust the detective and the relationship did not properly develop.

Then Kenny Noye had a bizarre break. He befriended a

blonde woman who was working as a civilian at a Kent police station, not far from West Kingsdown. Noye persuaded the woman to meet for a drink after work one night. They began a passionate affair and she unwittingly provided him with information about his local police. When Noye discovered he was sharing the woman's affections with a senior detective that made the affair even more exciting. The detective, of course, knew nothing of what was going on.

Noye soon befriended more detectives in the area. He was even asked to CID functions and parties held inside one particular police station.

'We all knew he was a bit of a rogue but I have to admit he was good company,' said one officer.

Noye's relationship with the woman went on for almost a year.

'Kenny Noye gleaned a lot of information about Kent police through that affair, although she actually believed he was in love with her,' added the detective.

Eventually the relationship fizzled out. Then the woman left her civilian job to become a full-time police officer serving at another station.

With his south London accent, gold bracelets and suits cut just a little too sharp, Kenny Noye undoubtedly had the respect of other criminals. But his attempts to maintain contacts in high places didn't always work. When Noye clumsily tried to revive the affair with the policewoman he was severely rebuffed.

'She didn't want to know once she joined the force. It was typical Kenny Noye behaviour. I'm certain her police work made her even more irresistible to Noye,' explained one detective.

Meanwhile Kenny Noye continued visiting Florida. His two Mafia associates even introduced him to a money launderer.

Once Noye flew to Miami with £50,000 in cash, which the two Americans invested for him in 90 acres of land.

Planning permission for two houses was obtained, and 50 acres were sold off at a vast profit — some $800,000 each for

Noye and his two associates.

Out and about at his favourite pubs in south-east London and Kent, Kenny Noye encountered a lot of second division criminals, many of whom became his drinking partners.

One robber-turned-cannabis dealer with a long criminal record, never forgot his first meeting with Noye. He explained: 'I first met Kenny in a pub in Dartford. I was a cocky young hoodlum in those days and I was a big lad. When Kenny walked in the place went quiet. I wasn't impressed so I started mouthing off at him. He smiled at me and then whispered gently. "I've got a couple of lions back at my house. I keep them as pets." I wasn't impressed and showed it.'

Noye looked annoyed. 'You're a cocky young bastard. You gotta problem?'

The criminal continued grinning at Noye defiantly.

Then Noye leant across and said quietly: 'I think I should feed you to me lions, don't you?'

There was no doubt he meant it.

'I was young and I was taking the piss, excuse my French but that's basically what I was doing,' the criminal later recalled. 'I was taking the mickey out of him. How did he react to me taking the piss? Well, basically, how would you react to a teenager mouthing off at you? I would say he reacted the right way, although he didn't clump me, which he should 'ave. I was a leery teenager at the time.'

But the criminal insisted: 'Kenny Noye wasn't a bully. He didn't have to be. He wasn't known as a thug. He was what we called a businessman.'

Back on those same mean streets of south-east London various 'firms' were carrying out armed robberies. They were considered the *crème de la crème* of criminals. And a street code of silence was essential.

As one robber explained: 'You'd keep your mouth shut and if you got caught you did your time and got out and started up again. Holding up people gave you a brilliant sense of power. You got respect from other villains and respect even from the police. They might have needed grasses to stop blokes going across the pavement, but they didn't respect them. A grass was scum.'

However, Kenny Noye wanted respect for different reasons. And as he continued picking up police reward money for tip-offs, so he also acquired a considerable criminal record.

Besides that conviction for receiving stolen cars when he was a teenager, there had been criminal convictions for shoplifting, assaulting the police, and failing to have a licence for a shotgun plus several charges of receiving stolen property. Not to mention that gun he'd brought in illegally from Florida. The list was hardly long enough to merit Noye's inclusion on a register of all-time major criminals, but it did indicate a fairly entrenched disregard for the law.

All his offences had occurred under the jurisdiction of Kent police, except for one.

The Metropolitan Police arrested Noye in 1977 for receiving stolen goods.

His reputation as a criminal with contacts had preceded him. But one Scotland Yard detective at the Met called Ray Adams decided that Noye was someone to nurture.

Unfortunately that relationship would eventually come back to haunt them both.

6: On the Square

In the late 1970s, Kenny Noye joined a Freemasons' lodge in West London following an introduction from Micky Lawson, who he'd met through his wife Brenda all those years earlier. The two men had become close friends and 'business' partners on a number of deals. According to one police source inside the Freemasons, Noye's membership was actually proposed and seconded by policemen.

The Freemasons' lodge that Noye joined included members who were police and dealers in gold bullion and other precious metals. Noye saw it as a perfect opportunity to ease his way into an important group of new contacts.

Membership of a Freemasons' lodge was a natural step for Kenny Noye, who was already boasting of a circle of acquaintances that crossed all social divides.

The Freemasons were a controversial society, not least because of the vast number of policemen who were members. Many look upon the Masons as a secretive organisation, but others claim they are nothing more than a very discreet gentlemen's club with tens of thousands of members across Britain. How much power and influence they wield among this country's politicians and lawmakers will probably never be known. But there was absolutely no doubt that it was the police who fuelled Kenny Noye's interest in Freemasonry.

As one police officer later explained: 'Kenny Noye cynically manoeuvred himself into the Masons as if it was the right pub for him to be seen in.'

Some police officer members of the west London lodge

were outraged by the presence of known criminals among their ranks. But others saw people like Noye as an opportunity to pick up a good informant.

Noye believed his membership was a further sanction of his status within that south-east London underworld.

On one occasion Noye wriggled out of an arrest thanks to his membership of the Masons.

'You've just nicked Kenny Noye and he's on the square,' a Mason detective told Noye's arresting officer at the police station.

'So?'

'Can't you help out?'

'Where are you coming from on this?'

'Oh, it's like that, is it?'

'Too bloody right it is.'

Noye even mastered the art of the Freemasons' handshake. This involved putting the thumb between the first and second finger and pressing the knuckle on the middle finger, which would indicate that the person in question was on the third degree, Mason-speak for being a member.

Whenever Noye met a policeman he thought was a Mason he would make a point of speaking to him very carefully to acertain his membership. The conversation would have bizarre overtones:

'You ever been taught to be cautious?'

'Yeah, well my mother always taught me to look left and right before I cross the road.'

If the person Noye was speaking to said yes, then he would follow up with passwords.

'Are you a regular attender?'

'Yeah.'

The moment someone said that back, Noye knew he had connected with a Mason.

However, despite the Masons and his immense wealth Kenny Noye still portrayed an image of the archetypal villain complete with jewel-encrusted Rolex watch, which he proudly claimed to change each year.

People meeting Noye for the first time sensed a wheeler-dealer prepared to cut corners to make money. It was an impression enhanced by his tough manner — he was a man who could have a frightening presence when he wished to make a point.

Back in West Kingsdown they still talk about the day Noye's Rottweiler dogs strayed into a neighbour's garden and a string of angry complaints ensued. Noye accosted one neighbour and accused him of being a 'nark' and threatened to 'bury' him. He never received any more complaints about the dogs.

Meanwhile many of Noye's contemporaries were starting to find security van hold-ups and bank robberies increasingly risky.

Armed guards were now being used to escort large quantities of cash. The biggest problem was the so-called supergrasses who'd become the key to police successes. Hard-hitting detectives from Scotland Yard's élite Flying Squad were even persuading members of close-knit gangs to inform on robberies in advance.

* * *

The Flying Squad had been in existence so long that the Squad's nickname in rhyming slang, the Sweeney (from Flying Squad/Sweeney Todd, the notorious Fleet Street barber who turned his customers into meat pies), was generally regarded as a cliché.

The Squad was set up at the end of World War I, when London experienced a crime wave as large numbers of men recently released from the armed forces emerged on to the streets of the capital, many of them hardened to violence after the carnage on the Western Front. Also, at that time, the use of motor vehicles in the course of crime began to increase.

A month before the war ended twelve specially selected detectives at Scotland Yard were informed that they were to become an experimental crime-fighting force. No longer would they be bound by regulations that prohibited police officers from crossing the border of a police division in which they were based to tackle crime. Instead they were given a roving commission and became the first fully mobile police squad in the country.

The title was impressive sounding, but the reality was a different matter. Instead of cars or even motorcycles transport for the fledgling group consisted of a covered horse-drawn wagon hired from the Great Western Railway. Despite this the Sweeney enjoyed rapid crime-busting success and by 1920 they were provided with two ex-Royal Flying Corps Crossley motor tenders, capable of a top speed of 35mph — the speed limit at the time was just 20mph. The vehicles were proof of the importance attached to the group's work — the entire Metropolitan Police force vehicle fleet at the time numbered just two cars and four dispatch vans.

Two months after the vehicles arrived, a *Daily Mail* journalist named W.G.T. Crook deemed the group worthy of a write-up, in the process referring to them as 'a flying squad of picked detectives'. The name stuck, and by 1921 Flying Squad had become their official title. They were the first motorised police force in the country and the first in radio contact with their base. Their equipment was so advanced that it was regularly borrowed by British intelligence agencies to eavesdrop on unauthorised transmissions emanating from Britain.

From the outset the men of the Flying Squad, with their swooping-eagle tie motif, were considered by the general public as something special. In the 1920s Edgar Wallace wrote a play about them and soon afterwards J. Ord Hume, a well-known composer, wrote a brass-band march for the squad. Their exploits went on to figure in a number of British films, and as late as the mid-1970s the squad was being eulogised in a TV series called *The Sweeney*, starring John Thaw and Dennis Waterman.

During the late 1960s, however, the image of Scotland Yard's detectives as courageous men dedicated to upholding the law took a bit of a battering. Over the following ten years, a climate arose in which Scotland Yard detectives were often viewed with as much suspicion as the criminals they dealt with.

The activities of a number of corrupt officers played straight into the hands of professional criminals, tainting the reputation of many of the Yard's most honest officers.

Police suspicions about the honesty of London's detectives force grew in 1969, when *The Times*, then a newspaper of the establishment, published a story accusing police of corruption.

Other scandals involving the Flying Squad soon followed.

In November 1971, the *Sunday People* ran a series of articles about the men behind London's burgeoning pornography trade, including a pornographer called Jimmy Humphreys. The paper accused them of corrupt dealings with officers from the Obscene Publications branch.

The same newspaper then revealed that Commander Kenneth Drury, head of the Flying Squad, had been on holiday in Cyprus where Humphreys, a man with nine convictions to his name including a spell in Dartmoor prison, had been his host.

Drury was served with disciplinary papers and suspended. He immediately resigned. Before doing so, however, he wrote an article for the *News of the World* claiming that Humphreys had been one of his informants.

The furious pornographer, aware of the effect that such a claim could have on his many contacts, responded a week later through the columns of the same paper, saying that the opposite was the case — he had never received any money from Drury but instead had wined and dined the police chief on a total of fifty-eight occasions and had always picked up the bill.

At his eventual trial Flying Squad Chief Drury said it was 'absolutely essential' for Flying Squad officers to mix socially with people connected with the criminal fraternity.

Drury claimed: 'During my career, I made a point of

mixing with criminals. It is essential that you do so. You cannot expect them to give information about crimes if you ostracise them except when you want information from them.'

As Drury wrote in his *News of the World* article: 'A good detective is only as good as his informants. And a copper's informants, by their very nature, are going to be villains or associates of villains. So where do you draw the line? You can't talk to a snout only when you want something out of him. He's got to know and trust you... all of which means that you've just got to mix with him socially, in his own surroundings, whether they be a scruffy little back-street caff or a plush restaurant or nightclub. You've got to be part of that scene.'

That, claimed Drury, was the way it would always have to be inside the Flying Squad. 'The lads are in and out all the time, getting around, being seen, keeping themselves in the know about what the underworld are up to.'

The problem with the Drury philosophy was that it left detectives wide open to accusations of corruption. Criminals, like Kenny Noye, would happily help police in an effort to divert attention from their own activities while at the same time obtaining, through the usefulness of the information given, a degree of protection from prosecution.

This was where corruption could occur, in the form of a detective either turning a blind eye to what was going on in return for a cut of the action or, if the information led to the recovery of stolen property, pocketing some of the reward money claimed by the detective on the informant's behalf.

Those are not, of course, the only possible opportunities for corruption among detectives. A strategically placed officer can, for a fee, ensure bail is granted, hold back evidence and details about past convictions from a court, or pass on to a person under investigation details of a case being made against him or warnings about police operations in which he could become compromised. Corrupt officers could also hold on to a proportion of whatever valuables they recovered during an inquiry.

By the late 1970s — as Kenny Noye's illegal activities continued to grow — it was the reward money that he and others occasionally collected for pointing the police in the right direction that enabled him to keep all his illegal activities going unhindered.

At this time, for a variety of reasons, the Flying Squad was completely overhauled. Instead of dealing with serious crimes in general, they would in future tackle only armed robberies, with the Squad's officers forming a central robbery squad run from a co-ordinating unit at Scotland Yard and four smaller groups strategically placed around London.

The newly appointed Deputy Assistant Commissioner David Powis also ordered a crackdown to stop corrupt policemen from creaming off reward money meant for informants. In future all payments amounting to more than £500 would be handed over by the DAC himself.

For the Kenny Noyes of this world it meant that every bit of information he fed to the police would have to serve a purpose for him rather than simply enable him to claim some extra cash. It didn't really bother Noye because he was more interested in scheming the downfall of his rivals than making a few extra bob.

He was trying to build an empire and no one seemed prepared to get in his way.

7: Flash Kenny

The spectre of corruption hung over Scotland Yard like a dense mist that would not disperse. 'Operation Countryman' was launched after a supergrass alleged that gangs who had carried out three armed robberies were linked to corrupt police officers.

It took nearly four years for the investigation to run its course and when it did, it ended in successful prosecutions against just three detectives, only one of them from the Metropolitan Force.

Members of the Operation Countryman team claimed their efforts to expose corruption had been 'nobbled' because so many detectives had skeletons in their cupboard.

By this time the problem of obtaining satisfactory evidence in some cases led disillusioned policemen to collect what little proof they could find, arrest a suspect and attribute to him remarks, partial admissions and sometimes full confessions that had never been made. This process became known as 'verballing'.

In court the defendant would deny ever making the remarks attributed to him and accuse the police of lying. But the police would often reap some benefits.

With the permission of the judge the prosecution would generally be allowed to tell the jury of the defendant's previous criminal convictions, which the police hoped would sway a case in their favour.

However, detectives who did not resort to 'verballing' were just as likely to have accusations of fabrication levelled against them as those who did — leaving the jury unable to distinguish between honest and dishonest officers and increasing the chance of acquittal for a guilty defendant.

Detectives who denied a suspect access to a solicitor for fear that inquiries might be hampered, would have this drawn to the jury's attention as further proof of unfair treatment. The provisions contained in the Police and Criminal Evidence Act of 1984 were introduced supposedly to ensure that defendants did have access to a solicitor within 36 hours of their arrest.

It is widely believed, rightly or wrongly, that the network of corrupt detectives known as the 'firm within a firm' still exists, flourishes and resists all efforts to expose it. Some allege that detectives have organised crime in London for years, planning and physically carrying out robberies and burglaries as well as stealing rewards and extorting money for bail, privileges and weakened prosecutions.

In the late 1970s, it was thought that London had the most corrupt detective force in the country, oiled by a handful of 'brokers' who linked criminals with corrupt policemen and in return received money and a licence to commit crime. All of these allegations may, or may not, have a basis in fact, or they may simply be the fantasies of convicted criminals.

But they fuelled the attitudes of people like Kenny Noye.

* * *

Around this time the first in a series of unexplained deaths of people connected to Kenny Noye occurred. These crimes could be entirely coincidental, but they none the less make for very disturbing reading.

Barbara Harrold, one of Noye's neighbours in West Kingsdown, suffered massive and fatal injuries in a bizarre parcel bomb attack in 1979.

Mrs Harrold, 55, was along with her husband Gordon, director of a firm that made packaging for military weapons and initially police suspected a terrorist link.

Then attention switched to Keith Cottingham, an

underworld associate of Kenny Noye, who had earlier bought a Costa Blanca villa from the Harrolds but fell out with them over a tax bill. Cottingham fled to Spain three days before the blast in the kitchen of Mrs Harrold's cottage at Ingtham, near Sevenoaks. Kent police named Cottingham as prime suspect in the murder of Mrs Harrold.

At that time the link to Kenny Noye seemed irrelevant to detectives, but attention would switch to him many years later.

* * *

One of Kenny Noye's greatest joys was that he was able to claim an energetic sex life as a legitimate working expense, part of the important business of establishing cover and hideouts.

For Noye was more than capable of ruthlessly exploiting his sexual conquests, although there has never been any evidence that he was calculating enough to make his initial approaches only in the line of duty. Doubtless there are women all over south-east London and elsewhere who went to bed with Noye and were not asked to store any of his merchandise or hide his gold or cash.

Throughout his marriage to Brenda, Noye always had at least two mistresses, although there were usually more than that. These women's homes were places of sanctuary, somewhere he could be assured, without warning, of getting a bed for the afternoon or early evening. He preferred not to stay out all night.

Many of these women were born and bred in Kent. Two of them were even the wives of Noye's childhood friends. Noye preferred familiar surroundings in more ways than one. He obviously felt safer dealing with people he already knew.

It was only in later life, as he became richer and more reckless, he would break that rule.

Noye was proud of his sexual conquests and many of his closest associates knew about them. He also always managed at least one night a week out with his male friends when he would drink Bacardi and lemonade and regale his pals with stories of his latest adventures.

However, it was the women who mattered most. They all found in Noye great charisma and charm.

By the early 1980s Noye would secretly meet at least two glamorous blonde girlfriends in hotels near his home. But in his newly acquired Rolls Royce he didn't exactly go unnoticed.

Back in West Kingsdown he maintained the image of a happily married, family man, living quietly with wife Brenda and their two sons Kevin and Brett.

In 1983, Noye bought wife Brenda a squash club in nearby Dartford for £100,000. It seemed the perfect way to keep her busy and make some money.

Noye also became a keen marksman. He liked shooting at a local range with several guns he'd purchased over the years. Despite his criminal record, Kenny Noye had no trouble getting firearms licences. He even turned up as guest marksman at one Kent police firing range.

However, at the village school in West Kingsdown, teachers continued to wonder exactly what wealthy Kenny Noye did for a living.

There was even talk of guns being sewn into curtains. What that actually meant no one really knew... or dared ask.

Among Kenny Noye's tight-knit circle of friends at this time were the Hedley family. Vic Hedley ran a haulage company similar to the one that Kenny had owned. He had also lived in West Kingsdown for most of his life.

Kenny, Brenda and the children would often go to the Hedleys' for Sunday lunch. However, the two families suddenly stopped seeing each other in the early 1980s. Neither of the wives knew the reason for this sudden fall out.

In fact, Noye and Hedley had argued about money Noye believed he was owed by Hedley over a supposed 'business deal' concerning the sale of some lorries.

Kenny Noye never forgot those who crossed him.

* * *

Kenny Noye's attitude towards the police baffled many of his underworld associates. Noye believed he could feed information to detectives and in exchange they would leave him alone. The problem was that most officers saw Noye as only a one-way ticket. They did not like the way he kept trying to make up the rules as he went along. Neither did many of the older south-east London villains.

'Careless talk costs lives and stuff like that,' says one south-east London criminal from the Krays' era. 'It was bred in you from the time you're a kid not to talk to the Old Bill. I don't even know any major informers from my age group.'

However, Noye was considerably younger than those who'd worked with or against the Krays and Richardsons. To him, informing was a currency that enabled him to thrive.

As the old timer added: 'They weren't brought up the same way as we were. We were taught that to be a Judas and inform on your own people was the ultimate sin.'

Kenny Noye wasn't interested in 'traditional' criminal behaviour. He had money to make.

* * *

Secret police records relating to Kenny Noye's criminal career up until this stage in his life were supplied by a police source to this author in March 2000. They provide a fascinating insight into Noye's activities in those early days.

On 10 October 1981 Noye appeared in Canterbury Crown Court for importation of a firearm, evasion of VAT, providing a counterfeit document after his arrest, making a false statement to the VAT and breaking the conditions of an earlier suspended sentence. He was extremely fortunate to get a suspended prison sentence plus a £2,500 fine. Some police officers to this day believe that Noye's 'friends' in the police helped him avoid incarceration.

But over the following couple of years police put Noye under regular surveillance in connection to many of his illicit activities — and even carried out a number of raids with search warrants on his premises in West Kingsdown. Detectives claimed in a highly secret Crime Intelligence Report that Noye was running a stolen motor vehicle parts ring which also involved exporting lorry equipment to Syria. The report referred to Noye's penchant for using an alias of Kenneth James and how he kept a luxury flat in Broomfield Road, Bexleyheath, where neighbours reported seeing him in the company of numerous women.

Detectives also recorded Noye's involvement with more than a dozen companies and his list of 'associates' read like a *Who's Who* of south east London and Kent criminals. At that time Noye was driving a Rolls Royce, a Chieftain Jeep and various Fords he was buying directly from Fords in Dagenham and then selling on for a mark-up.

One of Noye's former employees at his yard in West Kingsdown told police he was terrified of Noye and stated that he had 'suffered violence at the hands of Noye in the past'. There is also mention of 'Noye buying and supplying drugs' and the passing over of £10,000 in cash to an unnamed man in the Black Swan pub, on the Mile End Road. The same informant also claimed that Noye handled money from a robbery in the Blackwall Tunnel.

The report also states: 'Noye allegedly puts up the money for organised crime, he being an associate of prominent London criminals. Noye travels to and from America and the Continent to allegedly change money.' Police were even told that Noye had provided hundreds of thousands of stolen bricks for the construction of a housing estate called The Hollies, in Gravesend.

But most ominous of all, the police report names an MP with whom Noye 'had a business association'. And the secret report concludes: 'Noye appears a good class criminal and appears to be currently involved in crime.' The report also featured Noye's full criminal record from before his most recent appearance at Canterbury Crown Court. It read as follows:

14.12.66   Old Street Magistrates Court. Found on

enclosed premises for unlawful purposes. 12 month conditional discharge and £2.20 costs.

20.6.67   South East London Q.S.

Receiving stolen vehicles. Receiving stolen property. Found on enclosed promises for unlawful purpose. Borstal Training.

20.5.75   Marlborough Street Magistrates Court.

Theft of sunglasses. Assault on police. Fined £50. Ordered to pay £15 costs. Also fined £15.

21.2.77   Croydon Crown Court.

Handling stolen property (5 cases). Possessing document with intent to deceive. Unlawful possession of a shotgun. For all the charges Noye was fined £2100 and ordered to pay almost £8,000 in compensation plus costs. He also got a two year suspended prison sentence.

21.3.79   Malling Magistrates Court.

Dishonestly abstracting electricity. Fined £250.

* * *

Back in West Kingsdown, Kenny Noye was finding the local council disappointingly incorruptible.

Village councillors insisted on inspecting a vast outbuilding in the grounds of Hollywood Cottage — it was actually an aircraft hangar-sized drive-in shed large enough to keep at least two articulated lorries under complete cover.

When Noye was asked why he would need such a huge building he replied: 'Well, it's me apple store, innit?'

'But where are the apples, Mr Noye?' asked one inquisitive councillor.

'Over there,' said Noye, pointing at about a dozen small apple trees growing in the front garden of Hollywood Cottage.

The councillors immediately concluded that Noye wanted to load and unload lorries without anyone else seeing what was happening.

Visitors to Hollywood Cottage also noted with amusement

the kennels that Noye's two Rottweiler dogs Cleo and Sam lived in. They were brick built, with tiled roofs and normal household plastic drainage all round. They even had tubular heating inside to keep the dogs warm during the winter.

However, it was Noye's security precautions that seemed to suggest he had a lot to hide. A public footpath that ran along the far side of the property and enabled anyone to walk on to his land was of major concern. Noye erected a seven-foot-high fence along the entire perimeter complete with razor-edged barbed wire.

Noye proudly told one neighbour that he kept the Hollywood Cottage pool at a temperature of ninety degrees all the time because Brenda liked it that way. He didn't bother mentioning that he was still stealing the electricity for the heating from the mains supply at the end of the road.

While Kenny Noye deliberately kept a low profile in West Kingsdown, his sister Hilary — a teacher married with two children — was a pillar of the local community in nearby Hever Avenue. She attended church most Sundays with her family and was even a member of the church council at one time.

Undoubtedly Kenny Noye was a good father to his children. He regularly played football with them in the grounds of Hollywood Cottage. On hot summer's nights he'd put up a tent with the boys and they'd sleep overnight in the garden.

To the outside world he gave an entirely different impression.

'You always got the feeling there was a hard man there. He could be soft underneath in his dealings with his family, but he knew exactly what he wanted and always seemed to get it,' says one associate.

Other disputes with neighbours in West Kingsdown included an argument over eighteen inches of his land after Noye had put that seven-foot-high fence around the entire 20-acre property. Noye turned up at the 'offending' neighbour's house with a bulldozer and both his Rottweiler dogs.

'You do realise that this does not represent the actual

markings of the plot?' the neighbour pointed out coldly.

Noye did not hesitate in his reply.

'Yes, that's quite right. You're the only one along here who's not registered.'

Noye had actually gone to the local council registry and checked out the deeds of every house surrounding his property.

The neighbour did not pursue the matter.

Yet, despite Noye's fondness for flashy cars and clothes he still had a reputation as a 'tight-arsed sod', as one of his relatives put it. The family member explained: 'Once we were in the pub and Kenny owed one of his cousins some money. I think it was 50p. It might not seem much now, but in those days it could buy two pints of bitter. Anyway Kenny pulled every trick in the book to avoid paying that money. It became a bit of a game with him. He got a kick out of avoiding paying.'

In 1980 a friend in the construction industry introduced Kenny Noye to a man named Lorenzo Ferreiro, who lived in Barcelona. Ferreiro, a mining engineer, was a technical adviser to the United Nations and travelled frequently to Africa, particularly Rwanda, from where he claimed he could arrange for gold to be smuggled. The following year, the smuggling started and Kenny Noye's construction industry friend arranged for the gold to be taken to the Al Humaidu company in Kuwait, where it was refined. It was Noye's first big breakthrough on the illicit gold market.

Noye, using the name Sidney Harris, put up £50,000 to finance the first deal. He was wary of investing more because of the risks of moving into a Third World country. In Noye's mind he could end up being shot or robbed. He didn't like that kind of vulnerability.

Following that first run, Al Humaidu drew up a contract with Ferreiro and 'Sidney Harris', guaranteeing the two of them commission if they could find purchasers for more of the company's gold.

Early in 1981, Noye set up an office and a smelter in Eindhoven, in the Netherlands, where he knew people through his transport business. Two Dutch colleagues ran the operation from a ground-floor office and a smelter brought from West Germany was installed in the basement. The gold arrived with a courier from Kuwait, who was paid in dollars from an Amsterdam bank.

Over the following four years, Noye received more than £3 million worth of gold from Kuwait at his office and smelters in Holland. He bought the gold at 3% under the fixed price, as no tax had been paid on it.

The dealers, based in Britain and abroad, then charged tax when selling it on to the open market and took that amount as their profit — of almost half a million pounds every year. Most of the gold was sold to one Noye contact on the Continent, a very shrewd 'frummer', as Noye called Jews.

In 1981 Noye's two American Mafia friends told Noye they had contacts in Brazil who were already smuggling gold into Belgium. They wanted him to use his operation in Holland to take in some of that same gold. Noye even discovered the company was being given financial aid by the Brazilian government who were trying to encourage all exports at the time.

As Noye later admitted: 'The government of Brazil at that time was a military government, and military governments are always on the fiddle. This one certainly was.'

Noye was soon exporting the Brazilian gold to his Dutch operation, once again agreeing to buy it at 3% under fixed price.

By 1982, Kenny Noye was running a gold-smuggling operation that was worth £20 million a year. His profit alone came to £1.3 million. The following year that total reached £32 million, although his profit only went up to £1.6 million. In 1984 it climbed to £35 million, although his profit that year dropped to £1.5 million.

Large quantities of that gold reached Britain, but Noye remained largely uninvolved in that end of the smuggling operation. It was left to people who'd already purchased the gold from him.

Despite his ever-increasing wealth, Noye continued

frequenting many of the most notorious pubs and clubs in south-east London. His favourite hang-out at this time was The Pink Elephant afterhours drinking club in Peckham.

In 1982, Kenny Noye confounded those who claimed he was a cold heartless criminal by showing the hand of kindness to a neighbour in distress. The Noyes offered West Kingsdown greengrocer Alan Cramer their sincere condolences when his 26-year-old son was killed in a car crash on nearby Death Hill.

Mr Cramer later explained: 'They sent me a nice letter with their condolences. It was one of the first we got. They said that if there was any help we needed we only had to ask and they would help in any way they could and they didn't mean money-wise. It was a nice thought.'

Many years later Mr Cramer returned their offer of kindness by staunchly sticking up for the Noyes when they faced problems with the police.

Noye also continued to show his real colours, including flashes of that short-fused temper.

In one pub he got into an argument with a man, charged out of the pub, went straight to his Rolls Royce and grabbed a shotgun he kept in the boot.

He walked back into the pub and went up to the man he'd been arguing with. Without saying a word he cocked the gun and pointed it straight at the other man. Then he lifted up the weapon and blasted it just above his head. It was almost a carbon copy of that earlier incident.

Nearer to West Kingsdown, Noye drank at The George in Bexley Village and The Sidney Arms in Chislehurst. At The George, Noye amused the locals when he announced one day he would no longer be driving his Rolls Royce to the pub.

'I've had enough of it being fucking keyed everytime I leave it in the car park here,' he told one regular, referring to the scratches that kept appearing on the bodywork.

From the following day, Noye turned up in an ancient, rusting Ford Escort van that had no MOT or tax.

'If the cozzers give me a hard time about it I'll call up one of my mates and get it sorted,' Noye told regulars at The

George.

Noye boasted to his cousin Michael Noye that he'd met numerous policemen when he attended a Freemasons' gala night with Brenda. He even had photographs taken to prove it. Noye gave the negatives of the pictures to his cousin to develop because his father owned a photo development business. He wanted some copies for his own photo album at home. Many years later Kenny Noye would demand them back with menace.

Despite increasingly close contact with various police officers, Kenny Noye continued to harbour a grudge against the same officer who'd tried to arrest him for a variety of petty offences since his younger days in Bexleyheath. The policeman had been promoted but still regularly bumped into Noye. He was well aware of Noye's attempts to ingratiate himself with other officers, but refused to be intimidated by him.

Others were far more wary of Noye for different reasons.

In 1980 one of the best-known robbers in London — Eastender John 'Little Legs' Lloyd — was warned off Kenny Noye by his criminal associates in south-east London. Lloyd and his common-law wife Jean Savage had bought Noye's bungalow from him in West Kingsdown a couple of years earlier.

'Noye wasn't considered one of us. He never wanted to get his fingers dirty. He thought he could get other people to do all his dirty work,' recalled one of Lloyd's friends.

Lloyd ignored the warning and even told Noye how he'd assembled an experienced London firm who were planning a huge job they believed could scoop them a fortune. It was a highly risky venture, but the rewards would entirely justify it.

However, none of them realised it would turn out to be the biggest robbery in British criminal history.

8: Men on a Mission

Outwardly there was little to commend Unit 7, a functional steel and brick box on a nondescript trading estate near London's Heathrow Airport. A second glance might pick out the surveillance cameras and spotlights mounted on the walls, and occasionally an errant alarm bell might attract the attention of curious passers-by.

It was only when, with a loud metallic crank, the huge orange-and-white armoured shutter doors rolled open that the building's real purpose was revealed. Then solidly built dark-blue vans, with barred and tinted black windows and a gold portcullis motif painted on each side, could be seen either entering or leaving the well-protected loading bay.

The Brink's-Mat security vans were a familiar sight on the trading estate, where the jokes and dreams about their cargoes had been overused long ago. Unit 7 wasn't Fort Knox or the Bank of England, but it did have one of Britain's biggest safes, used to store hugely valuable cargoes of currency, precious metals and other high-risk consignments often en route through Heathrow Airport.

That morning of 26 November 1983 was still pitch black and icy cold as the Saturday shift of workers waited outside to begin the new day. The men kicked their heels as they blew clouds of mist, waiting for 6.30am to arrive. Then the automatic timer would neutralise the sophisticated alarm

67

system, allowing the keys to be inserted without triggering flashing lights, bells and alarms linked with the local police station and other security companies.

Security guard Richard Holliday had been the first to arrive in his beige Ford Consul and he was quickly followed by another guard, Ron Clarke, on his moped. Guards Peter Bentley and Robin Riseley pulled up moments later, and the four men mumbled greetings to one another. A fifth guard rostered for duty, Tony Black, was late and still hadn't arrived when the man who would supervise the day's work drove up. Michael Scouse, 37, a former special constable, was the longest serving guard on duty that day, with twelve years on the Brink's-Mat payroll. His seniority singled him out that morning as the 'keyman'.

Scouse entered the unit alone and locked the door behind him, leaving the crew outside while he collected from the safe in a downstairs office another key with which he switched off the alarm system covering the perimeter walls and windows.

Scouse then went back to the main door to allow the crew in. The outside door was relocked from the inside, then Scouse reactivated the alarm system, climbed the stairs and walked through to the radio-control room to look through the paperwork for the day's duties. Meanwhile the four guards went into the rest room to take off their coats, Holliday paused briefly to switch on the radio-room aerials and the surveillance cameras before joining his mates.

Just then the doorbell rang. It was Black, not unusually ten minutes late, and the guards heard Scouse go downstairs to let him in.

'You look a bit rough,' called Bentley, as Black walked into the rest room. The 31-year-old guard did indeed look pale, unkempt and apprehensive, as if he had just clambered out of bed and raced to work. He confirmed Bentley's suspicion that he had overslept, then, mumbling something about having to use the toilet, he disappeared downstairs again.

Guard Riseley glanced at his watch, a casual reaction to

the late arrival of Tony Black. It was 6.40am.

* * *

'Get on the floor or you're fucking dead!'

The masked figure filling the doorway of the rest room spat out the words in a harsh Cockney accent, motioning urgently to the stunned guards with his 9mm Browning automatic pistol. Riseley dived from his chair to the floor, quickly followed by Clarke and Holliday.

On the floor Riseley could see a white man, perhaps 5 feet 8 inches tall and clean shaven, wearing a trilby and a dark coat or anorak over a black blazer, black trousers and a black tie. He might have been dressed for a funeral but for the yellow balaclava that he quickly hitched up to cover all but his eyes.

For a second or two nothing happened, then the gunman made a move that was to earn him the nickname 'The Bully' among the guards. Without a word he jerked his gun arm upwards and then, a silver blazer button glinting in the light, smashed the weapon down on the back of Peter Bentley's head. Standing by the sink making the tea, the guard had been slow to react when the door crashed open, believing it to be a colleague playing one of their regular practical jokes. As he fell, Bentley's head hit the table and then the floor, dazing him momentarily and opening two bloody gashes in his scalp. The attacker then beckoned through the open door to someone waiting outside, and another three, maybe four, robbers rushed into the room.

'Lie still and be quiet,' ordered The Bully, as his henchmen began to immobilise the terrified guards, yanking their arms behind their backs and handcuffing them, then locking their legs together at the shins with heavy-duty tape. Cloth bags with strings were then pulled down over the guards' heads and fastened around their necks.

One of the other guards managed a close look at the gunman, close enough to distinguish the herring-bone pattern of the tweed hat and the crispness of the starched white shirt. He even saw a lock of fair hair protruding from the balaclava as the bag was placed over his head.

Bentley could feel rough hands pulling at the house and car keys at his belt, then his watch was snatched off and thrown across the room. Blood from his throbbing head wound trickled down his face and neck.

A moment later a voice, sounding almost sympathetic, asked whether he was OK and loosened the drawstring a little.

Then Holliday found it difficult to breathe. Thrashing about on the floor, he managed to attract the attention of one of the robbers, who bent down and untied the drawstring, pulling the bag back to clear his upper lip. To ease the discomfort further he was turned on his back. Ron Clarke was similarly treated, first roughly bound then casually asked whether he was in any distress.

Moments later another man spoke, this time with no discernible accent, who was obviously used to giving orders. 'Get that radio tuned in. If you hear anything, tell us,' he commanded. The guards all immediately realised that this man was the boss.

Seconds later several men left the room. Then a radio crackled through frequencies as it tuned in to a Metropolitan Police wavelength. There was precious little happening outside the Brink's-Mat warehouse — two police officers could be heard discussing a spot-check on a vehicle but nothing more.

Several members of the gang then returned and hauled Holliday to his feet, dragging him down the corridor into the locker room. He was lowered to the floor and pushed back against a girder. They tried to handcuff him to the steel strut but failed because it was too large for his arms to encircle. He was handcuffed to a radiator instead. He was joined by Ron Clarke and they were left to listen to the noises echoing in the vault directly below them.

Senior guard Scouse was then hoisted to his feet and dragged outside into the corridor, where he was thrown against a wall.

'Breathe in,' ordered one of the robbers.

Scouse felt his shirt pulled up to his chin and then a hand tugged violently at his waistband.

'Breathe in deeply or you'll get cut.' Just then the knife sliced through his belted jeans from the buckle to the crutch. As Scouse filled his lungs he became aware of an overpowering smell. A rag had been waved under his nose.

'Do you recognise the smell?'

It was unmistakable. The next instant he felt petrol being poured over his genitals.

'You'd better do as I say or I'll put a match to the petrol and a bullet through your head. I know where you live. You live in a flat in Ruislip High Street above a TV rental shop. We've been watching you for nine months and setting this up for twelve. Now, let's go through the procedure. You have two numbers.'

It was all over in moments. Still with a gun in his back, Scouse looked over his shoulder and declared that the alarms were now neutralised. They were in.

In Unit 7's vault shortly before 7am that morning, the fluorescent lighting revealed nothing more than a carpet of drab grey containers, no bigger than shoeboxes, bound with metal straps and bearing handwritten identification codes. There were sixty boxes, containing altogether 2,670 kilos of gold worth £26,369,778. Also in the vault at Unit 7 were several hundred thousand pounds in used banknotes locked in three safes. One pouch contained traveller's cheques worth $250,000. In the other were polished and rough diamonds valued at £113,000.

As box after box was opened, an El Dorado of treasure was revealed. The atmosphere was electrified as, with scarcely concealed excitement, the gang then moved the gold out to the side of the loading-bay and into their waiting vans.

The Brink's-Mat gang had expected rich pickings, but not fabulous wealth. Their audacious plot, ruthless in its conception and brilliant in its execution, had just landed them the biggest haul in British criminal history.

* * *

Scotland Yard Commander Frank Cater needed the Brink's-Mat job like he needed the proverbial hole in the head. Months before this raid, another 'firm' had coolly taken £6 million in used banknotes during an Easter raid on a Security Express depot in London's East End. On that occasion a guard had also been doused in petrol. That robbery had been dubbed the 'Crime of the Decade' by the tabloids. Cater wondered whether the same gang was also responsible for what was eventually going to be called 'The Crime of the Century'.

After all, before these two raids, the previous holder of the title, had been the Great Train Robbery near Leighton Buzzard in Bedfordshire in 1963 and that had netted just £2 million.

Of the six Brink's-Mat guards one man stuck out like a sore thumb. He was the guard who had been out of the sight of the others in the minutes before the raid, and now the humming computers and buzzing telephone produced some damning intelligence. This guard, Tony Black, had a brother-in-law who was a well-known name on the south London criminal circuit. Brian Robinson had convictions for assaults on two policemen.

In the previous two years he had also beaten two armed robbery charges. One was thrown out by a magistrate because of insufficient evidence; the other, for handling money taken in an armed raid, was dropped when the Director of Public Prosecutions decided there was not enough evidence to offer to a court.

Meanwhile, within 48 hours of the robbery, Lloyds of London announced they were prepared to pay £2 million for information leading to the return of the Brink's-Mat gold, which had already leapt in value by more than £20 an ounce since the robbery.

It was only when detectives decided to reconstruct the

events of the robbery to test all the guards' evidence that they were able to nail Tony Black.

At 8am on Sunday 4 December, just eight days after the Brink's-Mat warehouse raid all six guards on duty that day were taken to Hounslow Police Station for questioning. Only Black was properly interrogated.

Six hours later Detective Inspector Tony Brightwell rose to his feet and told Tony Black: 'There are certain points that have arisen as a result of the original statement that you made, the video reconstruction of events and during this interview... to put it bluntly, we are not happy with your story. We will leave you to have a rethink.'

The detectives then let him sweat for more than an hour while they discussed his story over coffee in the canteen, eventually returning to the interview room at 4.52pm. They were certain of their ground, and the investigators delivered what they hoped would be their *coup de grâce*.

One detective sergeant eventually spent more than eight hours taking down Black's twenty-one page statement.

Black even admitted to investigators: 'I'm feeling much better now. It's like a weight off my mind. It was just too big. I couldn't handle it. There's one thing though. I'm worried about these people, what they're going to do.'

Minutes later Commander Frank Cater entered the room and waved the three detectives out. They believed they already knew the identity of Robinson's accomplices. Black had said that he thought the surname of the big man, Tony, was White.

Criminal intelligence had already confirmed that a Tony White and a younger man, Micky McAvoy, were known acquaintances of Brian Robinson. It was also known that White owned a vehicle similar to the car seen leaving the trading estate soon after the robbery.

The detectives went downstairs to collect the mugshots they had already taken from police files. There were two folders, each containing twelve photographs of various individuals. In each batch they had placed mugshots of McAvoy and White.

Shortly before midnight, after Commander Cater had finished with Black, DS Branch pushed the folders under Black's nose. The first file was opened, and the pictures spread across the table. Black immediately pointed to one.

'That's Mick,' he said. He had confirmed the detectives' suspicions. The photograph he pointed to was of The Bully, McAvoy.

They pushed the second folder over the table and Black again picked one out immediately. 'That's Tony,' he declared. It was a photograph of a man called Tony White.

In the early hours of Tuesday 6 December, Tony Black was led back to his cell.

But the Brink's-Mat investigation was only just beginning...

9: The Aftermath

Just a short while after the Brink's-Mat raid, residents in Jenton Avenue, Bexleyheath, began noticing some strange activity at the house owned by Kenny Noye's parents.

Almost every Saturday for years Noye and Brenda had visited his mother and father with their sons Kevin and Brett. However, early in 1984, Brenda began turning up at the bungalow at least an hour before Noye arrived in his Ford pick-up. Noye was then seen by neighbours carrying what looked like very heavy batteries through to the garage next to the Noye house.

An hour or so later, Noye would emerge from the bungalow with more 'batteries' which he carefully laid on the flatbed of the pickup truck before driving off. Brenda and the children followed shortly afterwards in the family Range Rover or Granada.

Noye went through exactly the same routine every Saturday morning for months.

It wasn't until a long time later that the neighbours put two and two together. And there is no doubt that his parents had no idea whatsoever of what was happening.

* * *

Meanwhile surveillance experts at Scotland Yard's specialist C11 group provided the detectives investigating Brink's-Mat with an intelligence package that gave them a head start on their suspects.

When that package was opened, the names of Brian Robinson and Micky McAvoy stood out. The C11 operation team had noted that McAvoy was cautious to the point of paranoia about his movements.

McAvoy, the Brink's-Mat team knew, would require particularly careful handling. Early in 1983 he had been arrested after his brother and another man were found with £250,000-worth of cocaine at Heathrow Airport. A search of various premises then revealed a large number of shotguns and pistols, as well as two chain saws. He was not just an armed robber, police believed, but an underworld armourer as well.

$$* \quad * \quad *$$

The gang who committed the Brink's-Mat robbery were well aware that Black had been picked up, but they faced a dilemma. If they stashed the gold and disappeared, it would be seen as clear confirmation that they had been on the raid. They decided instead to stay put.

In doing so they pinned their hopes on two factors. The first was the alibis that they had all set up as a precaution to cover their tracks. The second was the belief that Black would not talk. They couldn't have been more wrong.

In the early hours of one cold December morning, eleven days after the bullion robbery, Tony White, Micky McAvoy and Brian Robinson were taken to separate police stations to ensure that they did not have any idea Black had grassed them up.

Tony White was surly and uncommunicative. He denied all knowledge of the robbery in the interrogation room at Heathrow Police Station. Police wanted to know why there were groceries in the boot of his car and packed suitcases in his bedroom. They also wanted to know why White's young son was not at home. Officers believed White had been expecting a visit when the police raid occurred and had sent his son away. They also reckoned he'd cleaned the house to remove any forensic evidence that might have linked him to the raid.

'If I sit here with my mouth shut, you haven't got fuck-all. I know that,' White told one officer.

At West Drayton Police Station, Brian Robinson was similarly cautioned. He gave them what appeared to be a cast-iron alibi.

At Chiswick Police Station Micky McAvoy was proving just as frustrating for police officers.

By the end of the following day, all the detectives involved in interrogating the three compared notes. One had politely denied any wrongdoing, another had been aggressively blunt in his dealings with the police, and the third had maintained a stony silence. The first had a detailed alibi involving his wife, his sick mother and a brother all of whom would have to be interviewed. The second man could bank only on the word of his wife to confirm a Saturday morning lie-in. The prisoner in Chiswick would not divulge his alibi unless his solicitor was there to hear it.

The police had the detailed confession of a guard who claimed that all three were undoubtedly to blame, but so far the only evidence was circumstantial and there was not much of that. In addition, all three men had refused to sign the contemporaneous notes of the interviews. They knew that the veracity of the unsigned records could therefore be questioned in court. Any mistakes they may have made, any slips that opened up a chink in their armour, could be dismissed as fabrication. Without signatures at the bottom of each page, all the records so far taken could be denied totally as 'verbals'.

Within a few days legal wrangles in the High Court began to release the suspects. The starring role went to a lawyer who was to later feature prominently in the life of Kenny Noye.

Tony White's lawyer, Henry Milner, was an engaging public school-educated man who specialised in representing people accused of serious crimes such as armed robbery. He had issued a writ of *habeas corpus* on behalf of seven people held by police in connection with the raid. They were Tony White and his wife Margaret, Micky McAvoy and his wife Jacqueline, Mrs Patricia Dalligan, who lived at 7 Tarves Way, the house where security guard Black claimed the plot had been discussed and her sons, Stephen, 23, and Mark, 17.

Victor Durand QC read to the court a sworn statement by Milner that, in effect, challenged the police to charge the prisoners or release them. At that time the law did not define clearly how long police were allowed to hold suspects in custody without a charge unless it was under the Prevention of Terrorism Act.

Durand informed the judge, Mr Justice Taylor, that all seven prisoners had been denied their right to legal advice, and Milner's statement read that he had repeatedly asked for access to the prisoners but had been stopped from seeing them by the Flying Squad.

When counsel representing Scotland Yard replied that the *habeas corpus* action would be defended, the case was adjourned until the next morning but it never re-opened. At 9.30 that night White was charged, followed by Robinson and McAvoy. The others were released. The next morning the three defendants were brought to Feltham magistrates' court and remanded in custody on the charge of stealing gold and other valuables worth £26 million.

* * *

Two-timing Brink's-Mat guard Tony Black was sentenced to six years imprisonment. With remission for good behaviour he would not serve more than four years and was likely to get parole after just two. The sentence was accompanied by a grim warning from Judge David Tudor-Price: 'Never again will your life be safe. In custody you will be segregated at all times, and you and your family will for ever be fugitives from those you so stupidly and so wickedly helped.'

Commander Frank Cater told the court that for the prisoner's own safety, he wanted Black to spend the time leading up to the trial of the three alleged robbers in police custody rather than prison. He was utterly determined that nothing should stop Black from giving evidence when the time came. The application, which had been sanctioned at a senior level after talks between Deputy Assistant Commissioner Kelland and the Home Office, was readily granted.

On Monday 25 October 1984 White, Robinson and McAvoy were brought before Judge Tudor-Price at the Central Criminal Court to answer two counts each, those of conspiring to commit robbery and of robbery itself. All three pleaded not guilty.

A month later Judge Tudor-Price summed up by explaining to the jury that he would be dividing the case into five parts. The first would be the robbery itself and the 'uncontroversial' testimony of the 'five honest guards'. That would be followed by his consideration of Tony Black's confessed involvement. Parts three, four and five would deal with the case against each of the accused.

At 10.42am on Thursday 29 November 1984, Tudor-Price brought to an end his careful and thoughtful summing up.

'Members of the jury,' he said, 'in this case allegations have flowed thick and fast, and it is for you to decide which ones have substance.'

It wasn't until the following Sunday at 3.19pm that the jury finally returned with a verdict — White was found not guilty, McAvoy and Robinson, however, were guilty of robbery. All verdicts were delivered with a majority of ten to two.

Next morning the two defendants were each sentenced to twenty-five years' imprisonment.

Without parole Robinson, 41, would be 66 when due for release and McAvoy, 33, would be 58. Yet both men replied to the sentences with a simple and polite 'Thank you.'

Back at his home in south-east London, Tony White broke his self-imposed silence. 'If I'm innocent, then the other two are innocent. The evidence was the same for all of us. None of the three of us was involved. The reason the police pulled us in was because they've wanted us for a long time and were waiting for something like this to get us.'

For Black, Robinson, McAvoy and White the Brink's-Mat job was over. For the police and Kenny Noye it was only just beginning.

* * *

Detectives investigating the Brink's-Mat robbery were now convinced that John 'Little Legs' Lloyd was also one of the original six members of the gang.

Lloyd — a legendary underworld hardman revered in criminal circles in his native East End — disappeared after he was tipped off that the police were on to him. When he finally resurfaced nine years later the Crown Prosecution Service announced there was insufficient evidence to proceed against him.

Indeed much of the time while he was a fugitive — taking advantage of his wealth by having shorts specially tailored to hide the spindly legs that earned him his nickname — Lloyd was actually back in Britain.

Yet such was his status in the East End that he drank and lived openly without the police ever being told. That was a measure of the criminal respect for Lloyd.

It was something his friend Kenny Noye had long admired.

10: Keeping a Low Profile

Among the criminal fraternity, the Brink's-Mat robbery was the stuff of legends. To stumble upon so much gold and then get away with enough to set dozens of people up financially for life was the sort of dreamscape scenario that few could ever hope for. But the sheer size of the Brink's-Mat haul of gold bullion created a huge problem for the criminals involved in the raid.

The gang needed a mechanism, a conduit down which the gold could travel. It had to be smelted and sold into industry before any of the huge amounts of cash could materialise.

There was also enormous paranoia in the London underworld about whether Robinson and McAvoy would turn supergrasses in exchange for lighter sentences.

The gang had to look outside their close circle of associates to find people to handle the gold.

This was the first big mistake of the Brink's-Mat firm. Here were villains who'd known each other for years and now they were having to put their trust in people such as Kenny Noye. He might have been known by John 'Little Legs' Lloyd but the rest of the gang had heard the whispers about criminals like Noye.

Kenny Noye and his criminal associates got close to the Brink's-Mat gang during this period even though they tried to ensure that the Brink's-Mat investigators did not observe them doing anything in connection with the stolen bullion.

Once during the early months of the investigation, Kenny Noye and a number of other 'faces' attended the marriage of the daughter of one of south-east London's best-known criminals. A wedding photographer started snapping away at Noye and some of the other 'faces'. Noye immediately lost his temper, pushed the photographer up against a wall and removed the film from his camera.

Kenny Noye had a particular aversion to having his photo taken, even at a public function such as a wedding. He suspected the photographer might have been a policeman in disguise.

As his cousin Michael later explained: 'Kenny didn't like any photos of himself to be floating around. He knew that if people outside his own circle didn't know what he looked like then he'd be able to move around much more easily.'

Yet Noye was considered a 'bit of bumpkin' by some of the Brink's-Mat robbery gang.

As Kathy McAvoy, Micky's second wife, explained: 'Noye wasn't from south-east London. He was from the suburbs and that just isn't the same. Bexleyheath ain't south-east London in the true sense. Noye wasn't the real thing and he knew the rest of us thought that.'

There was also a feeling among some of the Brink's-Mat 'faces' that Kenny Noye would not keep the code of honour that existed between the team involved in the robbery.

At that same wedding Noye also spent some time with Brian Reader, one of south-east London's most notorious burglars. The two men had done some business together in 1981 that ended up earning them both at least £200,000 each. Naturally, the subject of Brink's-Mat came up.

On 24 May 1984 Noye flew to Jersey clutching a suitcase containing £50,000 in £50 notes. Turning up unannounced at the Charterhouse Japhet (Jersey) Ltd bank in St Helier, he said he wanted to purchase gold worth about £100,000, which worked out at eleven one-kilo bars.

A surprised bank official told him that he couldn't just walk in off the street and buy gold — references would have to be taken up with his bank, and he would also have to open up an account at Charterhouse Japhet. Noye immediately opened an account in his own and his wife Brenda's name.

He was then told a cash deposit would be needed before negotiations could begin.

Noye then agreed to deposit the £50,000 in the company's account at the Midland Bank adding that, once back in England, he would arrange the transfer of the outstanding £47,322.50 from his own bank account.

Further purchases, he told the bank staff, would follow.

'It's an investment for my son,' Noye told bank staff.

'Once we've cleared it all I want to pick up the gold,' added Noye, much to amazement of the bank staff who thought that sounded like a highly risky move.

'There could be some security problems with you carrying such a valuable amount of gold, Sir.'

'Don't worry about that,' replied an increasingly cool Noye.

Then Noye hesitated.

'Will the serial numbers on the bars be shown on my receipts?' asked a puzzled Noye.

'No, Sir.'

Noye smiled.

Eight days later Noye returned to Jersey, travelling under the name of K. Swan and collected the bullion. This time he claimed the gold was to minimise his possible tax liabilities in England.

'Are you sure you feel safe carrying that amount around, Sir?'

Noye didn't bat an eyelid.

'No problem. In any case I want to make sure there's no connection between the bank and me.'

The bank staff continued with their work, then Noye made a strange request.

'Have you got something I could take the bars away in?'

A plastic shopping bag was provided.

'No one will suspect that I've got all this gold in 'ere,' chuckled Noye, as he picked up the straining plastic bag and walked casually out of the bank.

Kenny Noye's naïvety in expecting the bank not to be suspicious about his dealings has always surprised both his enemies and his friends.

Charterhouse Japhet immediately contacted Jersey detective DCI Charles Quinn, the Glasgow-born head of the island's CID.

Earlier that very same morning, Quinn had received a call from criminal intelligence contacts in London, tipping him off that Noye was arriving on a flight from Gatwick Airport. Quinn was even requested to put Noye under surveillance.

Special Branch officers at Jersey Airport spotted Noye as soon as he left the plane and CID officers watched as he went to collect the gold.

When he emerged 25 minutes later he was followed on foot to the TSB bank. There Noye hired a safe-deposit box, where he stored the gold after obtaining a form that allowed his wife access to the box. When he left the bank, detectives continued to follow him through St Helier but eventually lost him.

An hour later Noye arrived at the airport from the bank to catch a plane home. He walked through the airport security screen when he was stopped by a Special Branch officer and asked to fill out an embarkation form.

For the first time Noye actually felt nervous. His animal instincts for survival told him that something was wrong.

Noye entered his correct name and address on the form but couldn't, or wouldn't, produce any documents to prove his identity. Then he presented his ticket, which carried the name of K. Swan.

'I got it cheap off a mate who works at the airline,' volunteered Noye.

'What have you been doing in Jersey, Mr Noye?' asked the Special Branch man.

Noye squinted and looked irritated.

'Business.'

'What kind of business?'

'Just business...'

A worried Noye then walked on to the plane. He knew he'd been sussed but he also knew that whoever it was had decided it was too early to 'pull' him. He had better be very careful.

Noye never returned to Jersey to pick up the gold he had deposited. If he had, then the authorities would have been informed immediately. For after that visit to the TSB his safe-deposit card had been marked in large letters: CARE: DO NOT ALERT THE CUSTOMER, with a warning that should either Noye or his wife appear at the counter, senior officials were to be told. They in turn were instructed to avoid acting suspiciously but to delay the customer for five to ten minutes while DCI Quinn was contacted, at his home if necessary.

Despite the Fraud Squad's letter to the Jersey Police, Kenny Noye's activities in Jersey were not deemed sufficiently interesting for any further police action to be taken.

It was some months before detectives realised they had made a big mistake. For Noye had obtained something he considered far more valuable than the gold locked away in the safe-deposit box: he had receipts showing that he had legitimately purchased eleven gold bullion bars.

Those receipts could be produced to explain away any stolen or smuggled gold he was found in possession of, provided it was eleven bars or less. It was an elaborate cover for future criminal transactions.

For some months Noye then went about his business without attracting any more attention.

In the middle of 1984 Kenny Noye went to his bank manager.

For many years the manager had been aware that Noye had been taking money out of the country in suitcases to deposit in one or other of his offshore banking funds. On two occasions earlier in 1984 Noye deposited a total of £600,000 at the bank, the cash handed over in plastic carrier bags.

Noye then asked for banker's draft orders totalling the same amount to be sent to an account in the Isle of Man. Noye even followed up these deposits with at least another £200,000 which was transferred to the Isle of Man from another bank.

The manager even suggested to Noye that it might be

more convenient and certainly safer if he sent the money through the bank. He also told Noye this could be done by telegraphic transfer orders, without it going through or being reflected in his bank account.

In September 1984 Kenny Noye walked into a branch of the Bank of Ireland in St Michael's Road, Croydon, south London.

Dressed in a smart blue suit and glistening with gold jewellery, he called himself 'Sidney Harris' and inquired about the various facilities offered by the bank and its subsidiaries in the Isle of Man, Dublin and Jersey.

Eventually, he opted for an offshore account in Dublin, which, he said, would be in joint names, the other being Brenda Tremain (his wife's maiden name). He did not, he added, want statements sent to him and left the branch no means of contacting him.

His first deposit on 4 September was of £200,999 delivered in a small, black executive briefcase full of new £50 notes, divided into bundles of £12,500. He was shown into a private room on the first floor of the bank and the money, which he claimed was the proceeds from property development, was fed into the bank's cash-counting machine.

Over the following four months four such deposits were made, earning something like 9% interest, the claim being that Kenny Noye was in the building trade but had made a killing on the stock market. On one occasion 'Sidney Harris' even joked about buying a cash-counting machine himself but then decided it would be too expensive.

In September 1984, £800,000 of the money that he had sent to the Isle of Man and £1 million that he'd deposited in the Bank of Ireland during September went through the bank account at his local bank.

Noye later claimed the money had been sent over by his Florida business partners. They controlled one of the accounts in the Isle of Man. That money had come from their large illicit profits from property and gold that they couldn't bank in the USA because of the law stating that all amounts over $10,000 must be reported to the authorities.

Investing in sterling in the Isle of Man was an attractive proposition because the dollar was low against the pound at the time.

In October 1984 Noye arrived at his local bank with £150,000 and asked for transfer orders covering the amount to be sent to a Swiss bank with instructions that the money should be retained until collection by a Mr I. M. Bottom, bearing a British passport number B158417 as identification.

A few weeks later Kenny Noye, travelling with a passport stolen from Essex lorry driver Ian Bottom, flew to Zürich, collected the money and then deposited it in a Swiss bank account.

The transaction did not show up on his bank statements, but the bank did keep a record of them.

Meanwhile Noye even got his mobster friends in Miami involved.

Noye gave the Americans his false passport made out in the name of Sidney Harris so they could deal with the huge amount of money in the Bank of Ireland account. It was a classic money laundering operation in the autumn of 1984.

However, Noye's name was once again connected to Brink's-Mat. A detective inspector in C11, who had extensive knowledge of the south-east London criminal fraternity, received intelligence that Noye was moving large amounts of gold. Noye was also seen with a man who also required further investigation. That acquaintance was Brian Reader who, despite having only one criminal conviction for handling stolen property, was generally regarded as one of the best and most ambitious burglars in London.

Reader, aged 47, had secretly re-entered Britain earlier that year after being on the run in Spain with his wife, Lynn.

His exile had been prompted by a burglary charge that he faced at the Old Bailey. While on bail he fled with his wife, but the couple were forced to return to Britain when Lynn's mother fell ill. Reader had met up with Noye earlier at that underworld wedding and now lived just 15 miles from him in a house owned by an old schoolfriend (then a publican) in Winn Road, Grove Park, another suburb of south-east

London, close to the A20, which continued through to West Kingsdown.

Although Reader was a wanted man, police were content to let him carry on his activities because they believed that he was a vital cog in the machinery of the team that was handling the Brink's-Mat gold.

In November 1984 Reader met up with Noye at Brenda Noye's squash club in Dartford and asked him whether he could supply smuggled gold.

They agreed the price would be 3% above the fixed price and that deliveries would start after Christmas. Because of the number of £50 forgeries flooding the market at the time, payment would be made in new £50 notes that could be easily verified. As Reader was happy to pay 3% above the fixed price, it was clear that a VAT fraud was being committed.

Noye knew that such an operation required high levels of organisation. It was a very large business that needed dozens of people to run it and Noye was convinced that in the end the authorities would catch up with it. He should have been perfectly happy making over one million pounds a year on his own operation, which he believed could go on for years without any hindrance. But he wanted more.

By December 1984 suspicions about Kenny Noye and his friend Brian Reader were so strong it was decided that both would be targeted in a full-scale police investigation.

Scotland Yard did not inform Kent police of their plans. If they had, they would have discovered that Noye was issued with four new shotgun licences by the Kent constabulary at the same time as his link with Brink's-Mat was being established.

* * *

In the middle of all this activity, Kenny Noye managed somehow to find time to start an affair with yet another woman — the wife of one of his oldest friends.

Jenny Bishop was tall, blonde and shapely — very similar in many ways to Brenda Noye. She was also married to

Kenny Noye's old friend Dave Bishop.

Noye was so smitten by Jenny Bishop that he even bought her a £50,000 townhouse in Dartford and spent more than £20,000 on furnishings from Harrods. Noye considered the property a good investment. It was also much cheaper and safer than a hotel.

Noye had his liaisons with Bishop in the mid-afternoons and early evenings. That way he believed Brenda would not get suspicious.

Noye's affairs with women seemed to represent some kind of release from the enormous pressure he was under due to his various illegal activities. He thrived on the excitement.

* * *

By early January 1985 Reader had received gold worth £3.66 million from Kenny Noye. The gold was often smuggled into Britain from Holland in the Tupperware lunchboxes of various lorry drivers.

The drivers took their vehicles to the quayside and left them to be shipped over to Britain unaccompanied, with the Tupperware boxes still on board.

British drivers then picked up the lorries when they arrived and took them to their destination. Reader took the gold back to his home in south-east London and Noye collected the contraband a few days later.

It was the perfect set-up. But greed would eventually spin the entire operation out of control.

11: The Experts

To mount an effective surveillance operation against Kenny Noye and Brian Reader, Scotland Yard needed carefully to reinforce their Brink's-Mat inquiry team.

By this stage it was down to just 20 officers following the successful convictions of Robinson and McAvoy. A new senior detective would have to be drafted in to take charge of the investigation and build up the squad to full strength once more.

That man was Acting Detective Chief Superintendent Brian Boyce, a former member of the anti-terrorist squad, who thought that promotion opportunities had long since passed him by.

The son of a West End barrow-boy, Boyce had one ambition on entering the police service — to become a top detective at Scotland Yard. Having achieved that aim (he was with Commander Frank Cater when the Kray twins were arrested) he had no desire to swap the gritty life of a detective out on the streets for the cosier confines of high office complete with never-ending bureaucracy and the shadow of Whitehall administration.

Brian Boyce's air of determined independence — he was an accomplished jazz musician, a mountaineer of considerable prowess and a man with a lasting interest in comparative religion — coupled with a professionalism born of sheer love for the job made him an officer who inspired great loyalty among Scotland Yard's élite detective force.

Boyce spent his National Service twenty-six years earlier in Cyprus, where he helped track down EOKA guerillas. He picked up some vital experience of surveillance and intelligence gathering — lessons that he was able to implement on the Brink's-Mat case.

Following some discreet inquiries among London gold dealers, police chief Brian Boyce put both Noye and Reader under constant surveillance, an operation that would initially involve only regular Flying Squad officers.

On Tuesday 8 January 1985 detectives moved into position in a row of bushes by the public road in West Kingsdown at the end of the long driveway to Noye's Hollywood Cottage.

Within minutes, at 9.05am, Brian Reader was observed leaving Noye's home in a green Cavalier and then driving back to his own house.

Twenty minutes later Reader left his house in Grove Park. He was shadowed by four unmarked Flying Squad cars to Cowcross Street in central London, close to Hatton Garden.

Reader parked up outside Farringdon Underground and mainline railway station and went to a telephone booth in the ticket hall to make a call.

One detective managed to walk close enough to Reader to see the phone number being dialled. It turned out to belong to a nearby shop.

Reader then walked out to the street, looked up and down, returned to the phone and dialled the number again. The same thing happened once more before Reader left the station and went into a café on the opposite side of the road.

Two detectives watched from a distance as Reader sat at a table in a booth with two other men. One of them was 24-year-old Thomas Adams, an asphalter by trade. The other was a well-known figure around Hatton Garden, a gold dealer named Christopher Weyman, who ran a business in Greville Street.

Reader wrote something on a piece of paper, which he then showed to the two men. Then the three of them left the café and walked across the road to Reader's car. Adams climbed in and took out an unusually heavy, oblong parcel about one foot long. The parcel was placed in the boot of a nearby white Mercedes sports car, which Adams and Weyman then drove away in.

Meanwhile at Hollywood Cottage other detectives saw a Ford Granada belonging to Michael Lawson drive up to the house. It was driven by a man aged about 20. The car left soon afterwards and was later spotted outside Noye's former home in Hever Avenue, just one mile away. That house was now owned by notorious East End gangster John 'Little Legs' Lloyd, a prime suspect in the Brink's-Mat bullion raid.

That Tuesday afternoon Noye was seen leaving Hollywood Cottage with another man in a blue Range Rover. Flying Squad officers followed from a discreet distance.

After 12 miles they watched as the Range Rover turned off the A20 Sidcup bypass into the secluded car park of the Beaverwood Club, a Spanish hacienda-style nightclub set back from the road behind a screen of trees.

Noye stayed for five minutes before driving off. Although the police did not realise it at the time, this was a secret rendezvous spot used by Noye to meet Reader away from any prying eyes.

Police knew for certain that Noye was the key to the distribution of the Brink's-Mat gold.

They were going to have to move closer to observe Noye and that would require a very specialised team of undercover officers, who could remain outside for long periods of time, no matter what the weather conditions.

That Wednesday, C11 officers from the Specialist Surveillance Unit took up position near the house. They were a handpicked group, no more than eight in total, whose instructors in reconnaissance and close-target surveillance included specialists from the SAS.

The C11 team training course even included hiding beneath floorboards, in a gap just 18 inches high, for three days at a time and spending a similar length of time dug into a hole in the ground in open countryside.

As Kenny Noye lived in Kent, approval had to be obtained from the Kent police force. But there was a problem. When the Met had arrested Noye in 1977 for receiving stolen goods, they had done so without the knowledge of the local force. It was decided that only the highest ranking Kent officers should be put fully in the picture.

The C11 surveillance team working in West Kingsdown established a command centre on a ground floor room in the Stacklands Retreat House, a convalescent home for Anglican clergymen opposite the entrance to Noye's home in quiet, woody School Lane.

A hideaway made from branches and leaves was then carefully constructed in bushes under an oak tree near the gates to the retreat so that round-the-clock observation could be carried out on Hollywood Cottage.

Just above the huge cast-iron gates that formed the entrance to the driveway to Noye's home, a video camera disguised as a birdbox was placed in an overhanging tree. On the road outside Reader's house in Grove Park a variety of vehicles were used to maintain observation.

At midday on the day after C11 had moved into position, Reader drove from his home in Grove Park to the Crest Hotel in Bexley where Noye was already waiting in his Range Rover.

As Reader's Cavalier approached, Noye did a U-turn and drove off towards London. Reader immediately followed. Not long afterwards the two vehicles turned into a side road and parked. C11 woman detective constable Myrna Yates, 36, shadowed the pair and, remaining hidden from view, watched as Noye handed Reader a black briefcase.

The following day Noye and Reader met at lunchtime in the car park of the Beaverwood Club. Fifteen minutes later, their police shadows followed Reader to the Royal National Hotel in Bedford Way, Bloomsbury, central London.

WDC Yates followed him into the hotel lobby to find Reader sitting at a table talking to Weyman and Adams —

the same men he'd met a few days earlier at Farringdon Station.

Ten minutes later they drove off in the same white Mercedes. C11 officers tailed the Mercedes via north London to Paddington railway station. Adams carried what appeared to be a very heavy brown briefcase. Both men seemed agitated. They made two telephone calls then bought two first-class rail tickets and boarded a train for Swindon, 80 miles west of London. On board the train with them were three surveillance officers.

On arrival in Swindon, Weyman made several phone calls. Then the two men sat and waited. Eventually they got up, shook hands and waved to each other as though they were about to part company.

One moved off only to be followed at a distance by the other, a deliberate ploy to try to establish whether someone was following them.

Further down the road the two men met up again and headed for a fish-and-chip bar in a street opposite the station.

Eventually a black Jaguar XJS pulled up. Inside were Garth Chappell — the 42-year-old managing director of bullion company Scadlynn based in North Street, Bedminster, a rundown area of Bristol — and Terence Patch, a Bristol businessman who worked for the company.

Adams and Weyman immediately placed the heavy briefcase in the boot of the Jaguar. It sped off, with detectives following, back to Scadlynn.

At about 6.30pm Adams and Weyman returned by train to Paddington Station. They were clutching another briefcase.

This time C11 shadows followed them as they got into the white Mercedes and drove to Russell Square in central London where Weyman handed the briefcase to Colin Reader.

The following day Reader made yet another visit to the car park of the Beaverwood Club. He made a phone call from a public call box and stayed in the car park for just eight minutes this time.

Then the trail went cold. None of the suspects did anything to alert the attention of the police surveillance operation until six days later when Reader made an evening visit to Noye's home at Hollywood Cottage. Then he drove to Cowcross Street where once again he was met by the white Mercedes.

This time a man leaned into Reader's car while he examined some papers, but their C11 shadows couldn't make out what was being said. Eventually the man at the window returned to the Mercedes and drove off. Police almost immediately lost the car in the thick London traffic.

Five days later Reader once again visited Cowcross Street where he met Adams in the café they had used before.

Twenty-five minutes later a taxi pulled up. Weyman and a man wearing a brown sheepskin jacket got out, both carrying boxes.

Adams emerged from the café and opened the boot of his sports car where the boxes were then left.

The group adjourned to the cafe for thirty minutes, then the boxes were transferred to the boot of Reader's car. Reader, followed by C11, then headed out of London towards Hollywood Cottage.

The following day Reader again returned to that same café in Cowcross Street. This time he was seen talking to an acquaintance who was a jeweller long-suspected by police of being a fence for stolen goods.

While the two men were talking the white Mercedes drew up and Weyman entered the café. Reader took a green Marks and Spencer's carrier bag from his pocket and placed it on the table between them, keeping his hands carefully resting on the package. Weyman handed an envelope to Reader, who immediately let go of the package.

Once again Reader then went to Noye's house where he stayed briefly before heading home.

Within fifteen minutes of arriving back at his own house he drove back to the Royal National Hotel. He rejoined the jeweller from earlier that day and they sat looking out of the window until the white Mercedes arrived again.

As soon as it pulled up, Reader and the jeweller left the hotel and joined Weyman. The three of them walked across to Reader's Cavalier. Adams — who had left his sports car to join them — was handed a large package wrapped in brown paper, which he dropped into his own car before moving off.

Adams then headed for the M4 motorway. An hour and a half later he took Junction 15, the Swindon turn-off, and 200 yards further on pulled into the car park of The Plough, a small country pub.

Adams parked directly behind the Jaguar previously seen by C11 outside Scadlynn Ltd run by Terence Patch.

The boots of both cars were opened and a group of men clustered around the Mercedes. Then two men lifted a heavy object out of the boot and transferred it to the Jaguar. Surveillance officers knew it had to be gold.

The Jaguar then left the pub car park and headed westwards, with C11 in discreet pursuit. The car took the Bath exit of the motorway but was soon lost in the twisting country lanes close to where one of the suspects lived. The next morning detctives saw it parked outside Scadlynn.

On the following Thursday evening Brian Reader once again visited the Royal National Hotel. This time Weyman appeared with a large brown leather briefcase with fold-over flaps. Reader took the case to Kenny Noye's house later that same night.

The police surveillance team knew that the Brink's-Mat gold was still on the move.

*　*　*

After almost three weeks of surveillance, Operational Commander Brian Boyce gave a briefing in a south London police station to the twenty or so officers who had so far been involved in the surveillance operation. Warrants were obtained from a London magistrate for raids on thirty-six addresses in Kent, London and the Bristol area.

Boyce believed that all or part of the £26 million worth of gold was at Hollywood Cottage, but he couldn't be absolutely certain because some of the Reader transactions had been somewhat confusing.

Reader had been seen handing over heavy packages, but he had also received some which he'd then taken to Noye's home. Was it possible that Reader was also acting as a conduit to Noye from some other source, delivering the gold to Hollywood Cottage for some kind of processing before handing it on further down the chain?

There was also another dilemma for Brian Boyce. If the Flying Squad postponed some of the raids, would those people remaining think they had escaped detection and unwittingly lead police at a later date to more of the Brink's-Mat bullion?

Boyce had three options:

1. He could pounce at West Kingsdown and then decide what to do about London and Bristol.
2. He could intercept the gold at Scadlynn and follow up with further raids in Kent and London.
3. He could move in while the gold was actually in transit and then decide which raids to carry out.

Boyce decided that it would be the movement of Reader and Noye that would determine which of these three options he chose. Meanwhile the special surveillance unit would continue their observation of Hollywood Cottage to provide the most detailed information possible on movements.

Teams of Flying Squad officers would cover other areas:

- One would be placed on standby at the clergyman's retreat to remain in contact with the C11 post.
- A second Flying Squad team would be posted close to Reader's home.
- A third team would be in place in central London.
- A fourth would take up positions in the M4 area, west of London.

- A smaller fifth unit was to be kept mobile, ready to give back-up when and where it was needed.

Boyce set a 72-hour time limit for the operation. That meant they had to move in at some point within that period, otherwise the operation would have to be aborted.

The cost of police overtime over a weekend made this a necessity. Also, seventy-two hours was the maximum time that a surveillance officer could be expected to remain hidden and continue to be competent.

Boyce and his senior officers also knew that Noye kept firearms at Hollywood Cottage. However, he decided that none of his men would be armed. Boyce saw no evidence that people's lives would be in danger. Noye's shotguns, he felt, were not kept for criminal purposes but were part of the country-squire image he had been trying to build for himself in West Kingsdown.

Brian Boyce knew that the Brink's-Mat robbers were violent men, but he believed that in this instance they were dealing with the middlemen, not the robbers.

Boyce's decision was also influenced by the outcry two years earlier when Stephen Waldorf, a film editor, had been shot five times and seriously wounded in a London street when mistaken for a violent criminal.

A C11 police officer had been subsequently accused of attempting to murder Waldorf. Although the officer was later acquitted, the incident had led to a massive reappraisal of the circumstances in which British police should be armed. Brian Boyce had been working at C11 at the time and was one of the officers party to authorising the arming of the officer in question.

There was also another factor behind Brian Boyce's decision. If an armed officer of one force entered the area of another, the Chief Constable of the second force had to be informed immediately and had to provide armed officers from among their own men as back-up. There was a real fear that someone might tip off Kenny Noye about the surveillance operation.

Boyce's other problem was that he couldn't get too closely involved in the actual execution of the raid because he was handling three other important cases at the same time.

So Brian Boyce put his deputy DCI Ken John in charge of co-ordinating the Noye operation from Scotland Yard.

One Flying Squad officer was appointed local controller of the observation team outside Noye's house and another was placed in a similar role outside Reader's home. They each had full authority to execute a search warrant on the premises for which they were responsible if they felt it necessary.

Members of the C11 specialist surveillance team were warned they might have to enter the grounds of Hollywood Cottage before the search party arrived.

Boyce remained unsure whether the gold was hidden in the house itself or somewhere in the grounds. He was aware there were a number of concrete bunkers in the garden where the gold might be hidden.

Another problem was that the gates to Noye's mansion were always kept locked and could be opened only by remote control once callers had been identified over a closed-circuit TV system. Boyce did not want to give the occupants warning of a raid. He feared that they would flee or hide incriminating evidence in the grounds while police were still trying to get in.

Boyce's observations to his C11 specialists struck them as nothing out of the ordinary. This was the kind of work they had been trained for. But in every plan there are always unforeseen circumstances.

12: Dogs of War

There was no activity at Hollywood Cottage in the morning of 26 January 1985, until the daytime surveillance team DC Russell Sinton and DC Stephen Matthews witnessed an innocent-looking domestic drama.

Brenda Noye was about to take the two boys Kevin and Brett to stay with her mother when the Ford Granada she intended to use failed to start.

Kenny Noye reckoned it was one of the battery terminals that needed cleaning, so he took a knife from the kitchen and tried to sort it out. When that failed he started the car with jump leads from the Range Rover parked alongside.

Brenda Noye and the two boys drove off in the Range Rover and Noye left moments later in the Granada, having tossed the knife into the footwell of the passenger side of the car.

Over at Brian Reader's home that same day there was no movement until 1.10pm when he was seen driving off in his Cavalier in the direction of Kenny Noye's house. Two Flying Squad officers — DS Anthony Yeoman and DC Bruce Finlayson — were close behind in a covert surveillance vehicle.

Four miles down the A20, Reader turned off into the car park of the Beaverwood Club. This time Kenny Noye was nowhere to be seen. Four minutes later Reader left the car park with Yeoman and his partner following at a discreet distance.

What those officers did not realise was that Reader

thought he'd arrived too early at the car park. Reader then drove up the A20 to the Ruxley Corner roundabout two miles away, where he turned and doubled back. The officers following feared they would be easily spotted by Reader and pulled back to such an extent that they lost him.

In fact, Reader had turned up at the Beaverwood Club too late for his meeting with Noye, which had been arranged for 1.00pm.

Noye, despite the problems with his car, had been there on time. He had waited some twenty minutes, even joining the AA at a nearby kiosk, before deciding that Reader wasn't going to show up.

It wasn't until 2.25pm that afternoon that Reader was next spotted outside the imposing gates to Hollywood Cottage. C11 officers Sinton and Matthews watched as Reader found that the gates were locked and no one was home, so he drove away.

A few miles away Kenny Noye was enjoying a secret liaison with his mistress Jenny Bishop. He was seen drinking in a pub with her and then they visited a mutual acquaintance before he stopped at her lovenest in Dartford for a couple of hours.

Later that afternoon Noye and Brenda arrived back at Hollywood Cottage separately.

At 6.12pm Brian Reader turned up at the house once again. Nearby a new surveillance team moved into position.

The watching police were convinced that Reader and Noye had missed an important rendezvous earlier that day.

Acting DI Robert Suckling was parked two miles away in a Flying Squad vehicle near the Brands Hatch motor-racing track. He immediately ordered the two-man surveillance team into the grounds of Hollywood Cottage.

The January evening was bitterly cold even by 6.15pm. The only sound was the hum of traffic from the motorway a mile away across the fields.

'Move in.'

DC John Fordham, 43, signalled to his younger partner DC Neil Murphy and they headed for the perimeter wall.

* * *

Fordham, a family man with three children from Romford in Essex, was the senior of the two. Called 'Gentleman John' by his friends and colleagues because of his old-fashioned good manners, Fordham had been in C11 for nine years. He'd even turned down promotion to remain at the sharp end of police work.

John Fordham was a late entrant into the police force, joining in his late twenties after a variety of jobs, including being a merchant seaman and a prison officer in New Zealand. He had also travelled extensively throughout Europe and Asia.

Once in the force, Fordham's professionalism, sense of responsibility and quiet self-confidence singled him out as an above average officer. Unusually for the Metropolitan Police, Fordham became a detective without even having to sit the customary formal examination.

He won four commendations for bravery and by the time he was assigned to the Brink's-Mat inquiry he had a reputation for being, in the words of one senior Scotland Yard officer, 'one of the most experienced and best-trained surveillance officers in the country'.

His partner and back-up man, bachelor Neil Murphy came from a close-knit mining family in a County Durham pit village. He had joined the Met nine years earlier in 1975 following a short career as a regular soldier.

Murphy loved solitary sports like skiing and windsurfing. He also had the degree of fitness and self-sufficiency necessary for the job. Murphy had something else, too — an actor's eye. Even when off-duty he would constantly study the mannerisms of people in an effort to improve his powers of disguise. In 1980 Murphy was recommended for a posting to C11.

Murphy's dedication to the job had so impressed John Fordham that, after his apprenticeship, they had continued working together and the teacher–pupil relationship developed over the years into one of real friendship, although it was always clear that Fordham was the senior partner.

* * *

Back outside Hollywood Cottage Fordham and Murphy emerged from their make-shift observation post hidden behind some bushes and crept across the quiet country lane until they reached the low wall at the front of the grounds. Both were dressed in rubber wetsuits, camouflage clothing and balaclavas.

Beyond the wall the two officers could see by the light of a string of mock-Victorian lamps more than a hundred yards of sweeping driveway. There were small copses and shrubbery to one side and an open lawn to the other, dotted with newly planted saplings.

At the top of the driveway were the lights of Hollywood Cottage. Seconds later — without a word being spoken between them — the two officers were over the wall and crouching low, waiting to see whether they had been spotted.

A minute later, satisfied that all was clear, they moved towards the house, leap-frogging forward, one of them advancing while the other held back as a look-out to warn if they had been seen.

Keeping close to the perimeter fence, they made for the copse and shrubbery in front of the large barn, known as the apple store. That would give them enough cover to watch events at the house undetected.

The two undercover officers communicated with police through two radios that each of them carried. Their experience had taught them that the tiny body-set radios usually worn by surveillance officers were often inadequate for good reception in rural areas. The proximity of the aerial to the ground tended to interfere with transmissions, particularly when they were sending messages. So they were each equipped with a larger set for sending messages using the smaller set for receiving.

Fordham and Murphy's contact man outside the grounds

was DS Robert Gurr, a crusty C11 veteran. The golden rule for such operations was that once they had taken up their close surveillance positions, they were effectively on their own.

Fordham and Murphy were carrying yeast tablets to pacify Noye's Rottweilers if required. But they knew that they did not always work.

Fordham was also equipped with a pair of light-intensifying night-sight binoculars, a webbing scarf, gloves, two balaclavas, a woollen helmet, a camouflage hood, a peaked, camouflage coloured forage cap and a green webbing harness to keep the larger radio set in position while crawling through the undergrowth.

Fordham and Murphy got to the cover of the shrubbery and copse surrounding the garage some 60 yards in front of the house. Fordham was in front on one knee beside a tree waiting for Murphy to move forward when one of Noye's Rottweilers appeared out of the darkness.

Murphy was startled, his hand flew to his pocket and he tried to feed the yeast tablets to the dogs, but they weren't interested. They were barking louder and louder. Fordham grabbed his radio set.

He whispered: 'Dogs! Hostile!' It was picked up by the other officers in the retreat across School Lane.

Inside the house, Noye took Reader into the kitchen to admire some photographs of the house, taken earlier that month, showing the cottage covered in snow. A cup of tea was made, then Noye had taken Brian Reader into his study to discuss business.

'What the fuck happened to you today, Brian? Why didn't you show?' started Noye angrily.

Just then he heard the dogs making a commotion outside. Noye opened the study door and shouted to Brenda.

'Brenda, what's happening with those dogs?'

Moments later Brenda appeared in the room.

'They're down by the barn. I'm not going down there. It's too dark.'

Noye grabbed his leather jacket from behind a chair and

headed for the front door.

Sixty yards away — after gesturing to Fordham — Murphy began to withdraw. He presumed Fordham would follow him.

The first maxim of a C11 officer is: 'Blow out rather than show out.'

In other words, if his presence is discovered he should withdraw. Failing that he should identify himself as a police officer. But in the case of such hostile dogs there was only one option.

At 6.25pm Murphy radioed to his colleagues: 'Neil out toward fence.'

He then walked through the shrubbery and made for the end of a wooden fence that separated Noye's land from another house in School Lane.

Outside Hollywood Cottage Kenny Noye found a torch in the Granada parked in the garage. He also grabbed the knife he'd been using earlier to clean the battery tops.

Holding both items in his left hand Noye went down the drive calling to the older of the dogs, Sam, and one of the puppies, Cassie. The other dog, Cleo, was still in the kitchen.

Reaching the apple store area, Noye saw the dogs on a pile of sand barking into the shrubbery. He swung the flashlight beam in the same direction.

Noye then moved into the wooded area, letting his torch pan light on to the ground.

At 6.27pm Fordham came on the radio.

'Somebody out, half way down drive, calling dogs.'

At the boundary fence, Murphy walked up to the end furthest from Hollywood Cottage and, using a tree for support, climbed up to balance on top to take stock of the situation.

Looking down to where he had last seen the Rottweilers, Murphy spotted a figure with a torch obviously searching in the shrubbery.

The light suddenly moved towards Murphy so the police officer dropped into the garden on the other side of the fence.

Murphy then tried to attract the attention of the dogs to help his partner. He shouted through the fence.

'Keep those dogs quiet!'

Perhaps Noye would think Murphy was an irate neighbour and call off the dogs or Noye would come down to the fence to see who was behind it, allowing Fordham to escape.

Noye was startled by the voice but then another noise to his left attracted his attention. He swung the beam of light in that direction.

The light instantly fell on a hooded figure just four or five feet away. Noye froze with horror. All he could see of the man were two eyeholes and a mask.

Noye later claimed the figure then struck him a blow across his face.

Immediately after being hit, Noye dropped the torch and put his left hand up to the other man's face and grabbed him.

'Brenda! Help!' he screamed in the direction of the house.

Then Noye used all his brute strength to smash his fists into the man over and over again. But still the man kept coming. He seemed huge to Noye, dressed in black and with that mask on. It was then that Noye began to plunge the knife into John Fordham's body.

In the tussle that followed both men fell to the ground.

Fordham came down on top of Noye, who struck him again and again. Noye then managed to break free and began running up the drive.

He looked back momentarily and saw the figure staggering to his feet and start moving towards the garden wall.

In Hollywood Cottage Brenda Noye rushed upstairs and took a shotgun from one of at least half a dozen the couple kept in their bedroom cupboard. She also grabbed four cartridges out of the same cabinet.

Loading the gun as she ran, Brenda Noye — in tracksuit and slippers — and Brian Reader headed down the drive in the direction of where they'd heard Noye shouting.

Half way down Noye ran towards them.

'There's a masked man down there,' shouted a breathless Noye.

He grabbed the gun, which was by now in Reader's hands.

Running back to the copse with Brenda and Reader close behind, Noye picked up the torch off the ground and made towards the gate.

Then Noye spotted the dogs surrounding the masked figure, lying slumped on the ground. He went straight to the man.

Just a few yards away, Fordham's partner Neil Murphy was walking back along the lane towards the wall at the front of the cottage grounds when he heard a woman screaming. Moving into some bushes beside the entrance to the retreat, Murphy looked into the grounds and saw two men and a woman. Both of the men were shouting and looking down at the ground, one of them was pointing something at Fordham.

Murphy immediately radioed in: 'Man compromising John. Stick/shotgun.'

Murphy later claimed that at one stage he saw one of the men step forward and kick the figure on the ground.

Murphy remained in his hiding place, transmitting back to the retreat everything he could see and hear. He was following classic C11 training. He was there in a surveillance role not an operational one.

'Who are you?' shouted Noye, angrily. 'Who are you?'

Fordham was still wearing his balaclava hood.

Noye noticed the policeman's night-sight binoculars. He later claimed he thought he was dealing with a rapist or a peeping tom.

'Who are you? Take that mask off!' shouted Noye.

No response from the masked figure.

'Who are you? Take it off!'

Noye pointed the shotgun at the man. There was no reaction.

'If you don't take that mask off and tell me who you are, I'll blow your head off,' threatened Noye.

Then, according to Noye's later testimony, Fordham

groaned and started to take off his hood.

'SAS.'

Silence.

'On manoeuvres.'

'Show us your ID then,' ordered Noye.

There was no reply. John Fordham looked deathly pale. Then Kenny Noye proved just how adept he is at thinking on his feet. He found he was bleeding from a cut near his eye and nose, injuries caused, he would later claim, during his struggle with Fordham. Kenny Noye believed he needed photographic evidence of the struggle.

'Get a camera Brenda, quick,' ordered Noye. Then, as an afterthought, 'You'd better call an ambulance for 'im.'

Noye stood by John Fordham for a few moments, looking down at the policeman.

Then he knelt down and opened Fordham's jacket to get a closer look at the wounds he had inflicted just moments earlier.

In a much quieter voice he asked Fordham: 'What on earth are you doing here?'

Fordham didn't answer. His head fell back awkwardly so Noye put his arm under him to get him into a better position. Then a police car drove through the gates to Hollywood Cottage.

The first men into the grounds were Flying Squad Detective Constables David Manning and John Childs. They had been in an unmarked police car in the retreat's drive, moving slowly forward, when the order came.

'All units AM,' came over the radio.

Childs and Manning tore into School Lane. The gates to Hollywood Cottage had been left partly open after Reader's arrival and they swept through them on to the driveway.

Within seconds the car's headlights illuminated a body collapsed on the ground with a figure armed with a shotgun next to him. The dogs were still pulling and tugging at Fordham.

'Stand by all units!' screamed John Childs into the car radio set. That meant they were not to enter the grounds at that point.

'I am a police officer,' shouted Manning at Noye holding up his warrant card.

Noye moved towards him, pointing the shotgun and yelled, 'Fuck off or I will do you as well.'

'Put the gun down and get those dogs away from the officer,' said Manning.

Moments later the Rottweilers turned on Manning snapping at his feet. One of them jumped up at him.

Manning took off his jacket and wrapped it around his arm while trying to knock the dogs away.

Ignoring the shotgun pointed in his direction, Manning then walked over to where Fordham was lying.

'He's done me. He's stabbed me,' muttered the wounded officer.

The Rottweilers then jumped up and tore at DC Childs' clothing, but he managed to struggle past them back to the car, from where he called an ambulance and ordered all Flying Squad units in.

Looking down at John Fordham, DC Manning could see blood on his chest and stomach, and he immediately began giving first aid, but Fordham quickly lost consciousness.

In the confusion that followed, Brian Reader fled from the scene by foot. He scrambled over garden fences and through private properties.

It was the start of the longest night of all those people's lives.

13: Between the Lines

Back at John Fordham's side DC Manning and Kenny Noye faced each other.

'He's a police officer,' Manning told Noye.

'The SAS man,' replied Noye. 'What are you on about — he's a police officer? Look at him! He's masked up!'

The dogs were getting in the way again. The third Rottweiler Cassie had joined them.

'Get those dogs out of the way,' said Manning.

'I can't get the dogs out of the way. They haven't got their collars on and they don't pay any attention to me anyway.'

'Go and get the leads.'

Noye moved off towards the house and bumped into Brenda coming down the drive. She had the camera, flash gun and mobile phone.

Noye took the camera and the flash off her, which he put in his pocket.

'I couldn't get through for the ambulance,' said Brenda.

Noye grabbed the mobile phone off her.

'Go and get the dogs' leads,' he ordered.

Noye then returned to the three police officers.

'My wife couldn't get through for an ambulance.'

'I've already got them,' said Childs.

The dogs were still barking and jumping up.

'Where are the dog leads?' asked Manning, growing increasingly agitated.

'I've sent my wife.'

Noye later claimed that he was ordered by Manning to take

the shotgun and leave it in a broken position up against the wall beside the front door to the house. Just after that another car pulled up and two men jumped out armed with what looked like baseball bats.

Those two men were DS Yeoman and DC Finlayson who had earlier that day followed Reader from his home to the Beaverwood Club and later trailed him to Hollywood Cottage. They had been stationed outside the Portobello Inn just half a mile from Noye's house.

Yeoman noticed Noye was carrying a camera over his shoulder.

'Come here, you,' he yelled.

Noye ignored them all and disappeared between the garage and the swimming pool building. When he reappeared some moments later, Finlayson grabbed Noye's left arm and said, 'Police.'

'I know,' replied an ice cool Kenny Noye.

'What's been happening?'

'I took the knife and did him. Old Bill or not, he had no fucking business being here.'

Noye was then cautioned by Finlayson. He did not reply. They started walking towards the front door of Hollywood Cottage. Meanwhile Suckling noticed Brenda Noye standing by the front of the house.

'You're being arrested,' he told her.

'Why?' she asked.

'A policeman has been very badly hurt here tonight. You're being arrested in connection with that.'

'He shouldn't have come here.'

Brenda Noye was put in the back of a police car. Meanwhile other policemen were pouring into the grounds of Hollywood Cottage. It was only then that officers noticed Brian Reader had disappeared.

'Where is he?' one officer asked Noye.

'Mind your own fucking business,' replied Noye.

'Do you realise that the police officer you stabbed is dying?' asked the officer.

'He shouldn't have been on my property. I hope he fucking

dies.'

The officer lunged at Noye and pushed him hard against the wall.

'What sort of animal are you?'

If another police officer hadn't appeared at the scene at that moment then he might have seriously injured Noye.

Throughout all this, other police officers continued trying to save the life of John Fordham.

'Let me go,' he moaned, as he drifted in and out of consciousness.

He was given cardiac massage, mouth-to-mouth and shortly after 7pm the ambulance arrived. Neil Murphy accompanied him on the journey to Queen Mary's Hospital in Sidcup. As the ambulance set off, Murphy helped ambulanceman Bryan Moore by holding the oxygen mask over Fordham's face. He thought he saw signs of life until the paramedic pointed out this was just the oxygen going in and out of Fordham's body. His pulse had already stopped.

Twelve minutes later they arrived at the hospital where Fordham was seen by duty surgeon Graham Ponting. He could detect no sign of a pulse, although tests showed there was still some electrical activity in the heart. He found at least ten stab wounds on the body.

A blood transfusion into Fordham's ankle was set up and an operation carried out. Several more attempts were made to get the heart going again, using direct injections of drugs and electrical shocks, but at 8.20pm Fordham was pronounced dead.

Pathologist Dr Rufus Crompton who examined the body the following morning found the stab wounds consistent with blows from a single-edged blade about one centimetre wide and seven centimetres long. Five of the wounds were on the front of the body, three were on the back, one was in the armpit and one was on the head.

The two wounds that were fatal both penetrated Fordham's heart. One was delivered with the force of a punch and severed the fifth rib to enter the left ventricle. The other, two centimetres below, had just nicked the right ventricle. In both cases the knife had been plunged in to a depth of seven centimetres and a small bruise beside the cutting edge of each wound suggested that the knife had been pushed in to the hilt.

The close proximity of the five wounds suggested that, after the first one all had been inflicted while Fordham was immobile. They were consistent with a right-handed assailant, face-to-face with the policeman, who had delivered the blows to the front and had then reached behind to stab Fordham in the back.

This clearly implicated Reader in the murder accusations. The suggestion was that Reader had held Fordham while Noye did the stabbing.

Fordham had sustained no defence wounds, commonly found on victims of knife attacks because a person being attacked receives cuts to his hands or arms as he tries to fend off the blade.

Three other wounds seemed to have been inflicted by a knife held like a dagger, indicating Fordham was still on his feet when he sustained them. Noye always insisted he never held a knife in that way.

The torso also had a bruise to the chest. It was consistent with a blow from a light object, a fall, a punch or a kick.

Half a mile away, Brian Reader eventually reached the main A20 road leading back to London at about 7.40pm. However, for a man at the centre of a gold bullion distribution chain he chose an extraordinary way to make good his escape — by trying to hitch a lift.

Just then, Det Sgt Barry McAllister spotted Reader standing by the side of the road on the outskirts of West Kingsdown just past a pub called The Gamecock. McAllister was fully aware of the description of the man missing from Hollywood Cottage.

Also travelling into West Kingsdown from the London direction as Reader stood thumbing a lift, were Flying Squad detectives Alan Branch and John Redgrave, also in an unmarked car.

Redgrave immediately recognised Reader from

surveillance duties he had carried out on 8 January outside Farringdon Street station while Branch knew him from the station and Russell Square two days earlier. Both detectives leapt from their vehicle to detain Reader, but by that time Reader was already running up to the Kent police car.

DC Paul Gladstone, in the passenger seat, wound down his window as Reader approached.

'Any chance of a lift to London?' asked Reader.

'Yes, get in,' replied Gladstone.

As the car pulled off Gladstone revealed that he and McAllister were policemen and asked Reader where he had come from.

'The pub,' replied Reader indicating The Gamecock.

'Where were you before that?'

'What's all this about?' asked an increasingly anxious Reader.

'We're looking for a man in connection with a serious incident tonight. Where were you before The Gamecock?'

Reader did not reply but shoved his right hand into his pocket.

Fearing that he might be armed, Gladstone asked to see what he was holding.

Reader showed him a few coins. He was then ordered to put his hands on top of the back of the front passenger seat.

Reader was handcuffed and driven back to the car park at The Portobello Inn, where other Kent CID men were waiting.

Told that he was being arrested on suspicion of assaulting a police officer earlier that night, Reader replied:

'What?'

The charges were then repeated.

'You must be joking!' he said.

That night Noye, Brenda and Reader were all taken to Swanley police station.

Kenny Noye harboured deep suspicions that evidence against him would be invented and statements concocted. As a result he immediately demanded his legal rights.

For more than 24 hours following his arrest he asked for Kent police to be involved. Noye was very wary of Scotland

Yard, particularly the Flying Squad.

Noye also insisted on pointing out his facial injuries. He knew they would be crucial in paving the way for a plea or self-defence.

One of the first policemen to see Noye in custody was station sergeant, David Columbine. He asked Noye whether he knew why he was being held.

'Haven't a clue,' responded Noye.

'You're here for the attempted murder or murder of a police officer,' said Columbine.

'Is that all?' Noye allegedly replied.

Then he was searched and nearly £850 in cash was found on him.

When Noye was asked to sign a form listing what had been taken, he at first refused, then appeared to do so but instead wrote down the name and address of a firm of solicitors.

At 11.30pm that evening PC Fred Bird went to Noye's cell (the female small cell at the station) to ask for his clothing for forensic examination. The officer had no idea what Noye was accused of because Noye would not even admit his own name at this stage.

'You are not having my clothing until I have seen my brief,' Noye replied, using the London slang word for his solicitor.

'I want this photographed,' he added, pointing to his eye and nose and the mud on his clothing.

'If I do, will you allow me to take your clothing?' asked Bird.

'Yes.'

Noye was escorted to a first floor room where the photographs were taken.

Then, on returning to his cell, Noye said: 'All right, you can have my clothes.'

As they were being taken from him he asked: 'Will I be moved to London?'

'No. The offence happened in Kent. You will be dealt with here,' he was told.

Bird was not lying. At that stage the killing remained a Kent police inquiry.

Then Noye blurted out: 'I didn't know he was a police officer. All I saw was a chap in camouflage gear and a balaclava mask. I wouldn't have stabbed him if I'd known he was a police officer.'

'I can't discuss this with you. Can I have your name?' asked Bird.

Noye wouldn't say.

Bird told him he was being silly and told him he could well be facing a murder charge.

The sombre warning seemed to work, for the next moment Noye stuck out his hand and said, 'My name is Kenny Noye.'

He then repeated that he hadn't known Fordham was a police officer.

Later that same night Noye was transferred from Swanley to Dartford police station.

As he sat in the back of a police car during the journey through Kent, Noye asked: 'Well, is he alive or dead?'

'No comment,' replied one of the police officers with him.

'What's the unofficial answer?' Noye persisted. But his escorts would not be drawn.

In the early hours of that Sunday morning, Noye was examined by police surgeon Dr Eugene Ganz. His attitude by then had become 'commanding'.

Ganz noted that Noye virtually ordered him to make a note of his injuries, which included a black left eye, also slightly cut, and a cut nostril. Both wounds were relatively trivial, but the doctor also noted that Noye's face was smeared with blood.

Noye also complained about a pain in the abdominal area and the back, saying he had been kicked, but there was no sign of bruising. There was swelling on the back of his right hand. When the doctor noticed the scratches on Noye's left hand he refused to allow it to be examined saying, 'That's nothing.'

Noye's first formal interview took place at lunchtime on the day after Fordham's death, Sunday 27 January 1985. He was seen by DCI Peter Humphrey, a Kent policeman and — as was the case at a number of the interviews involving Noye, his wife and Reader — another detective made a note of all the questions and answers throughout.

That first interview lasted just seven minutes. Noye refused to answer questions unless his solicitor was present.

'I was promised my solicitor when I got to Swanley last night. Now it's Sunday, one o'clock, and I still haven't seen him.'

DCI Humphrey was unmoved. 'Has anyone told you that the man you stabbed last night has died?' he asked.

'No reply unless my solicitor is present,' responded Noye.

Noye then named Scotland Yard Detective Chief Superintendent Ray Adams, who had investigated Noye a decade earlier, as someone who would vouch for the fact he 'was not a violent man or a killer'.

At the end of that first interview, a short statement was drawn up of what Noye had said. Noye requested that the letters 'pm' be inserted after the time 'one o'clock'.

He then asked that a line be drawn from the end of the last word on each line to the edge of the page to prevent anything being inserted later.

That afternoon his request for a solicitor was granted. Raymond Burrough, his legal representative for twelve years, was ushered into the cell to see Noye.

Burrough had earlier reacted with amazement when told about the incident at Hollywood Cottage. The Kenny Noye he knew was a 'jovial sort of fellow, gregarious'.

The Kenny Noye who greeted his brief that afternoon was very agitated and distressed. Noye insisted he had been defending himself and he was extremely worried about Brenda. He briefly began outlining what had happened, but the solicitor cut him short. The cell door had been kept open a foot or two by officers guarding Noye and two of them remained outside within hearing distance.

Burrough didn't think it was a suitable location to listen to his client's instructions. He later described it as thus: 'One could almost cut the atmosphere with a knife.'

Noye didn't even realise that Brian Reader had also been transferred from Swanley to Dartford police station and was actually in a cell next to Noye.

At 3.15 that Sunday afternoon Reader was seen by Detective Superintendent David Tully of the Kent police force.

Reader immediately expressed concern about his wife who was a diabetic and due to go into hospital the next day for treatment to her pancreas.

'Where's my wife?' demanded Reader.

He was told that she had been arrested and was at Gravesend police station.

'I want you to know, Mr Tully, that she is a very sick woman and needs medical attention,' said Reader.

Tully assured Reader he would personally go to Gravesend to make certain she was all right.

'Thank you,' said Reader. 'She needs special food, like boiled fish, otherwise she gets ill.'

Tully got back to the subject at hand.

'At some stage you will be interviewed about the incident at Mr Noye's home on Saturday evening. You understand that you have been detained in connection with that incident?' asked Tully.

Reader tried to look concerned.

'It's a very serious matter. I know a police officer has been murdered and I was told I was responsible. I want you to know, Mr Tully, that I do not know anything about it and I did not have anything to do with it,' said Reader.

Reader then said he would not answer any questions without his solicitor being present. His brief's name was Stanley Beller of Beller Jarvis, based in Oxford Street, central London.

'You must understand,' said Tully. 'A large amount of money was found at your house when your wife was arrested and she, as you well know, will be asked to account for the possession of that money.'

'That money is mine. It's nothing to do with my wife,' said Reader.

That Sunday afternoon at Hollywood Cottage the most significant piece of evidence linking Noye and Reader to the Brink's-Mat bullion case was discovered.

Lying in a shallow gully beside the garage wall and hidden from view by a tin of paint covered by a rubber mat, was a red-and-white piece of material. Inside the cloth were eleven gold bars, amounting to some 13 kilogrammes, at that time worth at least £100,000.

The roughly cast bars were all of a similar size, three inches long, one inch high and one inch wide. Some of the same red and white material was later discovered in Noye's Ford Granada. Operating instructions for the model of a furnace bought by Noye's friend Michael Lawson thirteen months before were then found in Noye's apple store.

The discovery of the gold enabled the Metropolitan Police formally to take over the DC Fordham murder investigation because it linked the case to the missing Brink's-Mat bullion. The decision was reached after a top-level meeting at Scotland Yard between Brian Worth, the Yard's Deputy Assistant Commissioner in charge of serious crime operations, Anthony Coe, Kent Police's Assistant Chief Constable in charge of operations, and Detective Chief Superintendent Duncan Gibbins, Head of Kent CID.

The inquiry was immediately placed in the hands of Commander Philip Corbett from C11. Running such an operation was usually outside the department's remit, but it was one of their officers who had been killed. Corbett had also received the relevant training in running an interforce inquiry and, after all, the investigation into Noye had been initiated largely by intelligence provided by C11. It made little odds, however, as C11 allowed the on-the-ground investigation to be handled by Brian Boyce and his Flying Squad officers.

In the criminal underworld there was a wave of sympathy for Noye that infuriated the police.

Former Krays' henchman Freddie Foreman epitomised the reaction from the Old Kent Road.

'Put yourself in Kenny's position. If you went into your back garden tonight and someone leaps out the ground in a mask and that, what would you think? You would suspect they was there to rob you and your family,' he says today.

There are two sides to every argument.

14: Uncomfortable Silences

At Hollywood Cottage police continued an inch-by-inch search, including an aerial reconnaissance by a helicopter equipped with infra-red devices capable of pin-pointing metal buried underground or hidden in buildings. The grounds were checked by a line of policemen moving slowly forward, shoulder to shoulder.

Very rapidly there were some significant discoveries:

- Numerous copper coins of the kind used in the re-smelting of gold were found in several rooms.
- A child's drawing pad containing a picture of a gold bar found in a kitchen drawer.
- A *Guinness Book of Records* from 1985 with a circle drawn around the entry of Brink's-Mat as the largest British robbery.

A police dog searching the area of woods behind Hollywood Cottage discovered a flick knife as well as a similar weapon inside Noye's Ford Granada. At the back of the house close to the corner of the swimming pool another knife was found that appeared to be the one used to stab John Fordham. The white-handled knife had its blade thrust into the ground at the foot of a tree. The knife and the soil were taken away for forensic examination, but no trace of blood was ever found on it. Noye later insisted the knife had been left there by one of his children, who sometimes used to sleep in a tent in the garden.

A camouflage hat worn by Fordham was also found close

to the shrubbery where he had hidden. Inside those same bushes police also found his peaked camouflage forage cap.

As police swept through the inside of Hollywood Cottage they came across a locked bedroom door. After a specialist officer was called, the lock was picked.

Inside the room, police found a cupboard filled with sex aids and black leather clothing plus a selection of hardcore pornographic videos.

One detective recalled: 'Noye was obviously into all sorts of sexual perversions. We were surprised because he had at least one mistress on the go. But he was obviously into all sorts of sick stuff at home as well.'

Many officers concluded that Noye, who'd been with his blonde mistress the afternoon of DC Fordham's death, was some kind of sex addict.

In the lounge, officers were astonished to discover that 'Goldfinger' by Shirley Bassey was primed to go off on the stereo system whenever anyone walked into the lounge. Close examination and forensic tests revealed globular fragments of gold, which would have been produced in a smelting process, on the boot mat of Noye's Ford Granada. Traces were also found on the boot mat of Brian Reader's Cavalier as well as the rear mat and rear floor area of Noye's pick-up truck parked near the apple store. Inside the store fragments were found on a leather apron and two gloves, as well as the front mat of a Cadillac parked nearby and on a pair of gloves found in Noye's Range Rover.

Gold particles left by drilling or machining also turned up in the back of a Ford Transit at Noye's house and in the back of the pick-up truck. A pair of driving gloves taken from the Granada and a pair of gloves taken from Noye at Swanley police station also had telltale traces. Particles were also discovered in a briefcase at Brian Reader's home.

At Hollywood Cottage a safe was hidden in the floor of one room. It contained a large quantity of jewellery and £2,500 in new £50 notes with the same prefix as those at Reader's house — A24.

The wood panelling in all the rooms was removed and

secret compartments were discovered. One was hidden at the back of a built-in bedroom cupboard and contained antique Meissen porcelain worth about £3,000, which had been stolen two years earlier from the home of Lord Darnley. Secret compartments were also found under a corridor leading to the swimming pool and in an alcove above the pool. Paving stones from the patio were torn up and tiles removed from the swimming pool, but no more gold bars were found.

Next to the houses in Hever Road where Noye's parents and his sister and her husband lived in West Kingsdown, neighbour Rosemary Ford discovered a bundle poking from beneath her back-garden fence in a green Marks and Spencer's carrier bag. It was crammed with £50,000 in £50 notes with the prefix A24.

At first Mrs Ford thought it was a practical joke, so she took it to another neighbour to inspect it. Realising it was the real thing, she immediately took it to the police at Hollywood Cottage. No member of Noye's family knew anything about the money.

Following the discovery of the gold bars in the grounds of Hollywood Cottage, the Metropolitan Police — now in charge of the investigation — decided to interview Reader and Noye immediately. It was claimed that senior Flying Squad detectives did not want any of the detainees to be allowed any more access to solicitors. Brian Boyce strongly believed that police inquiries could be jeopardised by the appearance of a third party.

Noye was interviewed by DI Anthony Brightwell, acting DCI Suckling and DC Michael Charman. For much of the time Noye stood close to the cell door, shouting intermittently that he did not want to be interviewed by Flying Squad detectives and that he wanted his solicitor present. The truth of what happened during that interview is disputed by both sides. But one moment summed up the differing accounts when Noye asked the officers whether they knew the dead officer. He was told that John Fordham was known to all of them, that he was married and had three children, a girl aged 12 and two boys who were older.

According to the officers present, Noye then said: 'You must hate me. I have killed one of your mates and there is no way out for me. All I want to do is make sure I go to prison for the rest of my life.'

Noye later emphatically denied most of the remarks he was alleged to have made during that first interview with the Met. He insisted that his replies to most questions had been: 'No reply unless my solicitor is present.'

At 7pm on Monday, 28 January, 1985, that same evening at Dartford police station, duty police officer John Laker was standing in the corridor outside the cells when he heard Kenny Noye call out to Brian Reader in the next door cell:

'Have you got a solicitor, Brian?'

Reader replied from his adjacent cell, 'Yes.'

'Don't tell them anything, Brian.'

'No, I haven't.'

Noye continued: 'No, don't tell them anything. They don't know about the other geezer.'

Reader replied, 'I don't know anything.'

But Noye persisted, 'No, well, don't say anything. They don't know about the other geezer yet.'

Kenny Noye seemed determined to confuse the police inquiries as much as he possibly could. Later that night the three Flying Squad officers returned to Noye's cell for another interview. According to their statements Noye told them his only concern was the death of that policeman.

'You could ask me a thousand questions and I could give you a thousand answers. The gold is nothing to what I have done. I am not interested in telling you about the gold. My only worry is the murder. If I tell you about the gold now, I'm only adding to it. It won't make any difference to what you charge me with, will it?'

When the interview ended, Noye was asked whether he wanted to see Detective Chief Superintendent Brian Boyce. According to the officers he replied, 'I'll leave that to you.'

Noye was also asked whether he wanted to make a written statement but was alleged to have replied, 'No, because whatever I say you will make it work against me. I don't trust you. I have seen some deals written up. You give me one of those and I'll be able to interpret it in four different ways. I will tell my story to the judge and jury.'

* * *

Also Dartford police station detectives had an equally frustrating interview with Brenda Noye. She had been allowed to see the Noye's family solicitor Raymond Burrough when the killing was still a Kent police inquiry. But once Scotland Yard took over the investigation she was refused further visits.

Flying Squad DS Kenneth O'Rourke first saw her at lunchtime on the Monday following DC Fordham's death.

'Do you know why you are here?' he asked Brenda.

'Yes,' she replied. 'A man was killed.'

'Yes, we know that, but how?'

'I don't know anything.'

'You must know something. There were three people there, and you were one of them.'

'I don't know about anyone else. I was in the house and didn't see anything.'

'There was a green Cavalier outside your home. The driver of that was a visitor. Who was that?'

'I don't know anything about a Cavalier or any visitor. I don't know what a Cavalier looks like.'

Brenda Noye then started sniffling. Not quite crying. She took out a handkerchief. O'Rourke paused for a few moments then continued.

'It's a light-green saloon car.'

'I have never seen a light-green saloon car at my house.'

'Don't be silly,' said O'Rourke. 'It was there when the police arrived, on your drive.'

'I didn't see it,' she replied. 'Anyway I know that I don't have to say anything to you. My solicitor told me.'

'That's correct,' said O'Rourke. 'Is there any reason why you shouldn't answer the questions?'

'No reason.'

'Does the name Brian Reader mean anything to you?'

'No, I have never heard that name.'

'Before the incident, not long before, you, your husband and Reader were seen near the boot of the Cavalier together. What have you got to say about that?' said O'Rourke. (It later transpired that his claim was incorrect.)

'I was in the house.'

'And you never saw anything regarding that incident where the man was murdered?'

'I told you, no.'

'You were heard screaming by officers nearby.'

'I don't want to answer.'

'You were seen running from the area where it happened back to the house.'

'I went to the phone.'

O'Rourke seized the opening.

'So you were out there. You did leave the house.'

There was no reply. O'Rourke tried to press home the advantage.

'You were a witness to a murder. Do you want to sit there and say nothing about it?'

Again no reply.

'The man was stabbed nine times. Did you stab him?'

'No.'

'There were only two other people there. Which one did?'

'I love my husband,' she replied.

'Are you saying that he did it, but you won't say so?' asked O'Rourke.

No reply.

O'Rourke continued: 'The green Cavalier has been seen at your house, with Reader driving, almost daily. This is the culmination of a year's work. We haven't just stumbled on you.'

'I realise that,' replied Brenda Noye.

'I'm sure you know more than you are saying. We'll continue this interview later,' said the detective. He then gave her a chance to check and sign the contemporaneous note that had been made, but she refused.

Some four hours later she faced another interview with the same officer.

'I can't help you,' she began.

'Can't or won't?' asked O'Rourke. He then told her the police believed her husband had carried out the killing of DC Fordham.

'Look, I can't help you,' she repeated.

Then she added, 'My husband couldn't do such a thing.'

'Are you saying it was the other man, Reader?' queried O'Rourke.

'I don't know his second name.'

'You won't know this,' said O'Rourke, 'but we have found a large quantity of gold on your premises. Is that the reason your husband went to the extremes he did?'

'You will have to ask him if he did it, why he did it,' she said.

'You did know he was dealing in stolen gold?'

'Why should I know?'

'He's your husband. You were seen at the boot of the green Cavalier that night. You live with him. You must have known. Why not tell us from the beginning what happened?'

'I can't, I just can't,' said Brenda Noye, adding, 'I'm not a hard bitch, like you think. My stomach is knotted up. My life is destroyed.'

Once again, at the end of the interview, she refused to check or sign the notes that were taken.

The Noyes certainly had their own agenda when it came to dealing with the police.

* * *

Brenda Noye later spoke openly about the night of her arrest. 'They took me down to Swanley police station and they took all my possessions off me — watch, wedding ring, everything. Then they took me to Dartford police station and I was kept there and they came in and handcuffed me and said I was being shifted. They put me in a police car and took me as a ridiculous speed down to Gravesend police station. The next morning they took me back down the road to Dartford.'

But she did, perhaps surprsingly, concede that not all the police were unsympathetic.

'There was a policewoman outside my door and she was a very nice woman, trying to comfort me, get me to eat something. She even said, "I'll send out and get something for you. I don't blame you for not wanting to eat the stuff they dish out here." But when I was in there I asked two Metropolitan officers for some clean clothes. It was absolutely ridiculous. I asked one of them to bring a tracksuit because that was the safest thing. They came back with the top of one and the bottom of another. Two odd shoes. No socks or tights.'

While Brenda remained in custody in Holloway for the next two months, the Noye children Kevin, 12, and Brett, 10, stayed with a procession of relatives. Brenda later claimed that journalists waited to talk to them outside their school.

Inside prison, Brenda was put to work as a cleaner and met several much older women in Holloway for offences such as shoflifting. She was struck by how many women hadn't got any relatives or friends in the outside world.

In some ways Brenda was a lot luckier than most.

15: Secret War

Police rapidly moved in on the other suspects in the Brink's-Mat gold bullion chain. Thirteen raids nationwide were carried out simultaneously.

Garth Chappell found fifty police officers on the doorstep of his country house near Bristol. Nearby, Terence Patch was arrested at his luxurious bungalow.

Scadlynn Ltd was raided and invoice books, papers, telephone books, bank paying-in books, petty cash accounts and even a picture of an island scene were removed from the offices for further examination. Among the paperwork were telephone numbers that proved a link with Reader and Noye. The safes were also inspected and silver trophies and gold watches removed.

Evidence of the Brink's-Mat gold ingots and a non-stop smelting operation were soon uncovered at various locations in the West Country.

At one smelting works the police had the following classic conversation with one of the suspects:

'I understand you have been smelting this morning. Is that right?' one detective asked a man just arrested.

'Yes.'

'What were you smelting?'

'I don't wish to say.'

'Why not?'

'I don't want to.'

Minutes later police uncovered two gold bars, still warm, on a sofa in the house next to the smelter. A shotgun and a rifle were taken from the same house.

In a truck parked outside they found another shotgun and a crucible with two large ingot moulds still hot enough to have caused condensation on the windows.

However, the most significant evidence was paperwork that proved the handlers were making vast sums of money by avoiding payments of VAT on the gold. An initial check of Scadlynn's records in the national VAT computer at Southend revealed a surprising picture. Since the summer of 1984 the company's fortunes had undergone a remarkable change. Millions of pounds worth of gold had been going from Scadlynn to an assay office in Sheffield, where its purity was officially calculated, then on to gold dealers on the open market. Scadlynn claimed this was scrap gold made up from jewellery that the company had bought, but the amounts were too large for that to be a credible explanation.

Also, the gold had been moved in very suspicious circumstances in a series of undercover early morning pick-ups. The ingots were so badly smelted that the assay office could not determine their true gold content without re-smelting them. They later compared the bars sent by Scadlynn to a badly mixed cake in which all the currants (the gold) ended up on one side, and few appeared anywhere else in the mix.

The suspicions of the customs officers increased after apparently routine visits to Scadlynn to inspect their VAT accounts revealed the names of dealers to whom they were selling on. Garth Chappell even admitted to one VAT inspector: 'I'm a dealer. I don't understand books. Books are all Chinese to me.' Two days later the customs officer returned to tell him he owed nearly £80,000 in outstanding VAT payments.

More checks showed that Scadlynn was paying the same for the gold as they were selling it for. It didn't make sense unless their paperwork was false. They were undoubtedly avoiding vast VAT payments.

In London police carried out similar raids on various

properties belonging to individuals linked to Reader and Noye.

* * *

On the Tuesday after Fordham's killing, Kenny Noye spent much of the day alone in his cell at Dartford police station.

Then Chief Investigator Brian Boyce appeared in his cell with three knives and asked him whether he recognised them.

'No reply unless my solicitor is present,' was Noye's only response.

Two and a half hours later Kenny Noye's brief Ray Burrough was allowed to see his client.

He immediately told Boyce: 'My client does not wish to say anything at this stage.'

Noye was then asked whether he would provide blood, saliva and hair samples for forensic analysis.

Burrough immediately interrupted.

'Permission is not given and will not be given until we have taken counsel's opinion on it.'

Later, Noye was also seen by another detective.

'How's my house?'

'What do you mean?' replied the police officer.

'I suppose you've wrecked it.'

The detective then mentioned that the police knew that there might be concrete bunkers dating back to World War II in the grounds.

'I can't find them,' said Noye. 'You'd be doing me a favour if your lot could. I've had a JCB in there and I don't know where they are.'

'What did you want to find them for? Was it to hide gear in?' he was asked.

'No, I was going to open one up for the kids to play in.'

Not long after this, officers visited Brian Reader in his cell. He allegedly admitted to the officers, 'I am sorry about what has happened.'

After about twenty minutes of detailed questioning,

during which Reader conceded little, he was asked: 'How long have you known Noye?'

Reader did not reply and the interview was brought to an end.

Later Reader was twice visited by Brian Boyce. On the first occasion he was told that he would be charged with murder and was shown three knives, which he said he did not recognise.

Reader did, however, agree to provide hair, saliva and blood samples for forensic examination.

On the second visit by Boyce he was seen with a solicitor present. Reader was asked whether he was prepared to answer any questions.

Reader's reply surprised no one. 'I don't wish to say anything.'

Meanwhile Brenda Noye was moved to Gravesend police station, where she was seen by DS O'Rourke once again. It was to prove a more productive meeting than the earlier ones.

According to police, O'Rourke went in with a sympathetic attitude.

'I appreciate that these are not the surroundings that you are used to, but we have to get to the bottom of this. A policeman has been murdered. A quantity of gold has been recovered from your house. After speaking to you yesterday, I think you want to tell us, but you are frightened of something or someone.'

Playing on Brenda Noye's fears did not seem to make much impression, police later claimed.

'I'm not frightened of anyone,' she said. 'I didn't see anything. I was out after. It had all happened by then.'

'All what?' asked Rourke.

Brenda Noye's defence was weakening.

'Whatever happened to him. I didn't take any part. The dogs were making a lot of noise, so Kenny went to see. He was out for a few minutes and the dogs were still barking, so Brian went out and a bit later Kenny came running in and got his shotgun. I knew then that something was wrong. I went down the drive and could see Ken and Brian standing over something. I got closer and could see it was a man. He didn't move.'

'Did you think he might be dead?'

'I didn't know what to think. I can remember becoming hysterical and shouting. I suppose I must have thought that. I was just shouting at the two of them. I can't remember what I said.'

A few more questions followed, then O'Rourke said: 'Let's talk about the gold. You did know they were shifting gold, didn't you?'

'Of course I did. You said yesterday, I am his wife.'

'Did you know it was stolen?'

'Obviously it must be.'

'Did you know from where?'

'No.'

O'Rourke then enlightened Brenda Noye.

'I think it's from the bullion robbery at Heathrow over a year ago, when £26 million was stolen,' he said.

The explanation surprised her. 'I never gave it much thought,' she said.

'How much has been moved from your house?'

'I don't know.'

'Who brings it?'

'I don't know. We've loads of cars coming and going all day.'

'Does your husband bring it to the house?'

'I don't know. My husband is just doing a favour.'

'Who for?'

'I don't know, he doesn't tell me.'

'How long has it been going on?'

'I'm not around all the time.'

'When do you think it started?'

'Some time before Christmas.'

'How long?'

'I don't know.'

'Every day?'

'I don't know. I told you. I wasn't there all the time.'

'How much was your husband getting?'

'I don't know,' replied Brenda Noye. She added: 'I have already said more than I should have done. I'm not answering any more of your questions. My solicitor told me that I don't have to if I don't want to. I didn't really want to talk to you in the first place. I understand that you have a job to do, but I mean it this time.'

The interview was at an end. Once again, according to O'Rourke, she was offered a chance to sign the notes of the interview, but again she refused. She later denied ever making any of the comments attributed to her by the police.

After her visit from O'Rourke, Brenda Noye was moved back to Dartford police station. On the afternoon of her arrival she was interviewed by Brian Boyce.

He told her she was to be charged with murder and gave her five minutes to consult alone with the Noye's family brief Ray Burrough.

Re-entering her cell, Brian Boyce asked her whether she was prepared to answer any questions.

Burrough told Brenda Noye: 'This is something you must decide. It must be your decision.'

'No, I don't wish to answer,' she replied. Asked whether she would provide blood, hair and saliva samples, she refused, saying she would seek counsel's advice.

Early on that same Tuesday evening, Kenny Noye and Brenda Noye and Brian Reader were all officially charged with murder.

Both Noyes exclaimed 'No!' when the charges were read out.

Brian Reader shouted, 'I'm innocent of that charge.'

16: A Man of his Word

The following day Kenny Noye was moved to Bromley police station where he was interviewed by Detectives Suckling and Charman.

'What we have to deal with now is the question of gold bullion found at your address and your involvement in the £26 million bullion robbery at Brink's-Mat.'

Noye was not impressed.

'I think that's the last thing I need to worry about at the moment, don't you?' he said defiantly.

'Well, we are going to ask you some questions about it, as you know,' said Suckling.

By this time questions about the gold were the only ones the police could actually put to Noye. He had been charged with Fordham's murder, which meant that they were not permitted to interrogate him again about the killings.

There was brief silence between police and their prisoner. Noye scratched his chin, considering his next move.

'Tell me, what happens when you leave here?'

'What do you mean?'

'Do you write all this down?'

'Yes, we make notes on what's been said.'

'I can't say anything then, can I?'

'Why?'

The reply Noye gave showed just how familiar he was with the Brink's-Mat story.

'That Black's a dead man, isn't he?' said Noye, referring to the guard whose evidence had brought Robinson and

McAvoy 25-year prison sentences.

'You lot wrote down what he had to say. Now everybody knows what he's done. He's a dead man when he comes out. You don't think I'm going to get myself killed because you've told people I've helped you.'

Charman interrupted Noye.

'Are you saying you've got things you can tell us about the gold if we don't write down what we say here?'

'The thing is,' continued Noye, 'what good is it going to do for me? I'm going away for a long time for what I've done. I don't see you can help me whether or not I tell you anything. They won't cut my sentence. It won't make any difference at all.'

Charman sensed that his prisoner was edging towards some kind of a deal.

'The things that have happened to you over the past few days cannot be altered in any way and it would be wrong if we suggested they could. We've arrested you with what I'm pretty sure is some of the Brink's-Mat gold. Our interest is to recover what's left of the £26 million worth that was stolen. You can help us. I'm convinced.'

Noye was scathing.

'I can help to get myself killed as well. You know what these situations involve. I'm a businessman. If I thought there was any way I could put things in my favour, I'd tell you as much as I know. But this is a pretty one-sided sort of deal, from what I can see.'

Noye was then told about the surveillance operation on Hollywood Cottage, including the day Reader left Noye's house with that heavy briefcase and went to central London.

'That was gold from the Brink's-Mat robbery, wasn't it?' pressed Charman.

'If I tell you anything, I'm on my own. What guarantees have I got that you'll help me?' asked Noye.

Suckling studiously avoided the question. He told Noye: 'On that day, I suppose, the gold must have gone down to Bristol, but — I will be honest with you — we didn't follow it, so I don't know. But we do know that, on other occasions, the gold has ended up in Bristol, at a bullion dealers called Scadlynn. It looks very much as if you are the organiser of this whole chain of events, leading up to the realisation of the Brink's-Mat gold.'

'Like you said, there's other people involved. I can't take the blame for what they do,' said Noye.

'Yes, but you're evading the issue. I'm not talking about what they do. I'm saying it all starts with you,' said Suckling.

Noye was shocked. 'It doesn't start with me, no. I've never done a robbery in my life.'

Noye was then asked how he paid for Hollywood Cottage. He immediately claimed it had been with money from an insurance claim and other money he had earned. Asked how long he had been helping to dispose of the gold bullion, he ingeniously replied, 'How long have you been watching me?'

'Since 8 January,' replied Suckling. 'But we know it goes back beyond that.'

'How?' asked Noye.

It seemed a brilliant ploy — the prisoner was interrogating his guards.

Suckling went on: 'Because of what people down in Bristol and Hatton Garden have said.' He then mentioned a fence who'd handled much of the gold.

'I don't know him. You haven't seen him with me, have you?' challenged Noye.

Charman answered, 'We'll accept that. Will you accept that not everybody is capable of disposing of or dealing in gold?'

'Yes, I'll accept that,' replied Noye.

'Will you accept that you have been to Jersey with others in a private plane and that you bought gold there?' continued the detective incorrectly (Noye had taken a chartered flight to Jersey.)

Noye smiled.

'Yes. So what?'

Suckling then told him they believed the gold was

bought to provide legitimate paperwork to cover the moving of stolen gold. He was also told that he had been watched at the Beaverwood Club handing gold over to Reader.

'Perhaps that was the gold I bought in Jersey?' he ventured.

'It wasn't,' replied Suckling. 'We know that gold is still in vaults in Jersey.'

Charman tried to drive home just how much the Flying Squad already knew about the gold run, saying: 'From what we've seen, the activity around you tends to indicate that you are the trusted middle-man who has got the contacts and the money to get what's necessary done.'

'I know what you want from me, but any business I do with you will get me done in,' was the dramatic reply.

'Aren't you exaggerating a bit?' asked Suckling.

'I know enough about the people involved to know that if I say what I know and anything happens after that, they'll know it can only have come from me. If I do anything to get you back that gold which they think belongs to them, then that's me done.'

'Well, two of them can't bother you, surely. They are locked up for twenty-five years,' said Charman.

Noye then began to voice suspicions about how the police had got on to him. He named a man who, detectives believed, had taken part in the original raid but whose involvement they had been unable to prove.

'He probably gave you the name because you gave him some help. He's made sure his share is all right. The only sort of deal I'll do will be businesslike — if it's all in writing and signed by the people concerned.'

With that Noye fell silent for a few moments, then told the detectives that he wanted to speak to Boyce.

'We will speak to Mr Boyce when we leave you,' promised Suckling. 'What can you tell us about Tony Black?' he added, picking up on Noye's remark at the start of the interview.

'I can tell you he's as good as dead,' said Kenny Noye. 'I

know all about false identities and all that, and I know that won't help him at all. They'll find him and they'll have him.'

'Who's going to have him, then?' asked Suckling.

'There's enough money from this to get anyone to do it. They don't need to get their hands dirty.'

'Do you know whether anyone has been hired or propositioned to do it?'

'No, but they'll get that sorted out. It's easy enough.'

Noye was then asked about instructions for the furnace, which were found in the apple store, and once again about where he got his money from.

'I'm a businessman. I told you what I am,' he insisted.

Noye's attempt to sound respectable annoyed Detective Charman intensely.

'What you are, Mr Noye, is a man well acquainted with villains, armed robbers and the sort of men who come into large amounts of money, who will come to you to launder their cash. You're trusted to keep your mouth shut and you share in the profits of crime by percentages, without having to put yourself up front.'

'I put myself up front the other night, didn't I?' Noye bitterly responded.

Charman continued: 'It always goes wrong for these people at one time or another. Why protect them? I suspect that if they were in your position, they wouldn't hesitate to put your name forward. In fact, there's something to bear in mind for the future. A lot of people have been arrested.'

The appeal failed. 'Then they will have to watch themselves like Black, won't they?' said Noye, coolly.

As the interview drew to a close, Noye inquired again about Fordham's family, asking how they were.

'I think you can guess that as well as we can,' said Suckling.

'If that hadn't happened, I think we could be talking now,' said Noye.

'What do you mean? What could we be talking about?' asked Suckling.

'All I'd have to worry about would be the gold and I

think perhaps I might have got a deal and you might have got what you wanted.'

Three hours later Kenny Noye was interviewed in his cell by Brian Boyce. Boyce entered the cell with his deputy, DCI Ken John. He immediately made a point of shaking Noye's hand using one of the secret grips by which Freemasons the world over recognise each other. Noye smiled. He believed he was talking to a brother Mason. Boyce explained that he wanted to ask questions about the gold found outside Hollywood Cottage. Boyce made a point of cautioning Noye in the usual manner that anything he said could be used as evidence later.

Noye then turned to the police chief.

'Mr Boyce, can I speak to you alone?'

'Yes, if you prefer,' responded the senior detective. DCI John immediately left the cell.

Noye continued: 'I want to speak to you off the record. I won't if you write anything down. Have you got a tape recorder going?'

Boyce replied that he had not. He even opened his brief case and emptied out his pockets to put the prisoner's mind at rest.

'I won't write anything down,' promised Boyce.

Noye began by asking Boyce whether he considered him to be a cold-blooded killer. Boyce said he didn't know, but there seemed to be nothing in his record to indicate that he was. Noye then asked Boyce what he thought would happen to him. Boyce said it was up to the court.

'Yes, but what you say can make or break me,' replied Noye.

Boyce emphasised that all he could do was to present the evidence. The rest was up to the court to decide. Noye then began by saying he was a very rich man and that he wanted to give some money to John Fordham's wife and family. Boyce said he understood. Noye turned to matters closer to home. If he went to prison for a long time, his life and that of his family would be destroyed.

Noye asked Boyce whether he had any family and was

told he had. Then Noye inquired when the detective was due to retire.

'I conclude some 30 years service in four years,' replied Boyce.

'I'll make sure you have a good retirement,' said Noye quietly but firmly. 'I'll ensure you have plenty of money when you leave the police. I'll put £1 million in a bank anywhere in the world that you tell me. No one will be able to trace it. I just want you to ensure I do not go to prison.'

Boyce's face showed no emotion or surprise.

'You're wasting your time talking to me this way.'

Then Boyce went on to say the only kind of help he wanted was for Noye to reveal the whereabouts of the Brink's-Mat bullion. Boyce re-emphasised his point. He told Noye he had better weigh up whether he was going to tell him where the bullion was.

Noye replied that he would think about it but that Boyce should remember his offer.

'I am a man of my word,' said Noye.

He then repeated his offer to compensate Fordham's widow and children. He also told Boyce to think about his £1 million offer.

Boyce said there was no question of accepting and repeated what he had said earlier. Noye also insisted to Boyce that Brenda knew nothing of his criminal activities and should not have been charged with murder. He admitted stabbing Fordham but said his wife took no part. He added that there was no point in Boyce sending anybody else to interview him, as his solicitor had advised him not to sign anything.

At the end of the conversation Noye made a point of mentioning that there had been no written record of their interview. He didn't look happy when Boyce informed him that the contents of the conversation would be written down immediately Boyce left the cell.

Noye then recovered his composure before Boyce left and told Boyce: 'You are on your own.'

He then offered the detective a bribe yet again.

Months later Boyce was accused in court of offering to get Noye a reduced sentence. He denied it categorically and related how the bribe offer was made.

'I couldn't be mistaken about being offered a million pounds,' said Boyce.

The following day, officers Suckling and Charman returned to Noye's cell again. This time they wanted to talk about the Meissen china that had been discovered in one of the compartments. It matched other pieces recovered by police at Noye's former house in Hever Avenue, now owned by John 'Little Legs' Lloyd. Noye was also told that fifty brand new £50 notes, in serial number sequence, had been found in his safe.

'That's not much,' he replied.

Asked where it came from, Noye said he couldn't remember. He was then told about the £50,000 that had been discovered next to his sister's home in West Kingsdown.

'What's that got to do with me?' he replied.

'The prefix number on the notes, all fifty notes, is the same as that on the notes in your safe — A24. What's more, they are all new notes.'

'So what? It's not mine,' said Noye.

He was then told that the prefix also corresponded to that found on fifty notes found at Reader's house and on people involved with the gold runs down to Bristol.

Suckling gently turned the screw further. 'You must admit that the series of fifty pound notes, like our observations of you and the others, seem to link all of the people concerned in the disposal of the gold.'

'I want to see my solicitor,' said Noye. 'It's gone far enough.'

Later that morning, Brian Reader and Kenny Noye were both charged with conspiracy to handle stolen bullion.

Noye's only response was: 'No reply until I see my solicitor.'

* * *

Over in Bexleyheath, Noye's parents Jim and Edith were moving out after almost forty years in Jenton Avenue.

They told neighbours their beloved son Kenny had built them a house at the end of a cul-de-sac in West Kingsdown next to where his sister Hilary lived. Mr and Mrs Noye even admitted it didn't matter whether or not they sold their bungalow because Kenny had already paid for their new property.

Just before they moved out, Mr and Mrs Noye allowed the police to search the house, garage and gardens thoroughly. Officers even dug up the Noye's vegetable patch in the search for some of the missing Brink's-Mat gold.

The only thing of interest the detectives did come across was hundreds of new telephones stored in the garage.

* * *

Four months later the murder charge against Brenda Noye was dismissed at a committal hearing at Lambeth magistrates' court in south London because of insufficient evidence against her.

The defence exercised its right to the hearing as an opportunity to discover what a number of prosecution witnesses were going to say about crucial issues in the case.

Magistrate George Bathurst-Norman told the court: 'The only evidence against her is her presence at the time Fordham was on the ground. It's not surprising she was at the scene. If someone comes to your premises, it is not surprising that you go to see who that person is.'

His remarks were a flavour of what was to come.

Then Brenda Noye was re-arrested as she left court and charged with conspiracy to handle stolen bullion.

* * *

Around this time another close friend and associate of Kenny Noye's called George Francis was wrongly linked by police to the Brink's-Mat robbery. A Flying Squad search of his extensive property in Kent drew a complete blank.

The wealthy scrap dealer first gained infamy in 1981 when he was cleared of involvement in a £2.5 million cannabis smuggling operation in which a Customs officer was shot dead.

Then in May, 1985, while Kenny Noye was in custody awaiting trial for the murder of DC John Fordham, Francis was holding court as usual behind the bar of his pub, The Henry VIII near Hever Castle in Kent.

A hooded gunman, dressed entirely in black, burst in and shot Francis at point-blank range. He survived after an operation to remove a 9mm bullet from his shoulder.

No one is suggesting that Kenny Noye was connected to the shooting but his association with Francis was noted with interest by police.

17: Self Defence

Kenny Noye's good friend Micky Lawson was believed by police to be one of the key figures in the handling of the Brink's-Mat gold bullion.

He purchased the smelter from William Allday and Co Ltd in Stouport-on-Severn and — most significantly — his car had been seen regularly at Noye's house. One of Lawson's fingerprints was even found inside Hollywood Cottage. Lawson was eventually arrested on suspicion of dishonestly handling stolen bullion.

At the police station where he was taken Lawson admitted to Flying Squad DS Cam Burnell that he was a friend of Noye. Their children were friends and their wives played squash together. But Lawson said he couldn't remember the last time he had seen Noye or been to his house.

Lawson insisted to police that the furnace had been bought by him on behalf of a mystery Arab who had taken it from him shortly after he purchased it eighteen months earlier.

'Can you explain how the operating instructions for the smelter you bought were found in Kenny Noye's shed?' asked Burnell.

'No, I can't,' replied Lawson.

At a later interview Lawson did admit he bought the furnace under a false name for VAT purposes.

It wasn't until after Kenneth Noye was charged with the bullion offences, that Lawson started co-operating.

'I've been thinking about this all night,' he told Burnell.

'And what have you decided?'

'It's difficult. I've been friends with Ken Noye for a long time. I just don't know what to do.'

'The best is just to tell the truth.'

'I want to but, like I said, it's difficult.'

'You got that smelter for Ken Noye, didn't you?' said Burnell.

'Not exactly.'

'What do you mean?'

'I knew where it was going.'

'To Noye?'

'Yes,' Lawson admitted resignedly.

Lawson had assumed the gold that was to be smelted was from the Brink's-Mat job. Later Lawson's barrister was to deny that the remarks attributed to his client were ever made.

* * *

Kenny Noye and Brian Reader's trial for the alleged murder of DC John Fordham took place at the Old Bailey in November 1985.

At the request of the defence, the gold bullion charges were deferred to a later date.

The drama was played out in front of a jury of seven men and five women, packed press benches and a public gallery filled with well-known faces from the criminal underworld. Security was so tight that each time Noye or Reader arrived or left in a prison van, streets around the court were closed off and armed police posted at various vantage points.

Surprisingly for a major Old Bailey murder trial there were no challenges when the jury was selected. Under British law a defendant had the right, generally exercised through defence counsel, to reject three jurors and demand replacements without giving any reason.

Over the years many defence lawyers had challenged anyone who looked remotely middle class. The belief being that the more affluent and 'respectable' a juror looks the more likely they are to accept the word of the police against a defendant.

Kenny Noye used his wealth to secure the services of John Mathew QC. He insisted that neither Noye or Reader had anything to fear from a middle-class jury because they had nothing to hide. Mathew went on to challenge virtually every police statement in his bid to prove Noye's innocence.

On day one of the trial, immediately after the jury had been sworn in, the court was cleared while the judge, Mr Justice Caulfield, outlined to the jurors the protection they were to receive, including around-the-clock police guard and the interception of all telephone calls to their homes.

Police fears were fuelled that first day when an old friend of Reader's turned up in the public gallery at the Old Bailey. Just a few years earlier he'd been sentenced for nobbling the jury in a trial.

The police mounted around-the-clock protection and surveillance, which even involved Scotland Yard officers visiting the jury at the end of each day's hearing to make sure there had been no approaches.

Detectives were well aware of the problems of jury nobbling at this time following an earlier incident in which a jury member had had his backside slashed from one side to another with a carving knife.

One juror in a south London suburb was approached while she was out shopping. The woman was immediately given two police guards.

There were also strict rules about the behaviour of policemen on jury protection squad duty.

Two officers were severely reprimanded when one woman they were guarding outside her house came out with some sandwiches and a bottle of whisky. They were later told that this breached all the standard regulations.

Seventy-two police officers were assigned to jury protection duty during the Noye and Reader trial. It was a huge show of force and seemed deliberately intended to tell the criminals that they should not even attempt to nobble them.

The start of the trial brought an immediate objection from the defence to the use of photographs of the house and grounds of Hollywood Cottage, which were to be distributed to the jury.

The photographs, Noye's QC Mathew pointed out, had been shot in daylight and could give a misleading impression as Noye's alleged murder of Fordham had occurred at night.

The judge agreed and asked whether the defence wanted the jury to see the property for themselves in conditions similar to those of the night in question. That offer was readily accepted. The court was adjourned and later that evening it reconvened in one of the most bizarre settings in legal history.

At 5.50pm, in darkness and during a heavy rain storm, three limousines ferried the jury to the gates of Hollywood Cottage. The jurors even pulled their coats over their faces to hide their identities from the waiting TV crews and press photographers.

Ten minutes later, with blue lights flashing, two police cars arrived. Behind them was a green prison van containing Noye with a police back-up Range Rover following. Brian Reader had decided against attending, which was his legal right.

On the tarmac apron outside the gates — just yards from where Fordham had been found by his colleagues — the Old Bailey clerk convened the court. The official shorthand writer beside him was sheltering under an umbrella while he painstakingly recorded everything that was said.

Then there was the judge, complete with bowler hat, Noye with an escort of four policemen and four prison officers, one of whom he was handcuffed to. The jury and a clutch of legal representatives were then shown the grounds.

Following at a discreet distance were more than thirty journalists, straining to hear every word.

Up at the house Brenda Noye and her two young sons

were grouped together at a lighted window waving forlornly to Kenny Noye, hemmed in on both sides by his burly escorts.

Brenda even handed out a coat and a pair of wellington boots for Noye to wear. They were thoroughly checked under torchlight by two police officers before he was allowed to put them on.

The expression on Noye's face was a combination of aggressive confidence mixed with injured innocence. It was the way he looked for much of the trial.

In the days of legal arguments that followed, Kenny Noye's decision to hire one of the best defence counsels in the land proved to be money well spent.

Mathew admitted that Noye had indeed carried out the stabbing, but insisted it was justified defence after Fordham had struck Noye in the face when he was discovered.

In that admission, much stress was laid on the way Fordham looked that dark night. Dressed in camouflage clothing and a balaclava, he would, said Mathew, 'have struck terror in the bravest of us'.

Noye's reaction, according to Mathew, had been 'shocked terror. He froze, terrified with fear. Then he was hit in the face, in the left eye — he didn't know with what, but he sprang to life, thinking in a flash that he had been struck with some kind of weapon and assumed that the other man was armed. He presumed he had seconds to live, he thought his end had come and in a blind panic stabbed and stabbed.'

Brian Reader's counsel also insisted there was no case to answer. Reader exercised his right not to give evidence at all during the trial. Just in case they thought this indicated he had something to hide, the judge reminded them that it was only since 1898 that a person charged with any offence, including murder, had the right under English law to give evidence.

Reader could be found guilty of murder only if, first, Noye was proved to have murdered and if he was proved to have given assistance or participated in an assault with the intention of killing Fordham or causing him serious injury.

Hence, in his case there was no pressure for a manslaughter option.

The court heard that Brian Reader had been seen to make a kicking motion by Fordham's colleague, Neil Murphy, but he did not see where the kick landed and his claim was made in a statement five months after Fordham's death.

In court, Noye's counsel was quite open about the criminal activities in which he and Reader had been engaged on the night of Fordham's killing. They were illegally dealing in gold. But they claimed it was gold that had nothing to do with the Brink's-Mat case.

The bullion found at Hollywood Cottage was the subject of proceedings to be dealt with separately, so in the interests of justice the full details of the involvement of Noye and Reader with the Brink's-Mat bullion were omitted.

The prosecution in the murder case could mention it only in explaining why the two defendants were under surveillance. With Brink's-Mat, it was alleged, the stakes were so high that Noye and Reader had no compunction about murdering anyone who might have jeopardised their activities.

In the witness box Noye openly admitted he'd been involved in numerous gold transactions. He said the gold was part of regular consignments he had been receiving, smuggled in from abroad to avoid VAT payments. The profit for Noye lay in how far below the fixed price he could buy gold for and how much he could mark up on top as the VAT he was supposedly going to pay HM Customs.

His counsel Mathew told the court that Noye had been regularly dealing in property for many years. He also bought land, obtained planning permission for building development and sold it.

The prosecution tried to suggest that Noye got only a 50% share of the profits from the sale of a garage for some £775,000 in the mid-1970s.

Noye then revealed his familiarity with setting up offshore banking companies. He claimed that the property deal had been spread over three years to stagger the tax payments and that the prosecution were only looking at one section of it.

Noye's investment in an American trailer home business was also mentioned. It was also stated that he earned a considerable fortune from the sale of his haulage business.

The prosecution said that Noye had millions of pounds in various bank accounts and referred to an account in Brenda's name at an Irish bank that contained £1.5 million.

'I have access to various bank accounts, but the money is not mine,' Noye told the court.

By admitting both the killing and the fact that he was engaged in a wholesale gold-smuggling operation, Noye was hardly presenting himself as a respectable figure to the jury at Old Bailey.

However, following those revelations, virtually every piece of the police evidence, including the interviews with the two defendants and Brenda Noye, was vigorously challenged.

Noye and his defence team insisted throughout that he killed Fordham in self-defence.

* * *

After twelve hours and thirty-seven minutes' deliberation, not guilty verdicts were returned against both Noye and Reader. The jury accepted that the killing had been in self-defence. As the jury foreman announced the verdicts, there were screams of delight from Brenda Noye and Lynn Reader in the public gallery.

Kenny Noye smiled, looked at his wife, then turned to the jury and said, 'Thank you very much. God bless you. Thank you for proving my innocence because that is what I am, not guilty.'

Beside him Reader turned to the jury and said, 'Thank you for proving my innocence.'

The impression was slightly spoiled a few moments later when Noye turned to the back of the court, by then packed with Flying Squad officers, and sneered and mouthed obscenities.

Noye left the dock grinning, although it had not all gone his way. The judge refused an application that his defence costs should be paid out of public funds — Reader was on legal aid. But to Noye it was money well spent.

Anne Fordham, the 38-year-old widow of the dead policeman left the court, where she had sat every day listening to evidence, in tears.

'I am too upset to make any comment,' she said.

Outside the Old Bailey Brenda Noye told waiting reporters: 'I feel marvellous. I just want to get home to my children and start smiling again. I am deeply, deeply sorry for the Fordham family, but the death is down to others.'

Brenda did not specifically blame the police operation, but repeated that 'other people' were responsible. She insisted her husband was deeply sorry for the Fordhams.

'He would say to Mrs Fordham that he was not responsible for what happened and it was the fault of other people,' said Brenda Noye.

She then retired to a nearby wine bar for a celebratory bottle of champagne. Noye had to stay in his cell because he was still facing charges connected with the Brink's-Mat gold.

Her solicitor later issued a statement: 'She is really relieved the trial is over, and she has never doubted the jury's decision from the word go. But she would ask you to consider the unfortunate Mrs Fordham and her children at this time, for whom she has great sympathy. She feels the responsibility for Mrs Fordham's death is on the shoulders of others and not her husband.'

Brian Reader's teenage son was rather more belligerent. 'We are very happy. The whole thing was a complete fit-up,' he said.

Later that same afternoon, John Dellow, Assistant Commissioner of the Metropolitan Police in charge of specialist operations, paid tribute to John Fordham:

'John Fordham had been engaged in many other

operations against very professional, organised criminals. He fulfilled his duties with bravery and with a quiet acceptance of the risks involved. There are many citizens alive in London today who owe their lives to John Fordham.'

Dellow added that because of the nature of Fordham's work, it had been impossible for him to be part of the 'public face' of the Metropolitan Police.

He declined to comment on the jury's verdict, saying it would be 'improper' to do so. And he refused to comment on the operation beyond saying that, despite the killing, there would be no change in police operational guidelines.

'I am satisfied that the operation was as professionally and properly conducted as it could have been,' he said.

That evening Fordham's widow Anne — a New Zealander who had met her husband when he twice visited New Zealand with a view to settling there — was ushered into an interview room at New Scotland Yard.

In a bid to win herself some privacy after the trial, she had agreed to a press conference. With her voice breaking and comforted from time to time by her 22-year-old son John, she described her husband as 'a professional policeman. The work that he did and the risks that he took were all for the good of the country.'

Asked if she believed the operation had involved him in unnecessary risks, she shook her head and said in a forced whisper: 'No.'

Her son intervened only once, when his mother was asked whether her husband would still be alive had the operation had been carried out differently.

'We can't say that,' he said firmly.

A reporter then asked her about the sympathy extended by Brenda Noye.

'*Not accepted*,' she whispered.

* * *

Brenda Noye visited her husband shortly after his acquittal

on the Fordham murder. She told him: 'They're going to get you, Ken, aren't they? If they don't get you here they're going to get you somewhere else. You're never going to live down the fact that you walked out of court on the murder.'

Noye knew his wife was right. He'd drastically changed his attitude since she'd been kept in custody following Fordham's death. As Brenda later conceded, 'After that he thought, Bloody hell if they're capable of doing that to her what the hell are they capable of doing to me?'

Brenda Noye has always insisted that the man she was married to was not the hardened criminal portrayed in the media. She claimed to many that Noye was deeply upset by the death of John Fordham and it was 'something he has to live with forever'. Brenda saw her husband as an extremely successful businessman who'd come up from nothing to be a multi-millionaire. And, claimed Brenda, that meant there were a lot of jealous people out there trying to stab her beloved Kenny in the back.

18: Off the Streets

It was a confident Kenny Noye who strolled back into the dock at the Old Bailey's Number Twelve court in May 1986 — five months after his acquittal for DC Fordham's murder.

He had spent the intervening time in a prison cell, but nothing had dampened his spirits following what he saw as a superb victory over his great enemies 'the cozzers'.

As Noye and Reader, Chappell, Patch, Adams, Lawson and elderly fence Matteo Constantinou lined up in the box, the small army of fourteen defence barristers was also optimistic.

The trial was expected to last two to three months. All the defendants denied handling the bullion, as they did a second charge that all but Lawson faced — conspiracy to evade VAT.

As far as the first more serious offence was concerned, Kenny Noye was the principal defendant, as he had been during the earlier murder trial.

The gold distribution chain had started with him and if the jury couldn't agree that he was guilty of conspiring to handle stolen gold bullion, then it certainly couldn't convict any of the others.

Judge Richard Lowry QC underlined this on day one of the trial, asking the jury to be 'fair, decisive and courageous' when reaching its verdicts.

Lowry seemed an ideal candidate for the case — his entry in Who's Who listed 'fossiking' (searching for gold in old, disused seams) as one of his hobbies.

Noye believed there was a crucial flaw in the prosecution

case — no tangible evidence that the gold he had been handling originally came from the Brink's-Mat haul.

But the police had made some very thorough inquiries into Noye's 'business dealings' following the death of John Fordham. They knew that after the Brink's-Mat robbery, Noye had deposited large amounts of money abroad, sometimes using a false name. They also had a record of all the replies he allegedly made while being interrogated by the police, together with Brian Reader's damning admission, shortly before he was charged, that the gold he was handling came from the Brink's-Mat haul.

However, probably the most significant piece of evidence against Noye were some jottings in one of his diaries, which showed the daily gold-price fixes at the time of the Heathrow robbery. Why would he have made those if he was not involved in handling the gold?

What Noye and the others did not realise was that a young barrister was sitting at the back of the court carefully noting down every single reference to where the gold might have ended up.

He was employed by Brink's-Mat insurers who were determined to recover as much of the gold as possible. Armed with that evidence they sent a team of private investigators to study the homes and offices of all the Brink's-Mat suspects.

Many people were targeted who had not even been prosecuted by police. It didn't matter to the insurers whether they had been charged or not. If they had used some of the money raised from that gold to improve their lifestyles then that made them legitimate targets. Files were opened on each and every person and company linked to the Brink's-Mat case. Documents were carefully assembled.

Kenny Noye and the others had made the mistake of thinking that it would be only the police who'd pursue them.

'They didn't know where we were coming from. They thought perhaps we had some sort of moral vendetta against them while in fact we just wanted to recover the stolen property,' insurance lawyer Bob McCunn explained.

Back at his trial, Noye talked about the gold-smuggling operation but refused to name any of the individuals involved and claimed that no records were ever kept of the various transactions.

Kenny Noye was unable to explain why the date of the Brink's-Mat raid had an asterisk placed against it in his wife's 1983 diary, with a doodle drawn alongside. An examination of Brenda Noye's 1984 diary showed a similar asterisk every 25 to 28 days. As defence counsel Mathew told the court: 'It is clear what those asterisks relate to.'

Even in the middle of his trial, Noye found time to flirt with an impressionable young blonde Fleet Street journalist who was reporting on the case. She later admitted, 'he had one of the most luminous smiles I have ever seen. In a second it turned him from a stony-faced hard man into a charismatic charmer.' As the case went on, Noye grew bolder in his flirting, even though Brenda was in the public gallery. Noye told the young journalist he was going to buy her dinner to celebrated his expected acquittal.

In his summing up to the court Mathew told the jury:

'Kenneth Noye may have been a wheeler-dealer, he may have evaded his tax responsibilities and he may have had trouble over the years (but not for some years) with the law, but at least one can say he has never been an idle lay-about. As he has said, "I don't do any transaction without a deal on the side." Not paying your taxes and smuggling, in this day and age, you may think possibly unhappily are looked upon by many as being in a totally different bracket to the offences of theft and handling stolen property. You may think that most of these people, if not all, who do not declare their profits or all their earnings for tax would probably cut their arms off before they would put their hand in the till and steal even a 10p piece.'

The court rose and the jury retired to consider its verdicts two and a half months after the trial began.

The eight men and four women jurors were informed that — under the supervision of court bailiffs — they would be looked after at an £80-a-night London hotel. No discussion of the case would be allowed outside the jury room.

It soon became clear that the verdict was not going to be arrived at quickly.

The loss adjusters handling the Brink's-Mat insurance claim for Lloyds were so concerned the defendants might be acquitted that they launched a civil action against them the following morning.

In a High Court action a judge agreed that the assets of all seven accused, including the £3 million officially owned by Kenny Noye, should be frozen pending an outcome of the civil hearings.

On Saturday morning, two days after retiring, messages were sent to the jurors' families to expect them home no earlier than Monday. They were promised a day out in the countryside the following day. But the judge refused a request from the predominantly young jury that they, not the court bailiffs, should decide what time they went to bed at night.

It wasn't until the following Wednesday that the verdicts were finally returned.

Noye, Reader and Chappell were found guilty both of the conspiracy to handle stolen bullion charge and the VAT charge.

By the time the last defendant Constantinou's conviction for evading VAT was announced, the judge had to shout to make himself heard. Patch, Adams and Lawson were all acquitted.

'I hope you all die of cancer,' screamed Kenny Noye at the jury as the truth sank in.

And Brenda Noye shouted across the court from the public gallery: 'Never has such an injustice been done. There is no fucking justice in this trial.'

Pointing to the jury, Brian Reader exploded.

'You have made one terrible mistake. You have got to live with that for the rest of your life.'

Reader's 20-year-old son Paul scuffled with police officers as he shouted: 'You have been fucking fixed up!' He was arrested for contempt of court and later bound over for the sum of £100 for twelve months to keep the peace.

Down in the cells beneath the Old Bailey, customs officers immediately slapped a £1 million writ on Kenny Noye for the VAT he had evaded. A six-page High Court writ was also served on him from the Inland Revenue, claiming nearly £1 million in back tax.

Even defence counsel Mathew was infuriated by the Noyes' outburst and told Noye his comments from the dock would not help when it came to sentencing.

The following day, in a bid to make amends, Kenny Noye, casually dressed in pale-blue sweater and open-necked shirt, apologised to the judge before sentencing was announced.

His outburst, he said, had been made 'in the heat of the moment'. Then he stood resignedly as Judge Lowry jailed him for thirteen years for plotting to handle the gold and fined him £250,000.

Noye was also fined a similar amount for evading VAT, plus an extra year's imprisonment, and ordered to pay £200,000 towards the cost of the case, which was estimated to be £2 million.

Noye then received another two years' imprisonment for failing to pay the two fines. He couldn't pay, as his assets had been frozen.

Judge Lowry said the fine could be considered 'paltry' compared with the sums of money involved in handling the gold.

Chappell was jailed for a total of ten years for both offences, fined £200,000 and ordered to pay £75,000 towards the cost of the prosecution, while Reader, described by Judge Lowry as Noye's 'vigorous right-hand man', was jailed for a total of nine years. Constantinou was given a year, suspended for two years, on the VAT fraud.

After the sentencing, Brenda Noye called from the public gallery: 'I love you, darling.'

Kenny Noye blew her a kiss and shouted: 'I love you too.'

Outside the Old Bailey, there were violent scenes as friends and relatives of Noye and the other defendants were surrounded by journalists.

Brenda Noye and four burly minders pushed their way thorough the crowds. Leslie Lee, a freelance photographer working for The Times, was knocked to the ground and kicked when he tried to take pictures.

The following day it was announced that Kenny and Brenda Noye plus two others would face trial over the Meissen china found in a secret compartment at Hollywood Cottage and at one of the houses in Hever Avenue.

The china, worth £3,000, was part of a haul stolen three years earlier.

As Noye's assets were frozen, he applied for and was granted legal aid.

Noye later received a four year concurrent sentence for receiving the stolen property. No evidence was offered in the case against Brenda Noye and she was discharged, but one of the other defendants pleaded guilty to assisting in the retention of stolen property and was fined £500 and ordered to pay £150 costs.

A charge of conspiracy to handle stolen bullion that had been hanging over Brenda Noye was dropped.

Noye's sister Hilary Wilder and her husband Richard, a legal executive, both of whom lived in West Kingsdown, also faced trial for receiving £50,000 from the proceeds of the Brink's-Mat gold. Both were later cleared, although the money was reclaimed by the Brink's-Mat insurers.

It was that utterance of Kenny Noye's about his wish that the entire jury should die of cancer that provided the most telling insight into the character of the man who had stabbed another man to death in self-defence.

* * *

In south-east London's underworld, reaction to the sentencing varied enormously.

Krays' henchman Freddie Foreman said: 'As far as the police were concerned this was the first opportunity they had to convict Kenny and so they made sure he got the maximum sentence. They couldn't have given him a day more.'

But some criminal 'faces' were annoyed that the death of undercover policeman Fordham had sparked an even more energetic probe into the dealings of every single person even vaguely linked with the Brink's-Mat bullion.

'There was no reason for Noye to kill that copper. He could have just let his dogs sort him out. It was such a stupid thing to do and it caused a lot of us problems we could have done without,' commented a member of one of south-east London's best-known criminal families.

* * *

Undercover police officer John Childs — first on the scene following Fordham's death — was shocked by the outcome of both Noye trials.

'We all thought the trial was just an open-and-shut case and that Noye was guilty of John's murder. We were all devastated when he was acquitted. The second trial seemed less important because Noye had been acquitted of the murder and that was totally, in my view, a miscarriage of justice.'

DC Fordham's partner Neil Murphy was convinced that Kenny Noye was not so innocent of causing the death of John Fordham.

'He was playing the very sincere quiet family man, you know, who just happened to go out into his garden and saw someone dressed like we were who jumped on him. So he says, "OK, I don't know what made me do it, but I picked up this knife and, OK, I stabbed him ten times and, OK, I don't know what made me do it, but I thought he was attacking me." I won't accept that that's what happened — ever.'

* * *

Enormous sums of Brink's-Mat money had been deposited in Irish banks in London, as well as banks in Jersey, the Isle of Man and Switzerland. On one occasion a married couple from Britain were stopped by German border guards at the

Swiss frontier, and £500,000 in new £50 notes was found in their car. It was part of a consignment of £710,000 that they planned to deposit in Switzerland.

As deposits were made, companies were set up in Panama, the Cayman Islands, Spain and London to purchase property. Money was then transferred from bank to bank until it arrived back in London to fund the purchases.

By 1986 between £6 and £7 million was floating around in myriad bank accounts and a trust fund in Liechtenstein.

That figure rapidly grew, however, after a series of impressive property deals in London's booming Docklands area. One plot bought for under £3 million was rapidly sold for more than £4 million.

However, not all the deals were so profitable. Some of the Brink's-Mat gang were being taken for a ride by other criminals.

Noye and three others invested $100,000 each in some oil fields in Texas. It wasn't until Brink's-Mat insurance investigators visited the area that they found that the oil wells had been dry for more than ten years.

In other deals financed by the Brink's-Mat bullion, an area of prime land was purchased in Sussex for more than a quarter of a million pounds. But the land had restricted planning permissions attached to it and no houses could be built on it. It was worthless. There was also $1 million paid out for some land in Flordia that was useless because it was in a swamp.

However, many of the Brink's-Mat gang bought themselves huge houses in Britain, which naturally alerted the authorities to their financial situations.

As one investigator explained: 'Being flash was the biggest mistake they all made. They had to spend the money. They couldn't just sit on it and invest it discreetly.'

Meanwhile Kenneth Noye was locked up in Albany maximum security prison on the Isle of Wight. Police even visited him at Albany to try to persuade him to help their investigations into a senior Scotland Yard detective.

The investigation, under the supervision of the

independent Police Complaints Authority, was prompted when a detective constable arrested a drug dealer in south-east London who made allegations against various officers.

In this case, the investigation centred on his relationship with his informants, one of whom allegedly was Kenny Noye. In fact, the two men had known each other since the mid-1970s.

Kenny Noye refused to help the police investigation, although he used the visit by Scotland Yard detectives as an excuse to complain about the conditions at Albany Prison.

* * *

In the summer of 1986, a memorial stone was unveiled to John Fordham in West Kingsdown.

Lord Denning, former Master of the Rolls, paid tribute to Fordham and said he had made the ultimate sacrifice in the line of duty.

Prime Minister Margaret Thatcher even sent a wreath with the message: 'In honour of John Fordham for his devotion and service. We share the sorrow with his family and friends.'

As senior police officers and local councillors attended a special ceremony, Brenda Noye and her children sunbathed in the grounds where Fordham had been stabbed to death by her husband.

From that day on Brenda Noye would have to pass that plaque on her way into the centre of West Kingsdown.

It bothered Brenda Noye so much that, when she visited her husband in Albany prison, she tried to persuade him to agree to sell Hollywood Cottage and find something that would not be connected to that fateful night.

Brenda Noye told her husband she was having to bring up their two sons alone in that huge property while he was in prison. Surely she had the right to decide where they lived?

Noye eventually bowed to the pressure and Hollywood Cottage was sold for more than £1 million. He also approved Brenda choice's of a £300,000 detached house in nearby Sevenoaks. It wasn't nearly as isolated and Noye made a massive profit of more than half a million pounds on the sale of Hollywood Cottage.

Sevenoaks, in the heart of Kent commuter country, would provide Brenda with the sanctuary she required. Brenda also had another subject on her agenda during those early visits to her husband at Albany Prison — their marriage.

Noye's affair with Jenny Bishop and their secret lovenest in Dartford had been exposed in the newspapers. Noye expected Brenda to be furious about it.

Instead Brenda took a somewhat philosophical viewpoint.

She even admitted to a friend: 'I told him I wasn't that bothered about a seedy affair and I would stick by him.'

Brenda Noye's priorities had been very firmly stated.

* * *

Out on the streets of south-east London the lucrative days of armed robberies were numbered. Security vans were monitored with radar by the police and it was virtually impossible to rob a bank in broad daylight. As a result, drugs were increasingly becoming the main currency to be turned into huge fortunes.

As one south-east London robber-turned-drug dealer explained:

'It was gettin' hard work going robbin'. Villains stopped wantin' to go robbin'. They became more interested in drug importation, like. Many of these villains had hit their forties and fifties and drugs provided the perfect retirement pension. Puff (cannabis) and coke were the favourites. You'd bung a few people at customs here and there and you'd get the stuff through the ports easy. Drugs were wiping out the armed robbery trade. It was obvious it would happen.'

* * *

Shortly after Kenny Noye was imprisoned yet another associate of his was murdered in mysterious circumstances. Ex-policeman Daniel Morgan was found with an axe embedded in his skull in a south London car park in 1987.

Detectives initially involved in the inquiry believed Mr Morgan was killed because he was about to expose police corruption.

Two of the detectives named by him were later acquitted of all illicit activities. One of the links between them and Morgan had been Kenny Noye. They all knew one of Noye's closest criminal associates, who later helped bring another crooked policeman to justice.

Knowing Kenny Noye was proving an increasingly dangerous occupation.

19: All Alone

In some ways, Brenda Noye was the ultimate victim of her husband's crimes. Not only had she been incarcerated after John Fordham's death, but she'd also faced the public humiliation of her marriage being disected in the face of Noye's womanising. Now she was left to bring up their two sons alone.

But despite all this, Brenda Noye's reaction to the public exposure of her husband's alleged affair with Jenny Bishop was similar to everything else she felt about her husband's activities. She later commented, 'What can I say? They say Princess Anne had a lover! Ken relates very well to women but he's no Casanova. If he had a girlfriend... well, I've been with that man since I was fifteen years old and twenty-three years we've been together, and he's slept with me every night and come home to me every night. We've got a good marriage and the children are stable and there's not many could go through all that and come out the way they have.'

Yet privately, Brenda Noye had been so appalled by the public reaction against her and her children following John Fordham's death that she had thought long and hard about changing her name. She even admitted to friends that if she hadn't got the children she would have just moved to the other end of the country and cut off all her links with the bad old days.

Remarkably, despite Noye's incarceration and undeniable involvement in organised crime, Brenda proudly taught their two sons to 'stand up, look people straight in the eye and say, "My dad is innocent." ' Both Kevin and Brett were, perhaps not surprisingly, getting a lot of stick at school. But Brenda Noye openly encouraged them not to retaliate. 'Come out and take your anger out on a punchbag or a football or something, don't retaliate,' she later said she told them.

Selling Hollywood Cottage had not proved easy, either. Amongst prospective buyers were journalists, and there was even one story being put round that the house was cursed. In the middle of all this, Brink's-Mat insurers continued to be regular visitors to the house whenever any new cars appeared in the driveway. On one occasion, the insurer's attention was drawn to three brand new Range Rovers parked in the Noyes' barn, just a few yards from where John Fordham had died. Brenda Noye insisted the vehicles did not belong to her or her incarcerated husband and that she was just housing them for some friends.

She continued to tell friends that her husband's costly defence fees were paid by her selling off some of the family's most valuable antiques.

Brenda Noye's attitude towards those who'd labelled her husband a master criminal was to try and explain their life together. As she told author Duncan Campbell in an interview for his book *That Was Business This Is Personal*, 'People ask how he came to have money. When I first met him he worked at night in the print and by day as a tipper driver. He would take a couple of hours' sleep and go out to work. He did that for about two years and then bought his own lorry and eventually got a fleet of about a dozen lorries. He bought a yard, sold a third of it for the price he paid for the whole of it, dealt in watches and jewellery, did property deals in Kent and got a place where the children could grow up without roaming the streets sniffing glue.

'We worked damn hard to get that house [Hollywood Cottage]. We had six holidays, I think, in eighteen years we were together, and two since he's been away. He was a workaholic. When he came home he would sit down and get his work out and see how many lorries he had on the road and hope to God they didn't get a puncture in Birmingham with this load.'

Brenda Noye did later concede to author Campbell that she knew Kenny Noye was smuggling gold, but claimed she had no idea where it came from. I never thought about him being arrested because you don't know what's going on. You're at home doing the housework and they're getting on with their working life. All Ken ever said about it is that he was smuggling the gold. I knew what he was like for avoiding paying his taxes, he could be a little bit of a bugger for that, but when it all came down I thought at the end of the day they'll sort this mess out and he'll probably end up with two years for not paying his tax and that is it. I never even believed it would get to court or anything like that.'

Even Brenda Noye's law-abiding parents got caught up in the atmosphere of distrust between the family and the police. Her mother refused to go on jury service because of the injustice she believed had been carried out against her son-in-law.

Then there were some of Brenda's friends who turned their backs on her and the family after Noye's imprisonment. She later recalled: 'The ones I honestly felt I could lean on I never saw. The ones you didn't know that long came to the front.'

She claimed that the costs of the two major cases had put her and the family in serious debt. With tongue firmly not in check she even told one associate: 'I just thank the gods that my husband was surrounded by a lot of genuine businessmen who have helped me an awful lot.'

∗   ∗   ∗

In the months following Noye's sentencing, Brenda Noye faced numerous threats to herself and her family. These included anonymous letters and even black-edged cards containing warnings about killing the two Noye boys. One day Brenda picked up the phone in Noye's office at Hollywood Cottage. A familiar voice at the other end of the line said, 'I've just lost a relative.'

'Oh, I'm very sorry,' replied Brenda Noye.

'I've got a tape recording of your husband threatening someone about the land. I'm going to the police with it,' said the caller.

Brenda took a deep breath but kept her cool. 'Well, you do that, I don't know what you're talking about.'

'I'm going to take it to the police and he'll get another four years.'

The line went dead.

The same man called Brenda Noye virtually every night for the next week. She was convinced that if she went to the police then the media would get hold of the story and blow it up out of all proportion.

A few days later Brenda visited Noye in prison on the Isle of Wight. During their two-hour chat the subject of the anonymous caller came up. Her husband insisted that he'd done nothing wrong. 'I only ever bought the land off one old person and I got him rehoused and bought him a colour television and a video and Christ knows what else,' explained Noye to his wife. Then he added: 'Just front it out and take it to the police.'

But Brenda wasn't convinced. 'I'm not going to because it'll just go to the press and they'll make it out the worse way they can.'

A few days later the same caller rang back yet again. 'This tape, how much are you going to give me for it?'

Brenda snapped back: 'You're sick, you're really sick and you need treatment.'

'You're not going to look so pretty when your husband comes out by the time I've finished with you.'

Brenda hung up and never heard from the man again.

* * *

Also during those months following Noye's sentencing, Brenda spent many sleepless nights brooding about what she considered was a gross miscarriage of justice regarding her husband's heavy sentencing for VAT fraud. She was angry that following his acquittal of the Fordham murder, Brenda was advised by lawyers to say nothing about her husband to anyone, not to retaliate and behave as if she was the quiet demure wife who was just happy that her husband's ordeal was over.

But Brenda believed she should have reacted in exactly the opposite way. As she later explained to journalist Duncan Campbell: 'I should have screamed and shouted and hollered about what happened and not accepted what the lawyers said. They're interested in you not rocking the boat. I should have started campaigning from that day on when I was given the chance. They told me right from the start, "You're wasting your time, you're fighting society. You're not in a position to fight it or get anywhere." '

But Brenda told legal advisors, including the ever-present Henry Milner, 'I will prove him innocent and when he comes out you'll all bloody well kiss his feet.'

The Noye defence team tried to be sympathetic to Brenda but she knew that once Noye went down they would have to move on to the next case. Brenda Noye's growing bitterness with the police and the press treatment of her husband had turned her into a much harder character. She even admitted to one associate: 'I'm very bitter. It's something that grows in you and you can't stop it.'

20: Code of Practice

Make no mistake about it, jail was not the place Kenny Noye or any of his criminal associates wanted to be. Prison was there to take away his liberty, to lock him up and keep him from his beloved family, away from society.

But Kenny Noye had to behave because he knew that the first man out of the gate was the cleverest man. He'd leave the trouble-making to other, lesser mortals.

All around him in prison were drug addicts, homosexuals and social misfits. He saw it as a den of vice. He watched as inmates injected themselves with filthy needles. He heard the gossip about who the 'girl-boys' were and those who'd just give blow jobs. None of it mattered to him because he had businesses to run. He was above the riff-raff and everyone knew it.

Noye's criminal brain worked overtime, even in prison.

As one former south-east London detective pointed out: 'Like other parts of life there's a pecking order in prisons, and the more successful the criminal is the higher up the pecking order he will be. He'll have an easier life because he'll have gophers running around doing his chores for him.'

Certainly, prison life was never that hard for Kenny Noye. His reputation as a hard man went before him and many of his fellow inmates were convinced he'd been 'fitted up' over the Brink's-Mat handling charges because of what had happened to DC John Fordham.

As one prison officer at Albany Prison on the Isle of Wight explained: 'From the day he arrived to the day he left no one laid a finger on him or even said a bad word to his face. Kenny Noye was revered.'

Before his arrival at Albany following his conviction, a vast dossier on Noye was forwarded to the governor telling him about every known habit of the prisoner.

Noye was a Category A prisoner, which meant he was considered dangerous and likely to try to escape. He had to be accompanied at all times by a prison officer. He was even obliged to carry his dossier, called a Category A book, everywhere he went, even to the lavatory.

Even at night the attention was unyielding — guards were ordered to make sure they saw Noye every fifteen minutes.

Kenny Noye just wanted to get on and serve his sentence with the minimum of fuss. He'd already calculated he could get out in less then eight years with remission, if he played his cards right.

But as a Category A prisoner Noye also carried a lot of weight among the other inmates and they were the people whose respect mattered most of all.

The screws knew all about Kenny Noye. Some treated him with disdain, while others hero-worshipped him in almost the same way as many of the prisoners.

Kenny Noye made a point of remembering all the names of the useful screws. Some of them made it clear that in exchange for a backhander they would ensure that he got pretty much whatever he wanted. Money spoke louder than words, even in prison.

Noye did not blatantly bribe prison officers because he knew it would cause no end of problems. The prison had numerous closed circuit TV cameras to record prisoners' movements. But he did arrange to deposit money into the bank accounts of a couple of officers.

Many screws simply wanted an easy life. They didn't want aggravation and Noye realised that if he was to sail through his long sentence without any problems, then he had to call a sort of truce between himself and the authorities inside prison.

It wasn't just about respect. Both sides just wanting an easier time. In some ways it was the same as the IRA and

UDA men inside Albany who had an unwritten rule not to fight each other inside jail. There was a definite code.

Noye also knew that prisoners such as himself with the so-called respect of many of the other inmates could be a help to the regime in charge. They had the sort of respect the staff could never command. Soon Noye was being consulted by both inmates and staff on numerous internal prison matters.

When he got sent to Frankland Prison near Durham, he and a member of one of the most notorious crime families in south-east London were regularly called into the governor's office and consulted about prison security.

Some screws did try to pull rank on Noye. They objected to Noye's power and influence inside prison. Once a prison officer falsely accused Noye of stealing from another inmate. Noye seethed with anger about the accusation, but somehow kept calm and the danger passed.

'His attitude was we're here for a quiet life. Let's get on with our bird and get out. We don't want no aggro,' explained one old lag.

The inmates looked up to Kenny Noye and if the prison staff took any liberties he was always one of the first ones knocking at the governor's door.

Police claim that around this time Noye confirmed his status as an informant by offering Scotland Yard information on his fellow Brink's-Mat criminals in exchange for a reduced sentence. However, when it was made clear there could be no reduction of his sentence his offer of information was withdrawn.

Many of Noye's criminal associates insist to this day that he was not an informant. One south-east London robber-turned-drug dealer commented: 'The police do not like it, it is obvious because he killed one of their officers and someone high up has got it in for Kenny Noye. They put this story about to damage him.'

* * *

Meanwhile others continued to pay a heavy price for knowing

Kenny Noye.

Nick Whiting, an old school friend and close associate of Noye, had been questioned by police over allegations that he was involved in laundering some of the proceeds of the Brink's-Mat gold.

A former saloon car racing champion, 43-year-old Whiting lived in palatial splendour at Ightham, Kent, and had built up a fortune of more than one million pounds, apparently from a garage business in nearby Wrotham.

In June 1990, Whiting's luck ran out. He was abducted from his garage by an armed gang and five top-of-the-range cars were also taken. The cars were all soon recovered from nearby locations, but there was no sign of Whiting.

Then surveyors carrying out preliminary investigations for a new theme park at Rainham Marshes, in Essex, stumbled across Whiting's body hidden in undergrowth.

The father of three had been stabbed nine times and then shot twice with a 9mm pistol. The two men eventually charged with his killing were later acquitted. Once again, being an acquaintance of Kenny Noye had proved extremely dangerous, but it should be pointed out there is no way of connecting Noye to the murder of Whiting.

Back in prison, Brink's-Mat insurance investigators visited Kenny Noye on at least three occasions. It was not an ideal setting for such delicate negotiations.

Noye told agents he was worried his conversations were being monitored and in the end he recommended that they deal directly through Brenda Noye or one of his legal representatives.

Investigators were putting increasing pressure on those associated with the Brink's-Mat robbery because they feared the money might disappear completely. They already believed that millions of Brink's-Mat pounds were being spent on investments in drugs.

Also, in 1990, 57-year-old ex-train robber Charlie Wilson was murdered by one of south-east London's most feared young gangsters Danny Roff.

Wilson had been dealing in huge quantities of drugs, much

of which was purchased with Brink's-Mat money. Roff was owed money by Wilson so he travelled to Spain, personally shot Wilson and then escaped, bizarrely, on a bicycle.

Both men had met and socialised with Kenny Noye over the years. Whether Noye was in any way directly connected to Wilson's death is impossible to say. But the list of victims of violent crime he'd been acquainted with didn't end there.

In 1990, 27-year-old Stephen Dalligan, brother-in-law of Brink's-Mat defendant Tony White, was gunned down in the Old Kent Road. Dalligan survived but refused to talk to police about his associates, who included Kenny Noye.

Kenny Noye eventually got a 'dream ticket' move to Latchmere House resettlement centre, located by the edge of leafy Richmond Common on the borders of south London and Surrey. Latchmere, an imposing white-washed Victorian mansion with outhouses occupied by the inmates, was known as the flagship of the penal system to most inmates because of its relaxed regime. 'It was an open prison that everyone wanted to go to,' said one ex-inmate.

Ironically Latchmere had been chosen during World War II as the safehouse where Hitler's deputy Rudolf Hess was first secretly kept following his bizarre decision to crash land his Messerschmitt in Scotland in May 1941.

By the time Kenny Noye arrived, the staff consisted of prison officers with many years' previous experience inside Britain's top security establishments.

The officers even had to call the inmates by their first names and show them a certain degree of respect. As one inmate explained: 'It really annoyed some of them to be charming to a load of villains like us.'

Inside Latchmere, inmates were expected to do their community service and gradually start the process of rehabilitation back into society before their eventual release.

Noye lived in a small six-man dormitory. He saw little of that room, however, as he was out of the prison for the best part of eighteen hours each day.

Prisoners were supposed to be back at the centre not a

minute later than their previously agreed time each day. Any breaking of those rules could result in an inmate being shipped back to a 'normal' prison.

As one officer explained: 'Noye thought he'd hit the fucking jackpot at Latchmere. I told him, "You're not at fucking home, son. You fucking make sure you come back here every evening or else!"'

Kenny Noye knew that one or two screws sounding off at him was a small price to pay for the freedom that Latchmere House gave him. Under the jail release work scheme Noye, by now 45, officially worked for a company called Skiphire, in Crayford, Kent. But he was rarely seen there. Noye left the resettlement centre in Richmond, Surrey, at 4.30am most mornings in a borrowed BMW.

On day-release from Latchmere Noye also regularly visited Brenda and his two sons at their new house in Sevenoaks.

One day Brenda caused quite a stir at Latchmere by turning up in a brand-new £35,000 K-registered Mercedes, which Kenny later proudly boasted to inmates was a Christmas present from him. But Brenda Noye wasn't the only woman who came to Latchmere House to take Noye out for the day.

'We used to lay bets on which blonde would arrive for Kenny Noye,' said one Latchmere prison officer. 'Most of them tended to favour the fur coat and black stockings look.'

Another time during his day release from Latchmere, Noye contacted his cousin Michael and arranged a meeting in a south London suburb to discuss some 'important business'.

Noye was irritated that a photo of him at a Masons' gala night had been turning up in the Press.

'I want the negatives to every photo you've got of me,' said Noye coldly.

Michael did not argue with his cousin.

As he later explained: 'I just did what he asked. I didn't want any aggro.'

Noye even started inquiring among his criminal associates about any potential drug deals that might be worth investing in.

His attitude towards drugs had changed when in prison. Noye knew about the risks of setting up such deals inside prison. He needed to know what level of surveillance he was under so he got in touch with another Kent associate and asked him whether he had any police contacts.

The man was an acquaintance of Michael Lawson, one of Noye's oldest friends and the person who bought the gold smelter that was connected to the Brink's-Mat affair. It was well known among a close-knit group of Kent criminals that Lawson's acquaintance had a senior detective called John Donald in his pocket.

While inside Latchmere, Noye began to get reports from the National Criminal Intelligence Service through his associate's police 'contact'.

He soon discovered he was being shadowed while out on day release. Noye now knew he had to be very careful but he was so confident he still went ahead and began setting up a £50,000 cocaine deal through his old contacts in the Mafia in Miami and New York.

But Noye's drug deal was monitored by the American Drug Enforcement Agency which was tapping the phones of the Mafia man. They were astonished to find that Noye was still serving a prison sentence. The DEA immediately informed Scotland Yard about Noye's activities. But within days, crooked detective John Donald — a sergeant at the National Crime Intelligence Service — leaked all the information about the DEA tip-off.

Noye was particularly anxious to know the exact level of the surveillance on him because he was about to hand over £50,000 to the Mafia's cocaine connection in America.

John Donald warned Noye that US Drug Enforcement agents had almost enough evidence to implicate him in the drugs deal.

Noye immediately pulled out of the deal and the NCIS realised they had been compromised. A six-month ongoing investigation into Kenny Noye had to be abandoned at a cost of tens of thousands of pounds. Other officers were later outraged that Detective John Donald had been helping Noye, who was considered an enemy of all policemen following the death of DC John Fordham in the grounds of Hollywood Cottage.

Noye's pleasant lifestyle at Latchmere was abruptly ended after his involvement in the Mafia cocaine deal was uncovered by police. Noye was furious that he had been named by the Kent criminal who acted as go-between with a crooked detective.

As a result Noye found himself unceremonially dumped into HMP Swaleside, on the Isle of Sheppey, in Kent.

Noye got a virtual hero's welcome in Swaleside where he encountered numerous familiar faces from the Old Kent Road pubs and clubs he'd frequented throughout his adult life.

Everyone inside Swaleside knew Kenny Noye was a millionaire and soon he had new friends and sidekicks offering their services.

Within weeks of arriving at Swaleside, Noye was given the best job inside the jail — as a gym orderly. This gave him access to a phone for incoming and outgoing calls. Soon he was running his entire life from the end of that phone.

Inside Swaleside Kenny Noye cut an impressive figure. He surrounded himself with younger, extremely fit inmates many of whom he met through his job as gym orderly. They looked to Noye for advice and guidance. They respected him and he rewarded their loyalty inside prison with promises to 'invest' in their activities once they got out. Noye never liked to get his own fingers dirty and here were criminals prepared to go out and commit crimes that he could benefit from.

Inside Swaleside, other prisoners even held all Noye's illicit belongings in their cells, so that he wouldn't face any disciplinary problems within the jail.

Noye continued cleverly to nuture the prison staff as well. By then he was getting porn magazines, vodka and cheap cigarettes on a regular basis.

When the wife of one officer celebrated her birthday, Noye bought her a £600 watch-bracelet. Noye and the officer even declared the gift to the governor.

'There was nothing the authorities could do about it because it was all done out in the open,' explained another officer. 'But we all obviously had a good chuckle about it because you couldn't help wondering why Noye would give out something as valuable as that.'

Noye had a vast supply of phone cards, so that he could use the main prison phone whenever required, although he preferred the privacy of the outside line at the gym.

'Kenny Noye was soon running things inside that prison. No one dared take him on,' said one Swaleside officer. 'He was a friendly, shrewd man. He never made us look foolish because that would be too easy.'

Noye even got his favourite cigars brought in for him by friendly officers.

A typical day inside Swaleside went as follows:

8am:	up for breakfast
9am:	start work
11.30am:	lunch then lock-up at 12.
1.30pm:	unlocked and back to work
4.30pm:	back on the wing
5pm:	tea
6pm:	association
8pm:	locked up again for the night

Besides his own TV in his cell, Noye also kept a desktop computer and stereo. Brenda Noye even brought her husband a brand new duvet for his bed.

Noye was also allowed to cook his own meals with pots and pans provided by Brenda. His pasta was soon renowned among the élite chosen few who became part of Noye's inner circle inside the prison.

'We didn't mind because it was good for prison morale, but there were times it felt like something out of *The Godfather*,' said another member of the prison staff.

Noye even got Brenda to buy him sports equipment, including boxing gloves, weightlifting belts, three tracksuits, badminton racquets and shuttlecocks. He donated it all to the prison gym, on condition he had first refusal to use any of the equipment.

Kenny Noye's cousin Graham visited Noye when he was in Swaleside. He immediately realised that his cousin was running things inside the jail.

Graham Noye recalled: 'Kenny asked me whether I wanted a cup of coffee when we sat down at a table in the visiting room. He came back three minutes later with the coffee and six Kit-Kats. Nobody bothered him. He seemed to have the run of the place.'

Noye and Graham spoke in detail about the Brink's-Mat job and the death of DC John Fordham. Noye never once swayed from the story he had told in court during his trial for the alleged murder of the undercover police officer.

'He jumped on me first, I swear it,' Noye insisted. 'I had no choice.'

Graham Noye later recalled: 'Kenny was very proud of his connection with Brink's-Mat and he reckoned that he'd do his bird and come out still young enough to enjoy himself.'

Graham Noye even sent Kenny a Christmas card inside prison that year, which featured a photo of the Bank of England, where he worked as a clerk. It was Graham who had first sparked Noye's interest in gold many years previously.

'Let me know when you want to come and see me here, Kenny,' wrote Graham, who has no doubt that his cousin was capable of anything he put his mind to.

Inside Swaleside Prison, fitness fanatic Noye eventually joined forces with one of the jail's most notorious inmates, Pat Tate, another of the gym orderlies.

Tate was already a well-known criminal who commanded respect in the London underworld after staging a daring escape from a magistrates' court in December 1988. Two policemen and a WPC who tried to stop him fleeing the court in Billericay, Essex, were injured in the process.

Heavily tattooed Tate, who also faced a charge of possessing cocaine, leapt on a 1,000cc motorbike driven by a pal and escaped.

The 18-stone villain had been charged with armed robbery after a knife gang held up a Happy Eater restaurant in Laindon, Essex, and stole £800.

Tate boasted that he'd fast tracked into Swaleside despite being at the beginning of a long sentence for a violence-related offence.

Inside Swaleside, Tate became Kenny Noye's personal body builder and minder. Among the bench presses and dumb-bells, Tate further convinced Noye there was a fortune to be made out of drugs.

As former Brink's-Mat investigation chief Brian Boyce pointed out: 'As the drugs explosion came about I think everyone turned to drugs and it was drugs that became the highway and conduit for all other criminal activities.'

Drugs were undoubtedly easy money compared to robbing and there were always middle men to take a fall if the law caught up with anyone.

Kenny Noye was shrewd enough to know that, if he wanted to replace all those millions frozen by the Brink's-Mat insurance agents, then drugs would be the answer.

21: The 'E' Game

Inside Swaleside Prison, Pat Tate told Kenny Noye all about the designer drug Ecstasy, which was taking off in Britain. Unlike heroin and cocaine, Ecstasy could be sold to teenagers as user-friendly. An amphetamine, it propelled the release of a chemical, serotonin, that gave an immediate rush to the brain.

The side-effects included panic-attacks, kidney, liver and heart problems. A Health Education Authority survey recently suggested that by the early 1990s, 31% of the 16–35 age group could not identify any health risk from taking Ecstasy.

Pat Tate convinced Noye to invest £30,000 in one of his early Ecstasy deals. It was just one of many occasions when Brink's-Mat cash helped flood Britain with Ecstasy in the late 1980s and early 1990s.

'Ecstasy provided the gang and their fences with a perfect investment opportunity,' explained one of the detectives involved in the Brink's-Mat inquiry. 'There is absolutely no doubt that the flood of Ecstasy into Britain was backed by Brink's-Mat cash that was floating round at the time.'

Kenny Noye was aware that some of his Brink's-Mat circle had invested money in cocaine and then moved on to Ecstasy because it was more profitable and far less risky. Some of Noye's robber associates even boasted to him that they had increased their fortunes tenfold with little effort.

And inside Swaleside, muscleman Pat Tate knew how much money Noye had available for 'suitable investments'.

Eventually, Noye came around to his way of thinking.

Kenny Noye had no problems getting the £30,000 needed to invest in Pat Tate's drug-peddling venture. Three months later the drugs had been purchased, distributed and Noye had been handed back a handsome £70,000 profit by Tate.

Once Kenny Noye tasted that profit, drugs became the backbone of his business opportunities inside prison. All it needed was a few phone calls and the money would come pouring in.

Noye had friends everywhere. He suspected he was still under surveillance inside prison, but believed that with his contacts he could continue all his activities just so long as he remained very careful.

The Pat Tate Ecstasy deal ensured that Noye was always one step removed from the purchase of the drugs. In other words it was actually easier for him to control the deal from inside prison because he had the ultimate alibi if anyone tried to finger him.

Inside Swaleside it seemed to other inmates and staff that Noye and his henchman Pat Tate were being given special privileges. At one stage Noye tried to pressurise prison authorities to allow Tate day-release visits to his girlfriend. Tate eventually made some day-release visits to her Essex home before his release.

Noye had teamed up with Pat Tate even though he was an extremely dangerous man with many scores to settle. One of Tate's former associates, 'Nipper' Ellis, upset the hardman with some remarks he made about his family. Tate immediately took out a £10,000 contract on Ellis' life, while Tate was in prison with Noye.

Ellis later explained: 'My family were told that Tate planned to snatch my little sister and take off her fingers one by one as a warning. She was only 15 and was terrified.'

While inside prison it became clear to Kenny Noye that the Brink's-Mat insurers were not going to stop chasing what legitimately belonged to them. Many of the Brink's-Mat criminals' bank accounts, including Noye's, had been frozen but much of the money was still missing. When Noye discovered that the Brink's-Mat investigators were not working in the pockets of the police, he decided to negotiate in order to get them off his and Brenda's back.

He knew that insurance agents had already spent months following Brenda near her Kent home. They had checked out everything from the money she spent on her weekly shopping for the family to the types of cars she bought, to the cost of the luxury holidays she regularly took while Noye was in prison.

Noye established that the insurers were prepared to negotiate in complete privacy because, ultimately, Brink's-Mat wanted its money back — nothing more, nothing less.

Eventually Noye's lawyers met up with insurance investigators and began trying to work out a deal. It would take time because Kenny Noye was determined not to be completely cleaned out. He wanted to stay in control of the situation even from inside prison.

The Brink's-Mat insurance representatives were relieved to find that dealing with Noye's lawyers and accountants was much easier than with many of the other Brink's-Mat circle.

As one of the investigators pointed out: 'With some of these characters you had to watch your back constantly to see who was sitting nearby. On one occasion a gun was shown tactfully just to remind us who they were dealing with.'

Kenny Noye would never show such disrespect. As far as he was concerned dealing with the Brink's-Mat investigators was just another aspect of his business. He'd got involved in a risky venture, so he needed to find a way out of this latest spot of bother.

However, he wasn't going to be hurried and the negotiating had only just begun.

* * *

In Swaleside Kenny Noye rapidly became one of the fittest

inmates thanks in part to a vigorous training programme supervised by bodybuilder Pat Tate. Noye also became personal weight training partner to one officer called Peter Askew.

Noye was also keen on playing badminton. It was a one-on-one sport and team games remained unappealing. Typically, Noye's regular playing partners included a number of prison officers, which helped nurture his close relationship with members of staff.

Following Pat Tate's release from Swaleside, Kenny Noye was introduced to Derek 'Del' Kandler, a black Caribbean 28-year-old murderer who'd been given life imprisonment on 25 November 1987. He'd just arrived from Wormwood Scrubs when he met Noye.

'Kenny and Del got on like a house on fire. They both had rapid-fire criminal minds and an impressive understanding of each other. They were like a mutual appreciation society,' explained one member of the prison staff.

Noye — steeped in a lot of old fashioned south-east London colour prejudice — was surprised to find that Kandler was a witty, bright criminal not unlike himself. The only difference was that he'd run out of luck and been found guilty of the ultimate crime — murder — after clashing with a business rival.

Kandler soon also became a gym orderly and was even given a Gucci watch by Noye. Clearly, Kandler was Noye's number one gopher.

However, there was another side to Kenny Noye, which some of the other inmates and staff never forgot.

'He had an uncontrollable temper if you ever crossed him,' explained one former Swaleside prison officer. 'He used people like Tate and Kandler as a buffer between himself and the other inmates because he didn't want to end up fighting with anyone. On one occasion Noye was approached by another inmate in the canteen. Noye's face went red with rage because this fellow had dared to talk to him without his permission,' explained the officer. 'He never made that same mistake again.'

At Swaleside, Noye had numerous visits from Brink's-Mat police detectives still trying to persuade him to tell them who was involved in the crime.

Noye showed complete and utter contempt towards the police. He said he wasn't interested in deals anymore. One time he even lost his temper with two detectives, thumped his hand on the table in front of him and warned them to 'Fuck off out of my life!'

As one of the detectives later recalled: 'That was when we saw Noye's true colours. He didn't like us putting him under pressure. He was not a pleasant man. He had a temper that was terrifying.'

In the early 1990s, Kenny Noye secretly purchased a two-acre plot of land that backed on to his parents' and sister's houses at the end of Hever Road in West Kingsdown. He orchestrated the purchase through phone calls to his accountant and solicitor from inside Swaleside Prison.

As one local explained: 'Kenny Noye seemed to want to own the entire area at the end of that cul-de-sac. Maybe he wanted his family to be able to see who was coming across the fields.'

The Noye houses were in such close proximity to one another that their security cameras panned from one house to the other to keep an eye out for unwanted visitors.

Around this time another of Kenny Noye's associates — London money launderer Donald Urquhart — was shot dead by a hired assassin in a London street. It later transpired that the gun used in the killing was supplied by another contact of Noye, policeman-turned-gun-dealer Sidney Wink.

There is no suggestion that Noye was connected to Urquhart's murder but knowing Kenny Noye continued to prove extremely dangerous.

In August 1992 Kenny Noye's old friend Jean Savage, wife of Brinks-Mat robber John 'Little Legs' Lloyd was jailed for five years for transferring £2.5 million during shopping trips to the same Bank of Ireland branch in Croydon where Noye opened an account during the Brink's-Mat inquiries.

Grandmother Savage, 48, had even been nicknamed Lady Goldfinger for painting her nails gold and wearing gold jewellery at her trial. Savage loyally refused further to implicate Noye, whose bungalow in West Kingsdown she and Lloyd had bought years before.

On 14 November 1992 Kenny Noye watched himself on TV from his prison cell in a TV film of the Brink's-Mat raid called *'Fool's Gold'*.

The amazing story of the raid had been made into a prime-time TV film starring Sean Bean as gang leader Micky McAvoy. Actor Larry Lamb portrayed Noye as a smooth-talking, gold jewellery-encrusted fence with a penchant for flashy clothing and expensive cars. It wasn't so far off the truth.

Noye quite liked Lamb's portrayal but was annoyed at the new round of publicity about Brink's-Mat, which inevitably sparked further activity from the police and insurance investigators still anxious to clear up 'one or two outstanding matters'.

While in Swaleside, Noye was also informed he was barred from membership of the Freemasons. It irritated Noye, as he was busily planning all sorts of new ventures for when he was released. He still needed that impressive network of contacts to ensure that he could continue his 'career' uninterrupted. But one setback wasn't going to stop him from keeping a lot of fingers in a lot of pies.

Eventually, Noye was transferred to the even easier regime at nearby Blantyre House prison.

Later Noye even paid out of his own pocket for the hire of a bouncy castle, trampoline and other play equipment to be set up in the grounds of Blantyre House one Saturday for inmates and their families during a special open day.

'A lot of us were surprised that Noye was allowed to pay for it, but there was nothing in the rules against it,' said one prison staff member.

It seemed like a remarkably kind gesture from Kenny Noye. But then he was determined to make himself indispensable in the eyes of the staff and inmates. Noye didn't want anyone even considering transferring him back to any of the high-security prisons.

He was on the home straight and knew that soon he'd be back in the big world breaking laws and making even more money.

22: Turkish Delight

Immediately after his release from prison in the summer of 1994, Kenny and Brenda Noye celebrated by spending a month on Northern Cyprus — the Turkish controlled part of the island. During the trip Noye visited the secluded mansion of runaway financier Asil Nadir, sought in Britain on fraud charges involving his Polly Peck business empire.

Nadir wanted Noye to head up his security team on the island and actually paid for Noye's accommodation at his Jasmine Court Hotel.

'Nadir was very impressed by Kenny Noye,' explained one detective involved in the surveillance of Noye. 'In many ways they were quite similar. Nadir was intrigued by Noye. There was a criminal aura that surrounded Noye and that made him an interesting character.'

Noye gave Nadir some free advice on whom he should contact back in Britain for security cover, but he didn't get involved because he wanted to keep a low profile having just been released from prison.

However, Nadir did encourage Noye to invest money in property in northern Cyprus. Nadir told Noye he believed that eventually the Turkish section of the island would become a major holiday destination for British tourists who were being priced out by the ever-increasing cost of Spain and other European countries. Three million visited the south of the island every year, but only 30,000 came to the north. An explosion of popularity was inevitable.

Noye tried to buy a house during his stay on the island.

He visited one secluded villa that belonged to a local restaurant owner. She had been entranced by the handsome English stranger from the moment he walked into her restaurant with his wife and two sons. Noye and his son Kevin visited the woman's property several times before backing out of the deal because the house didn't have a swimming pool and was too far from the sea.

However, they did put down a £30,000 deposit on a penthouse apartment being built just a few hundred yards up the coast from the Jasmine Court Hotel in Kyrenia. It overlooked the sea and Noye put it in Kevin's name. Noye adored Kyrenia not least because it had a port with direct access by ferry to the Turkish mainland.

Throughout his stay on the island all Noye's movements and phone calls were monitored by British secret service agents in collusion with the Metropolitan Police.

'That's how we know he met Nadir. Kenny Noye couldn't make a move or a phone call from that island without us knowing about it,' explained one detective.

If Noye knew he was being watched he certainly didn't seem to care. In northern Cyprus, his entrepreneurial spirit knew few boundaries. Half way through the holiday, Noye found a stretch of isolated coast line on the east side of the island just north of the port of Famagusta. It was cheap and seemed the perfect location to make a business investment. Noye wanted to create a timeshare holiday complex. He'd seen others make a fortune out of such developments on sunshine islands elsewhere, so now it was his turn.

Timeshare was a relatively new development on northern Cyprus. The scheme would cater for tourists wanting to reserve for themselves several weeks each year in an island villa.

During that trip Noye allegedly decided to invest in the development and Brian Reader's brother Colin also got involved. It was to be called the Long Beach Country Club.

Timeshare's attraction, as Noye had already noted, was that by selling individual weeks in a villa, the amount made from all the weekly bookings would be much greater than the actual real-estate value of the property.

Noye helped finance the project by selling some of his gold stock and a number of other properties, including a business in Florida. He even got one associate to fly some cash out to him in northern Cyprus.

He believed that, within five years the Long Beach Country Club would be booming. With an investment in dozens of timeshare villas, the sale of the weekly units would bring in a vast profit.

The sales technique was a familiar one used by a number of timeshare development companies in the USA, Britain, Spain and Portugal. A sales army of more than a dozen touts, mostly British youngsters, would be employed to lure prospective buyers off the streets. The money they were going to pay would then be banked offshore on the Isle of Man.

It seemed like yet another great business opportunity for Kenny Noye.

Whilst they were at the plush Jasmine Court Hotel, Noye and Brenda even befriended a disabled holidaymaker called David Williams from Milton Keynes. Noye was impressed by Williams' spirit and even took him out for dinner with Brenda on at least three occasions. Williams never forgot the kindness shown to him by the 'other side' of Kenny Noye.

* * *

Back in London, another of Kenny Noye's associates hit the headlines.

Ex-Metropolitan Police officer Sidney Wink was a gunsmith and weapons dealer. His speciality, although never proved in a court of law, was renumbering illegal weapons, including those used by members of the Brink's-Mat gang.

Wink was also strongly suspected of supplying the guns used in two murders — the 1992 contract killing of Noye's London money launderer Donald Urquhart and the shooting of PC Patrick Dunne by three Yardie gunmen.

In August 1994, a week after officers investigating PC Dunne's murder raided his Essex home, Wink put a pistol to his head and pulled the trigger.

Another death of someone linked to Kenny Noye. When would it end?

* * *

Not long after Kenny Noye was released from prison he decided to recruit some more law and order officials to his payroll to try to avoid the way he had been almost caught out over that cocaine-smuggling operation when he was in Latchmere House.

Noye began casting around his contacts inside and outside the police to find out whether he could 'buy' the services of a hard-up British intelligence officer.

He knew that MI5 and MI6 had recently joined forces with the police in mounting complex surveillance operations and he wanted to know when he was under watch.

Many ex-spies suffered from personal and money problems, making them especially vulnerable to the very kind of tempting offers Kenny Noye had available.

'Noye actually believed he could buy anyone if the price was right and he didn't like the way we were still trying to shut down his operations,' explained one detective.

Eventually Noye made contact with an ex-intelligence officer whose security clearance had been withdrawn but still had access to certain computers and was happy to keep Noye informed for a price. The agent was bitter about the way the intelligence services had treated him.

What Kenny Noye did not realise was that the 'agent' had been planted inside Noye's operation.

'The idea was to monitor Noye's activities. We knew he was well aware of our surveillance, so this seemed the best way of keeping an eye on him without him knowing,' explained one detective.

The ex-intelligence agent was astonished to discover

Kenny Noye was paying out large sums of money to numerous police contacts and even recruited one police officer who gave him details of phone taps still being carried out on his home.

Police had also been tapping phones belonging to Michael Lawson, Noye's associate and good friend who bought the smelter that was found in Noye's house by the Brink's-Mat investigators. The police taps were also made on offices, mobile and hotel telephones used by both men.

At one stage Noye was receiving weekly transcripts of telephone conversations picked up on his telephone, in a warrant signed by the then Home Secretary Michael Howard.

What Noye didn't allow for was that Customs and Excise officials had also continued monitoring his movements and he had no one inside that particular enforcement agency.

* * *

Kenny Noye proved just how strong his influence had been inside Swaleside Prison soon after his release. Three prison officers and Noye's best friend inside the prison, convicted murderer Derek Kandler, visited Noye's new home near Sevenoaks on 11 September 1994.

The warders had earlier escorted prisoner Kandler to a weightlifting competition in Birmingham in a prison Montego and were returning to the Isle of Sheppey when they found they had some time to kill. Kandler made a call to Noye and the unlikely foursome were invited round to Noye's home.

The security breach came to light only because Customs and Excise officers had Noye under surveillance and traced the prison officers' car registration number to Swaleside Prison.

Prisoner B83180 Kandler was unhandcuffed throughout the visit to Noye.

In confidential prison documents leaked exclusively to this author by a dissatisfied member of the staff at Swaleside Prison, the full story of this extraordinary incident can be told for the first time.

They reveal that Kandler was not even strip-searched before going to the weightlifting competition and not forced to wear handcuffs.

As the three prison officers and their inmate drove down the M40 they saw a signpost for Sevenoaks.

'That's where Ken Noye lives. Why don't we nip in and see him?' asked Derek Kandler.

Two of the prison officers looked at each other and shrugged their shoulders and pulled off at the next public telephone box. Kandler and one of his guards then made a call to Kenny Noye.

Brenda Noye told the convicted murderer and his guards on the phone that Noye was out but due back at any moment. They headed straight for his house.

None of the prison officers realised that the house was under constant surveillance.

At between 5.30 and 6pm the murderer and his guards reached Noye's house in Sevenoaks and were welcomed in by Brenda Noye. They were shown into the living room and offered a cup of tea.

The watching Customs and Excise surveillance officers were astonished.

Noye eventually turned up with a friend of his called Mick. The men exchanged pleasantries about the weightlifting and training in general. Noye then told them to follow him in his car to a Thai restaurant.

Noye's friend Mick ordered all the food because none of the others had ever been in a Thai restaurant before in their lives. Another man then turned up with three women and they all sat down to enjoy their meal.

Wine and beer was served throughout the meal, and convicted murderer Del Kandler knocked back numerous drinks. Noye kept saying to one officer that he wanted to meet him for a game of badminton. Noye also openly referred to his close relationship with many other prison officers.

Noye paid for the entire meal that day.

In that secret prison report there is a specific document relating to Kenny Noye's prison record. It reads as follows:

HM PRISON SWALESIDE
SOCIAL/CRIMINAL HISTORY

NAME:

Kenneth Noye
Reg No: B73876
Category: A: 01.03.85
            B: 25.01.91
            C: 15.01.92

BORN:

24.05.47 in Abbey Wood,
London

ETHNIC GROUP:

White European

SENTENCE:

14 years on 24.07.86 & 4 years concurrent
on 15.05.87

OFFENCES:

1. Conspiracy to handle stolen goods
2. Conspiracy to avoid payment of VAT
3. Handling Stolen Goods

PRISON WORK ALLOCATION:
Gymnasium Orderly

STATUS:

Married to Brenda Noye with two children

HOME ADDRESS:

Hollywood Cottage, School Lane,
West KIngston(sic), Kent

EDR:

Released on EDR of
28.05.94

* * *

Also out of prison, Noye's former Swaleside henchman Pat
Tate found that dealing in Ecstacy was not always a safe
occupation. Someone tried to kill Tate at his £250,000
bungalow in Basildon in December 1994.

It all began when a brick was thrown through the toilet
window while Tate was in there. When he peered outside a
gunman opened fire with a revolver from close range.

Tate raised his right arm to shield his face. The bullet hit
him in the wrist, travelled up his arm, and smashed bones in
his elbow.

Tate later told his mother that his own murderous habits
may have provoked the attack. He had even hidden a gun
under the hospital bed where he'd been taken following the
shooting.

Tate admitted that just a few months earlier he'd
ambushed a drug dealer called Kevin Whitaker, 27, and
killed him with a poison jab. Whitaker had been working for
a rival gang of drug pushers in Romford, Essex.

First Tate and an associate paralysed Whitaker by forcing
him to snort large quantities of a substance called Ketamine.
Vets use it to numb horses before castration, but it is known
in the underworld as 'Special K'.

Tate's associate then snatched a bag containing £60,000-
worth of cannabis.

As helpless Whitaker's muscles froze, the laughing
gangsters pierced his groin with a syringe and pumped a
deadly concoction into his blood. After he died, they

dumped his body in a ditch near Basildon in Essex.

Pat Tate's fearsome reputation was growing by the day.

Around this time, Kenny Noye made a rare public appearance with his family when he attended the funeral of his uncle, the father of his boyhood friends, cousins Michael and Graham Noye.

'He looked real flash and turned up in an expensive motor with all the trimmings. We hardly spoke but at least he bothered to come, I suppose,' recalls Graham Noye.

Noye did talk to his other cousin Michael at the wake held in a local pub following the funeral. He told Michael he was enjoying life and had no intention of going inside ever again.

'He meant it,' recalled Michael. 'And when Kenny said something like that you knew he'd keep his word.'

Meanwhile the bid to recover the Brink's-Mat proceeds continued. The insurers even brought a civil action against a suspected Brink's-Mat robber.

In June 1995, with all this pressure mounting, Kenny Noye finally agreed to return nearly £3 million of the proceeds from the Brink's-Mat robbery. In a confidential settlement, Noye gave back laundered money to the underwriters. Investigators had traced £2.8 million in bank accounts to him in Britain and Ireland.

Noye also gave up claim to the eleven bars of Brink's-Mat gold worth £110,000 found under the patio of Hollywood Cottage.

Noye submitted to the deal after underwriters agreed to make no claims against the £300,000 mansion in Sevenoaks, which was now in Brenda Noye's name.

Loss adjusters Bishop International were increasingly confident that the majority of the £26 million would eventually be recovered.

* * *

At a pub just off the Old Kent Road, a small and dirty enough place to keep most ordinary punters out and therefore chosen for its privacy by a number of south-east London faces, Noye met up with John 'Little Legs' Lloyd. Lloyd said he was planning a cash card cloning scheme he believed would net them a huge fortune.

Cash dispensers were the key to this daring crime and Lloyd — common-law husband of jailed Brink's-Mat handler Jean 'Lady Goldfinger' Savage — was looking for backers to set up the audacious crime. He'd already recruited Noye's south-east London hero Billy Hayward.

Kenny Noye immediately decided he wanted a piece of the action. The hole-in-the-wall job (also known as the ATM scam) was potentially the biggest crime ever committed, as it involved stealing one billion pounds from cashpoint machines.

Noye gave financial backing to the team of villains who had spent many months planning the crime. He also used his own extensive prison contacts to scout around for some technical recruits to the team.

They were going to tap into the latest banking technology and an army of corrupt communications engineers and computer experts would be needed to make huge numbers of cloned cashpoint cards.

These would then be used to empty cash from the bank accounts of thousands of ordinary people. If they pulled it off it would throw the entire British banking system into total chaos.

Eventually computer boffin Martin Grant was recruited from inside Blantyre House open prison in Kent where he'd earlier met Noye. He had been jailed for attempting to murder his wife and child.

In prison, Grant had studied for a degree in electronic communications. Grant was then allowed out on day-release for work experience at a van hire business owned by Paul Kidd, another villain involved in the cash card cloning scheme.

The hole-in-the-wall gang even planned to enter British Telecom exchanges with a team of corrupt engineers to put telephone taps on the lines and memory boards. This information was then to be transferred to the gang's computer.

Although Noye's role was purely as an 'investor' he knew that once again he'd inevitably become the conduit through which much of the proceeds would travel. Noye was so convinced that this crime would overshadow Brink's-Mat that he hosted a lavish celebration before the job had been carried out.

In the mid-summer of 1995 the hole-in-the-wall criminals enjoyed a champagne dinner at a Kent hotel followed by six prostitutes hired for £3,000 for the entire night to service them.

Unknown to the gang, computer wizard Martin Grant, who was plainly out of his depth amongst the hardmen of the hole-in-the-wall gang, was already feeding information about the credit card scam to police.

He'd confessed to a prison chaplain about the planned robbery and later made a statement of over 300 pages in length to Scotland Yard detectives.

On the evening that the men were supposed to have sex with the prostitutes, Grant got cold feet. He didn't want to sleep with any hookers, let alone the ones specially recruited from London by Kenny Noye.

Noye became infuriated with Grant when he turned down one of the girls. Tension had been building between the two men for weeks. Noye had agreed to keep Grant on the team only because his computer knowledge was invaluable.

Grant was doubly nervous because he was a police informant. Eventually he forced himself to sleep with one girl in case it gave him away as a grass. It was a disaster and the other gang members made fun of him because of his failure to perform.

Meanwhile, Kenny Noye had sex with every one of the women.

'When Noye paid for anything he expected good value for money and he certainly got it that night,' explained one detective who later interrogated Grant.

Noye remained furious with Grant. He was suspicious

about his behaviour. Eventually his instincts proved entirely correct.

On 25 July 1995 Kenny Noye's old pal Billy Hayward's home in Yalding, Kent, was raided by detectives investigating the hole-in-the-wall scam. Officers seized more than 70,000 blank cash cards at Hayward's home plus 28 computer disks. They immediately arrested Hayward and four other suspected members of the firm.

Detectives didn't have enough evidence to nail Kenny Noye, but they knew that he'd invested some of his own money in the scheme.

A murder contract was put out on computer boffin Martin Grant the moment he began singing.

As Roy Ramm, one of the senior detectives involved in the case, explained: 'The ATM scam was a classic example of a group of south London robbers and villains who saw an opportunity to make a great deal of money, but did not have the technical expertise so they worked outside their circle and brought in somebody who eventually destroyed them.'

At Blantyre House prison, a warder was arrested in July 1995 by police investigating the hole-in-the-wall scam.

An inmate was also arrested and at least six other prisoners were moved from the prison following nationwide raids by Scotland Yard's Cheque and Credit Card Squad.

The hole-in-the-wall scam had been uncovered before it had been put into operation, but Kenny Noye had avoided being legally implicated in the crime.

＊　＊　＊

Hole-in-the-wall computer boffin Martin Grant eventually revealed what it was like dealing with so-called master criminal Kenneth Noye. 'Noye and Lloyd were just names to me at first. They meant nothing. But people inside Blantrye House talked about them as if they were gods. When I tried to sabotage the scam by saying it wouldn't work they got heavy. One inmate told me if I wasn't careful

I'd lose my eye. That's when I contacted the police.'

Grant said he attended one meeting with the gang where Noye produced prison paperwork on his (Grant's) record and family background. Those details included the addresses of Grant's mother and brother. Then, in a chilling incident, John Lloyd drove Grant up to his mother's house and walked him through the front door and even introduced himself to Grant's mother 'just to let me know he knew where she lived'.

Grant added: 'John Lloyd then phoned Kenny Noye to say he had met my mum. I was so scared.'

But Grant conceded that the first time he met Noye 'he was charming to me. A real gentleman. But if ever anything went wrong with the equipment I saw the aggressive side of him come out. I could see how he could lose his temper and him and Lloyd told stories about hijacking vehicles in the early days and what they did to people who crossed them.'

Grant said that during the time he was involved with Noye, he made continual references to other criminal associates in Spain and the United States. Grant also confirmed that a number of other London criminal families invested funds in the hole-in-the-wall scam. He said that when he decided to go to the police about the scam he was too scared to report anything to staff at Blantyre House because some of the staff were 'so close to Noye'.

Grant says that Noye became very threatening towards him once he and Lloyd began suspecting he might have grassed on them. One time they got a bunch of other villains to follow me back to prison to make sure I wasn't in touch with the police,' he said. He also recalled an incident when Noye and Lloyd almost came to blows after they had a problem with the computers they were using as part of the scam. 'I saw Noye lose his temper with Lloyd and it wasn't a pleasant sight,' is all he will say.

Grant claimed that while still in Blantyre House he was given £50,000 by an inmate who was handed it by a visitor who was a contact of Kenny Noye's. The cash was supposed to secure Grant's role in the scam but instead he claims he threw it away in disgust. 'I didn't want the money but it shows just how powerful Kenny Noye was that he could get that money to me inside jail,' said Grant. Then Noye even opened a building society account in Grant's name and started dropping small amounts of cash into it. After the arrest of the hole-in-the-wall suspects, Martin Grant was put into police custody away from the prison for his own protection. Detectives were so worried that Noye and his associates might harm Grant that they put him in a safe house with armed officers 24 hours a day and only moved him by helicopter. Grant concluded: 'I know they hold a grudge against me and I'm very nervous about it. Remember, I have seen the other side of Kenny Noye, not so much against me, but against others who have mucked him about. Although he can be a very nice chap he is quite capabale of turning into an aggressor.'

Grant had absolutely no idea what he was letting himself in for when he signed up on the witness protection programme. There are two distinct categories of protected witnesses. The first is the innocent bystander. If they agree they are given every privilege imaginable and are helped to set up a new life. The second category are professional criminals like Martin Grant who turn grass because it is their only choice if they want to avoid more prison sentences. And the police tend never to let such people forget they are criminals. Rather than being kept in a hotel or safe house, they are more likely to spend their time being moved between special protective prison units and police stations. As Grant later recalled: 'It was worse than the open prison I was already in.'

At the time of writing Martin Grant was still in hiding, afraid that Noye and his associates might still wish to do him harm.

23: Deadly Medicine

10 November 1995 was a Friday night like any other in Raquel's nightclub in Basildon, Essex. It was also the night that a youth bought four Ecstasy tablets, one of which killed schoolgirl Leah Betts. The death of Leah sparked a nationwide debate on the dangers of Ecstasy as well as outrage against the evil drug dealers who supplied those pills.

Now, it can be revealed that Kenny Noye helped finance the purchase of the consignment of those drugs through his friend and former Swaleside prison henchman 18-stone muscleman Pat Tate. Nightclub boss Tony Tucker was Tate's right-hand man along with another steroid freak Craig Rolfe.

At Raquel's the piano bar had been transformed into the neon-lit Buzz Bar, complete with piped jungle music. Chart music and slow dances had given way to house music and garage nights to bring in the young crowds.

Tate — nicknamed the Enforcer — and Tony Tucker were themselves living life on the edge with constant rounds of drug cocktails of cocaine, Ketamine and Ecstasy. They started to suffer violent mood swings and, on one occasion, Tate got into an argument at a pizza restaurant in Basildon, Essex, over the topping he wanted. The manager was punched and then had his head smashed down on a glass plate. He was too scared to make a statement to police. But none of this seemed to bother Kenny Noye who happily bankrolled Tate and Tucker's drug deals.

'The link between Noye and Tate was significant. They formed a partnership in prison and it developed into a major drug-smuggling operation by the time they were both out,' explains one detective.

The Ecstasy tablets supplied that night by Tate and Tucker were called Apples. Four of them were obtained by a youth who gave one of them to his friend Leah Betts for her birthday the following night. The young man bought them in good faith, without being told that they were double strength. They cost Leah Betts her life and sparked nationwide outrage.

None of this concerned Kenny Noye, however. His only priority was making money and the deals with Tate were easy because he could distance himself from them and the profits were vast. Conservative estimates put the value of the Ecstasy business in Britain by the mid-1990s at more than £500 million per year. The Ecstasy trade adhered to the classic economic rule — buy cheap, sell expensive. Most of the Ecstasy flooding into Britain could be bought for as little as £1 or £2 a tablet, mainly from The Netherlands where Noye still had close contacts from his earlier gold-smelting activities. It was then sold on the street through people like Tucker and Tate for sometimes as much as £20 a tablet, a vast mark-up.

Noye knew that the sheer scale of the production of Ecstasy meant that there was a vast supply network and he found it a much easier option than smuggling gold, which had effectively ended with his prison sentence in 1986. From manufacture in Europe to use in Britain, the Ecstasy trade chain was complex, with up to fifty pairs of hands often involved. Noye cut that down to just five or six and saw his profits leap.

Most of the Ecstasy came in through ports like Dover in Kent and Harwich in Essex, as well as illicitly landing on the beaches of the south coast. Freedom of movement under EU laws meant that it was difficult for customs officers to track down the Ecstasy traffickers who were capable of smuggling thousands of tablets in something as small as a briefcase.

From English ports the Ecstasy was quickly moved to a warehouse in London that Noye rented specifically for the distribution. It was then taken to wholesale suppliers in the main cities of Essex, Kent and East Anglia — Kenny Noye's territories. That was where his old friend Pat Tate came in. Tate was in charge of ensuring that tens of thousands of tablets every weekend got into the hands of small-time dealers who were essential to the entire process.

Not everyone in the criminal underworld approved of the switch from robbing banks and security vans to dealing in drugs.

Former Krays' henchman Freddie Foreman pointed out: 'Drugs were becoming like heavy gangsterism. There were too many people involved. It became widespread. There was also a stigma in dealing drugs. Also, people would name so-called drug dealers to police just to get them off the streets. All the people I know and associate with are from the old school and they don't want to know about drugs at all. People like Pat Tate got involved in the drug scene to his error.

But Kenny Noye wasn't interested in what the old-timers thought — he was in it for the money.

* * *

South-east London underworld figure Tony White — long suspected of direct involvement in the Brink's-Mat raid — was furious with Kenny Noye for settling those insurers' claims on the missing gold bullion. For White was then ordered by the High Court to repay £2,188,600 and his wife Margaret £1,084,344 in compensation and he was convinced it was because Noye had paid up so easily.

The High Court Judge Mr Justice Rimmer even told the court that White did participate in the planning of the Brink's-Mat robbery and said: 'Mr White is a dishonest man with an appalling criminal record.' The judge also pointed out that White's earlier acquittal on the Brink's-Mat charges at the Old Bailey in 1984 meant only that the jury was not satisfied that White was guilty according to the standard of proof required.

Brink's-Mat insurers continued their efforts to recover the remainder of the proceeds from the bullion. They even established that some of the gold bullion proceeds had been laundered in Miami by a money launderer with strong Mafia connections who knew Kenny Noye.

'This character was laundering all sorts of proceeds from crimes and the Brink's-Mat bullion proceeds was just a small part of his operation,' explained one insurance investigator. 'But this was a crucial development because it showed just how wide an area we would have to cover in order to get back all the proceeds of the robbery.'

In fact, Noye had met this same man during numerous trips to Florida in the 1970s and early 1980s. He was also an associate of the men involved with Noye in his trailer-park business north of Miami.

The Brink's-Mat insurance investigators travelled across the world, to Scotland, the Isle of Man, Ireland, Denmark, Germany, Spain, Cyprus, Greece, Hong Kong and the Far East.

And there were yet more attempts at intimidation by some members of the Brink's-Mat gang. One agent had heroin planted on him to try to get him arrested when he arrived back in Britain following some surveillance work abroad on one of the gang.

Investigators also found a huge sum of money in one bank account in the Middle East after continual surveillance on it for months.

In Britain, Noye found himself yet another mistress and even bought her a £150,000 house in a small Kent village. It was conveniently situated for afternoon love trysts whenever he could slip out of the family house in nearby Sevenoaks. As with all his previous (and in some cases still current) mistresses, Noye also happily splashed out thousands of pounds on the house's furnishings.

To Kenny Noye it was definitely the controlling aspect of such secret relationships that appealed to him. Although, as he had already proved with the prostitutes he hired for the hole-in-the-wall gang, there were times when he simply couldn't control his urges.

Whatever Brenda's true feelings on the subject it was clear she had chosen to ignore her husband's infidelities. In exchange, she enjoyed a luxurious lifestyle and a future that would never see her short of money whatever happened to her husband.

Kenny Noye's appetite for illicit sexual encounters came a close second to his obsession with wealth, although, as with everything else in his life, he sometimes managed to combine the two to devastating effect.

In 1995, Noye became friendly with two women who were living in a rented house in Brigden Road, Bexleyheath. The women held a series of regular, very noisy parties at the house. These social gatherings were on most Fridays throughout the second half of 1995 and the first few months of 1996.

Guests at the parties spanned the typical range of Kenny Noye associates and included policemen, criminals and many who inhabited that grey area in between.

'They were wild parties and Kenny Noye called all the shots,' one detective later recalled.

The motive behind Kenny Noye's involvement in those parties soon became clear. Noye actively encouraged the girls to entertain guests, so that he would have even more favours to call in with the police, customs or whoever else might pose any threat to his many illicit operations.

The police knew all about the parties but there was little they could do about them, as no laws were being broken.

* * *

An unknown Range Rover was parked in front of padlocked gates leading to a fishing lake rented out to anglers by Ken Jiggins and Peter Theobald, who ran the nearby 130-acre Whitehouse Farm, near Rottendon in Essex.

The two men were puzzled by the car parked on the lonely farm track blanketed with snow on that cold December day in 1995. At first, the two men didn't even notice that one of the rear windows was shattered.

The Range Rover was blocking their route so they climbed out of their Landrover and tapped on the window to ask the occupants to move. There was no response. They looked so peaceful that Ken Jiggins thought they were all asleep. Then Jiggins noticed that the driver was slumped to one side with blood running from his nose and mouth and his eyes were closed. The passenger was sitting bolt upright with blood all over his face and chest. Jiggins immediately called the police on his mobile phone.

His friend came running back from the Range Rover to say there was a third dead body slumped in the back seat. It was Kenny Noye's old friend Pat Tate and he had been blasted twice in the head and once in the chest. Neither of the men could see any footprints leading away from the vehicle in the snow.

Within less than an hour the place was crawling with police as the Range Rover — registration number F424 NPE — was covered with a tarpaulin and loaded onto a police lorry with the bodies of Pat Tate, Tony Tucker and Craig Rolfe still inside.

Forensic experts spent the rest of the day combing the track and surrounding area for clues. Overhead a helicopter scanned the fields with a heat-seeking camera for any more evidence of what had happened.

Police believed Rolfe, Tate and Tucker were lured to their death by the promise of a massive drugs deal. All three men were pumped up on steroids the entire time. Tate never went anywhere without his mobile phone in his hand and a gun in his pocket. It wasn't until detectives started digging that they uncovered the Ecstasy connection between Kenny Noye and Pat Tate.

Privately, detectives spent many months trying to prove a link between Noye and the deaths of Tate and his two criminal associates. But two other men were eventually charged in connection with the murders.

'Noye's involvement in Ecstasy through Pat Tate is without doubt. But we could not establish he was involved in the killing of Tate and the other two,' one of the investigators later explained.

It later emerged that Tate, Tucker and Rolfe had been invited to meet and inspect a landing site for a light plane that was due to bring in hundreds of thousands of pounds worth of Ecstasy. Their 'host' was another person who knew Noye, Michael Steele, aged 55. Steele met the other three men in a pub and climbed into the back of their Range Rover alongside Tate, who was so relaxed about the meet he didn't even bother bringing along a gun. But as the car turned into a quiet lane off the A130, it had to stop at a closed gate where Steele's accomplice, Jack Whomes, was hiding. Steele opened the back door of the Range Rover to get out and open the gate as Whomes rose from the ground and ran towards the car blasting away with a shotgun.

Only Tate had time to put up his hands and crouch down — Tucker and Rolfe were killed instantly. After Whomes reloaded, Steele is believed to have taken the gun from him and then shoot each of the men behind their ears 'just to make sure'.

But to this day, police privately believe that another more powerful figure commissioned the hit.

'We have our suspicions about the involvement of others,' said one detective.

It also emerged that Tate, just like his friend Kenny Noye, wasn't averse to horse trading with police if required.

As one Essex drug insider later explained: 'Pat Tate thought he was a clever bastard. There were rumours that he'd been feeding the Old Bill with info to keep them off his back.'

Was Kenny Noye's involvement in the Ecstasy trade one of the 'tit-bits' Tate offered the police?

'If it was, then Kenny Noye would have gone fucking bananas,' added the Essex drug insider.

* * *

Back in Kent, Kenny Noye added yet another mistress to his collection. Blonde divorcée Sue McNichol-Outch, 44, lived in a £250,000 four-bedroom town house in Bromley, Kent.

Noye's blue and grey Land Rover Discovery was frequently seen parked outside McNichol-Outch's home by neighbours.

She and Noye began a passionate affair eighteen months

after Noye's release from prison. They had known each other for almost thirty years, as Sue had been married to one of Noye's Bexleyheath school pals, estate agent John McNichol-Outch, for nearly 17 years until their divorce in 1988.

From 10–17 April 1996, Noye even took his blonde mistress to northern Cyprus while he oversaw the development of that timeshare business on the island. The couple spent the first night at the Jasmine Court Hotel where he'd stayed at Asil Nadir's expense just after his release from prison almost two years earlier.

They had orginally planned to stay in the penthouse apartment just along the coast from the hotel, which Noye had bought in his son Kevin's name, but it had not been completed.

Again Noye had drinks with Asil Nadir who remained keen to recruit Noye as his security adviser. And again, Noye turned down Nadir's offer. Then he moved eastwards across the island to the Long Beach timeshare development near Famagusta. Construction work was slow but Noye could afford to wait for the development to be completed because he knew he'd get such a massive return on his investment.

After staying in one of the few constructed villas for a few days Noye and Sue flew back to London.

Once back in Britain, Kenny Noye became involved in a plan to import a brand-new designer drug into Britain.

He had spent the previous few months in high-level negotiations to buy vast quantities of the hallucinogen Khat from African drug barons. Although legal in its raw form, Khat leaves were processed by some dealers into capsules of oil, which did breach British drug laws.

Noye was persuaded by some criminal associates that it would be possible to make even bigger profits than he did from Ecstasy if the market was saturated immediately. He was seriously considering investing as much as £500,000 in the drug over the following eighteen months, but he was concerned that no one had tried a similar operation before.

Noye was shrewd enough to know that there must have been a good reason, so he decided to wait and see whether

Khat had the impact on the British drugs scene that everyone kept telling him it would. In the end it never properly materialised on the open market. Kenny Noye's instincts had saved him a lot of money.

Around this time Noye's tame 'secret service agent' was dropped by him because Noye didn't trust him. In fact, Noye was rapidly dropping many of his associates. His dwindling circle of trustworthy friends was shrinking by the week. He was starting to believe he was a marked man.

He was finding it increasingly difficult to operate on a criminal level. The police kept turning up at his home demanding answers to questions about crimes he was (and in some cases was not) involved with. Noye kept his cool, but he told Brenda that it might make sense to live abroad. Certainly that would be the plan after his 50th birthday in May 1997. He'd always promised himself he'd retire then.

He still had a vast fortune, but he wanted more. Pressure was mounting and his patience was wearing thin.

24. Sudden Fury

M25/M20 INTERSECTION, SWANLEY, KENT, 1.15PM, MAY 19, 1996

Kenny Noye had things to do and people to see when a small red van swerved in front of him as he headed at speed down the motorway slip road. He angrily flashed the full beams of his Land Rover Discovery at the Bedford Rascal and blasted his horn as the vehicle slowed down for the first set of traffic lights on the busy intersection near Swanley in Kent.

As the lights turned green, Noye swung his L registered Discovery across the two-lane roundabout to pursue the van. He was infuriated and had decided to teach the driver a lesson. Inside the Bedford minivan, electrician Stephen Cameron, 21, and pretty blonde fiancée Danielle Cable, 19, had minutes earlier set off from their nearby homes to get some bagels for a late Sunday breakfast. Danielle had no idea that her driving had just sparked a tirade of abuse from the motorist in the Discovery.

Just then Noye cut them up again and Danielle was forced to brake hard to avoid a collision. 'That was stupid,' said Stephen Cameron, sitting next to his fiancée in the van. He looked across at the driver of the Discovery and shook his head. The two vehicles moved on to the next set of traffic lights just a couple of hundred feet further along the busy roundabout. This time the Land Rover pulled up sharply in front of them. Noye got out. He was wearing jeans and a T-shirt and a short jacket with a zip. Witnesses later said he seemed to be looking for something in the pocket of that jacket. Cameron, almost six foot in height, stepped out of the van as Noye approached.

Kenny Noye came face-to-face with Cameron. They exchanged a few words and Noye punched Cameron hard in the face. As he recovered his balance, Cameron noticed something glinting in the other man's hand. He immediately tried to kick whatever it was out of his grasp. 'Get in the van. Get in the van,' Danielle Cable shouted at her fiancé.

But by now the two men were struggling and Noye twice plunged a knife into Cameron's heart and liver. In the middle of all this, Danielle Cable frantically tried to stop the stream of passing traffic. 'Help. Please help us,' she screamed. Meanwhile Cameron, despite his injuries, was trying to kick the knife out of Noye's hand. As she turned she saw the four-inch blade glinting in the daylight.

No one stopped to help.

Then Danielle moved towards her fiancé, Stephen Cameron, as he staggered towards her. He was clutching his chest.

It was only then she noticed the blood all over him.

Cameron told her: 'He's stabbed me. Dan, get his number plate.' Danielle looked across at the driver of the Land Rover. Kenny Noye was walking back to his car still carrying the knife in his hand. Another motorist later said he saw Noye smiling.

'Help. Somebody please help us,' screamed Danielle Cable as she once more looked at her fiancé, covered in his own blood. He collapsed in her arms. Nearby, the Discovery's tyres screeched as Noye drove off at high speed.

Minutes later an ambulance arrived but it was already too late. Cameron never recovered consciousness and was pronounced dead at a nearby hospital at 2.10pm.

* * *

Kenneth Noye had a bloodied nose and swollen eyes. He shot back onto the M25, swerving to avoid at least two other motorists. He needed time to think what to do. After driving around for more than half an hour he realised he had to break cover and use his mobile phone. He immediately made a flurry of frantic calls in an effort to rally his associates so he could hatch an escape plan. He was convinced there was no point in waiting around for the police to come calling.

Noye spoke to family and friends a total of 17 times in the nine hours following the killing of the motorist that tragic Sunday lunchtime.

Noye's mobile went silent for the following two days until his son Kevin made a brief call. It was never used again.

Meanwhile less than 24 hours after Noye's attack on Cameron, he flew a close 'business associate's' private helicopter from a field in Bristol to a golf course in Caen, in Normandy, France. From there he took a private jet to Madrid, Spain.

Noye knew that the moment police worked out he was the man involved in the roadrage death of Stephen Cameron he'd become the most wanted man in Britain.

So, until they made that connection, he had to use every available moment to ensure he put as many miles as possible between himself and his police pursuers.

* * *

Just as Noye's helicopter was rising above the countryside just outside Bristol his Land Rover Discovery, still containing the knife he'd used to kill Stephen Cameron, was being driven in a bizarre three-car convoy to Dartford, Kent. The last car had the number plate TOM 1E. This was owned by one of Noye's closest friends, skip yard owner Tommy Lee. The middle vehicle, Noye's Land Rover Discovery, turned into Lee's yard and minutes later was crushed into a compressed box of jagged steel.

A passing motorist who'd seen the convoy drive into the yard immediately mentioned it to her husband who was sitting alongside her and they both 'had a conversation about the stabbing incident the previous day.'

Meanwhile, an identical L-reg Land Rover Discovery was purchased for £20,000 cash and parked in the driveway of Kenny Noye's Sevenoaks home to confuse any curious policemen.

Noye's cronies were already playing a significant part in helping Noye to cover his tracks.

25. On the Run

The murder of hard-working electrical engineer Stephen Cameron shocked the nation. Headlines the following day included POLICE HUNT FOR ROADRAGE KILLER and HORROR OF MOTORWAY ROADRAGE MURDER.

Across the country there was stunned disbelief that one motorist could take the life of another motorist just because of a row over their driving.

The only clue to the identity of the Land Rover Discovery driver was a description from heartbroken Danielle Cable. She told police that he was about 5ft 10in, slim with brown collar-length hair. He was also clean shaven, wearing jeans and a dark bomber jacket.

Other witnesses who passed the scene along the overhead motorway provided police with the first part of the Discovery's registration number and officers were hoping that video cameras by the motorway might yield some clues.

Within days police announced they were planning to check 1,000 drivers of L-registered Land Rover Discovery vehicles.

Unfortunately, video camera footage from nearby security cameras revealed no clues to the identity of the killer. But an E-fit image of the killer was published in newspapers. It prompted various names to be put forward by members of the public as possible suspects. But still there were no concrete clues.

Meanwhile police were very careful not to reveal the

identity of Cameron's fiancée Danielle Cable, as she was the only real witness to the entire incident.

There were genuine fears that the killer might come after her if he knew where to find her. Not surprisingly the Cameron family and friends were having great difficulty coming to terms with what had happened.

At a heartbreaking press conference given three days after the killing, Cameron's brother Michael said: 'He was the kindest and most affectionate person. We are absolutely crushed and I don't have the words to express it. The family is so close and there is so much love generated that we are going to get through this.'

* * *

Three days after Cameron's killing, police were told about the Land Rover Discovery having been seen driven into a Dartford scrapyard owned by Noye's old friend Tommy Lee the day after the incident. Officers immediately raided the premises and found an AA card in Noye's name.

Then police closely studied the computer image of the roadrage killer and recognised a definite physical resemblance to Kenny Noye.

Not only was there an uncanny likeness, but Noye's house was not far from the scene of the murder. The team set about making discreet inquiries and discovered that Noye had left the country the day after the roadrage killing. The connection was gaining credibility.

More than a week after the killing of Stephen Cameron police raided Noye's home in Sevenoaks looking for evidence that might link him to the roadrage crime. They took away papers, clothes and a Range Rover, as well as closely quizzing Brenda Noye.

What they did not realise was that Noye was actually being shadowed at the time of the roadrage killing by undercover detectives from a different force investigating his criminal activities. However, they had not followed him on the Sunday of the murder.

Incredibly, the surveillance team monitored his departure from Britain the day after the murder without realising the possible significance of his flight abroad.

As one detective later admitted: 'It was just one of those things. No one realised he was wanted for questioning about the roadrage killing because the police had not identified him by that early stage.'

Behind the scenes, detectives tried to find Kenny Noye before news of his link to the roadrage killing became public. News of his possible involvement was not released to other police forces immediately because detectives feared that Noye might find out.

'Noye was lucky. His continued relationship with some policemen had left many officers deeply untrusting of their colleagues and that helped him slip through the net,' explained one Kent detective.

It wasn't until some time later that Kent police realised Kenny Noye had not vanished into thin air.

On 9 June 1996 Kenny Noye was publicly revealed as a suspect in the roadrage death of Stephen Cameron in a huge splash story in the *News of the World*.

It was a blow for police who had hoped they could keep his alleged involvement under wraps until they located him.

COP KILLER NOYE TO BE QUIZZED OVER ROADRAGE MURDER screamed the headlines in Britain's most popular Sunday tabloid. The story began:

Detectives are hunting cop-killer Kenneth Noye and a pal to quiz them about the M25 roadrage murder. They believe the Brink's-Mat bullion raid crook can help track down the fiend who stabbed 21-year-old Stephen Cameron to death.

Noye, who knifed to death an undercover cop investigating the 1983 gold robbery, was named by a police informant. Police have questioned a large number of criminals about the motorway killing that shocked Britain.

A police source said: 'Noye has the contacts to help the inquiry. There's no one he doesn't know. He's a nasty criminal, but if you met him you'd think he was a charmer.'

It was a confusing report provided by an unnamed source who'd blown the whistle on what had been until then a very secretive police operation to find Noye.

However, the most interesting aspect was the response when the *News of the World* sent a reporter down to Noye's family home in Sevenoaks to seek a reaction from Brenda and other family members. With yet another new Mercedes — registration number 3KN — parked in the driveway, the front door to the house was answered by a burly man.

At first he was reasonable with the journalist.

'I'm sorry. I don't know where Kenny is.'

Then the man was asked his name and he immediately became aggressive towards the reporter.

He snapped: 'He's not here. I haven't seen him for some time and I don't have a number you can call him on.' Menacingly, he added: 'I think you should go.'

Superintendent Nick Biddiss, the Kent police officer leading the hunt for the killer of Stephen Cameron was clearly concerned that news of the Noye connection had been made public.

'Who told you that?' he asked a *News of the World* journalist. 'I have made a policy decision. I'm not discussing my lines of inquiry for obvious reasons, or anybody that might be affected by them. If you're talking in terms of how our inquiries are going, we are continuing to eliminate Land Rover Discovery owners. There are a number of people I'd like to speak to. It's not helpful having people named.'

The police were furious that the Noye link had been exposed because they knew it would make Noye even more difficult to locate.

At the same time that Kenny Noye disappeared, car dealer John Marshall was found dead in his black Range Rover in Sydenham, south London. Marshall supplied Noye with stolen vehicle licence plates, including the registration plates used on the Land Rover Discovery linked to the roadrage killing of Stephen Cameron. Tattooed Marshall, 34, vanished after leaving his £250,000 home at Little Burstead, Essex, to meet business contacts.

He was found in his car, shot in the head and chest. Marshall had also been a close friend of executed Pat Tate and his brother Russell and had worked as a courier for Noye's Ecstasy runs from Holland.

Once again there is no suggestion that Kenny Noye was connected with this murder. But just knowing Noye seemed to put a lot of people at risk.

On the day after Kenny Noye's name was officially linked to the roadrage murder for the first time, Stephen Cameron's heartbroken fiancée Danielle made an emotional appeal to the public to help find his killer.

'I wish he had stabbed me as well so I could have died with Stephen and we could still be together.'

By this time police were also convinced that the Discovery used in the attack had been either destroyed or given new registration plates.

On 11 June, Kent police encouraged Interpol officially to send out a worldwide alert on Kenny Noye, admitting he was urgently wanted for questioning by Kent police over the M25 roadrage murder of Stephen Cameron.

Every one of the 176 countries who were members of Interpol were sent a 'blue warrant' asking them for information and to alert the Kent police murder room at Dartford if Noye was seen.

Detectives then announced that another character called Anthony Francis was wanted for questioning in connection with the roadrage attack. In fact the name was simply a popular pseudonym used by Kenny Noye and a number of his other Kent criminal associates.

'Anthony Francis', registered owner of the Land Rover Discovery L794 JTF, 'lived' at the house in Brigden Road, Bexleyheath, where Kenny Noye had attended those parties earlier that year and during 1995.

DS Nick Biddis, leading the hunt for Cameron's killer, told reporters: 'We have got to find Mr Francis who is shown as the registered owner of the vehicle.'

At the police press conference — when Kent police were still insisting they simply wanted to eliminate Noye from their inquiries — Biddiss was inadvertently photographed sitting in front of a large-scale map of Noye's house. He became highly agitated when this was pointed out to him.

Meanwhile neighbours at the modest house in Brigden Road, Bexleyheath, given in the registration details of 'Mr Francis', confirmed that they regularly saw a car similar to Noye's Discovery parked outside the property. Both the girls who rented the house moved out shortly after the roadrage attack and the Discovery had not been seen there since the killing.

Police eventually interviewed both the women who'd been living at the house. They also dug up part of the back garden just in case any of the missing Brink's-Mat bullion was anywhere to be found. Nothing was located.

Noye had actually left his first destination, Spain, and arrived in northern Cyprus approximately a week after the roadrage incident. He slipped into the familiar surroundings of the port of Kyrenia. Turkish Cypriot police even had concrete evidence of Noye arriving by ship.

It would be practically impossible to get him extradited, as Britain did not even officially recognise the self-proclaimed Turkish republic. As the northern Cyprus foreign minister later admitted: 'If he had done nothing wrong in our country why should we ask him to leave?'

Noye even managed a few rounds of golf with his associate Asil Nadir. Nadir knew nothing of the roadrage killing at this time, as it had received no coverage in Cyprus.

Noye had planned to stay at his son Kevin's apartment in Kyrenia, but that was still being completed by construction workers. So Noye drove across to the east side of the island near Famagusta where the Long Beach Country Club timeshare development was still being constructed by local builders. Noye spent a few days in one of the completed villas. The timeshare development should have been the perfect refuge — except that too many people knew of his connection with it.

Development manager Colin Reader, brother of Brink's-Mat co-defendant Brian, was less than helpful when approached on the development site some months later.

'Fuck off,' were the only words he'd utter in response to questions about Kenny Noye.

It was then made very clear to this author that it would be advisable to leave the development immediately or face physical intimidation.

Noye moved from the half-completed timeshare development to the Hotel Sema in nearby Famagusta. Within days he left the island.

Just after this, northern Cyprus police detectives received a faxed message, through unofficial channels set up between them and British police for joint action on drug trafficking, from Scotland Yard requesting assistance in tracing and handing over Noye.

However, by that time Noye had already headed back to Spain.

In Swanley, Kent, the family and friends of roadrage victim Stephen Cameron attended his funeral service. His fiancée, the only person who actually saw the killer, told the packed gathering: 'I thought it was forever, that we were going to get married and have children. I close my eyes and picture Steve. The sound, the smell, the love. I will never forget him. He was so cruelly snatched away. When he died a part of me died, too. Please God, tell me why it was my Steve who had to die.'

It was a measure of the shock within the community and across the country that so many people turned up for the funeral service and crowds even stood outside the church listening to the service on loudspeakers. More than 120 floral tributes surrounded Stephen Cameron's grave. His brother sent a wreath shaped like a golf club. There was one shaped like a screw driver from his pals at the engineering factory where he worked.

Just one mile away at the spot where Cameron was killed by the M25 motorway, a dozen red roses and a birthday card from Danielle stood against the side of the road.

The note read: 'You are not here with me to give you a birthday kiss. But I send these red roses as a token of my love for you. You will be forever in my heart, sweetheart, and I will love you always.'

After the service at St Mary the Virgin church, DS Nick Biddiss said he believed that 'associates' of the criminal community could have information about the killer and his vehicle. He said that they may be withholding evidence 'through fear or misplaced loyalty'.

He added: 'I am talking about people who may have associations in the criminal community and more than likely in the Kent area. We are well aware that there are people who have knowledge about the disposal of vehicles that we have been seeking. Some people may feel they are returning a favour or equalling an old score by protecting someone who could be involved.'

It was the nearest Biddiss would come to referring to the fact that someone on the criminal level of Kenny Noye was involved.

26. Hot Air

At 2.30pm on Wednesday June 13 1996, thirty armed French police officers, tipped off by Kent police, swooped on a private plane as it landed at Paris's Le Bourget airport. Four squad cars swept across the runway as gendarmes surrounded the Learjet 55. It had stopped at Paris for refuelling *en route* to Tenerife. The previous day the Learjet had flown from Bristol to St Petersburg.

The plane and some baggage were searched and five men were allowed to leave two hours later. Noye was not amongst them.

Over the preceding month since the roadrage killing of Stephen Cameron that same jet had made a series of flights, some of which detectives believed involved Kenny Noye:

20 MAY: MOSCOW–BRUSSELS–PARIS– MADRID–TENERIFE

24 MAY: TENERIFE–STANSTED –BRISTOL

28 MAY: BRISTOL–STANSTED–PARIS– TENERIFE (FLIGHT DELAYED FROM PREVIOUS DAY)

31 MAY: TENERIFE–PARIS –STANSTED–BRISTOL

4 JUNE:	BRISTOL–STANSTED –TENERIFE
6-7 JUNE:	TENERIFE–FARO –STANSTED–BRISTOL
11 JUNE:	BRISTOL–ST PETERSBURG
12 JUNE:	MOSCOW–PARIS–TENERIFE

Back at the Noye family house in Sevenoaks, Brenda Noye was refusing to speak about her husband's disappearance.

Her gleaming £30,000 silver Mercedes (N483 EKN) stood in the driveway to the house, which was protected by numerous security cameras and Noye's beloved Rottweiler dogs.

Meanwhile police established that the number plate they had narrowed down to the Discovery used by the roadrage killer — L794 JTF — had been carried on two other vehicles that also had links to Noye and his criminal associates.

On 28 June Noye allegedly flew into Britain and lunched at the China Gardens restaurant in West Kingsdown. It was a sensational development since it seemed to indicate that Noye was trying to taunt detectives. *'Come and get me if you can,'* seemed to be the message.

It wasn't until the end of July that police officers even bothered to visit restaurant manager Malcolm Edwards to quiz him about Noye's supposed visit. Within a few months the China Gardens restaurant had mysteriously closed down.

Kent Detectives also flew to Tenerife to check out alleged sightings of Noye on the island. But their inquiries drew a complete blank.

The police increasingly relied on intelligence information to try to track down Noye. Noye knew that and was now creating all sorts of smokescreens to confuse his pursuers.

Scraps of information came in to police from Noye's criminal contacts. It was clear there were many who would rather he was not at liberty because it was attracting police attention to their own illicit activities.

Many of Noye's one-time friends were still seething about how he'd settled the £3 million out-of-court claim on the Brink's-Mat bullion he handled.

'It was all right for him, he still had loads of money but many of the rest of the Brink's-Mat crew couldn't even afford what the insurance people were after,' said one south east London criminal.

At least five other key players implicated in the bullion raid, but never found guilty of taking part in it, had been forced to make similar-sized settlements.

By this time rumours even began circulating that victim Stephen Cameron knew his killer. It was completely untrue, but the lack of hard facts in the case had the knock-on effect of encouraging wild rumours to spread.

There was also the possibility that someone who had his own agenda and disapproved of Noye's involvement with the police was maliciously putting his name forward, knowing that he lived in the area and had a volatile temper.

Equally, in a case that could eventually hang on the question of identity, Noye could argue that the juxtaposition of his face with the identikit compiled with Danielle Cable's help also damaged his chances of a fair hearing.

At the end of June, Kent detectives revealed that they wanted to speak to a close friend of Kenny Noye. This man drove a Mitsubishi Shogun similar in appearance to the Land Rover Discovery identified by Cameron's fiancée as the vehicle used by the killer.

On 2 July 1996, police questioned another of Noye's oldest criminal associates. The man denied all knowledge of Noye but, privately, officers were convinced that he had helped Noye flee the country more than a month earlier.

Then Kenny Noye allegedly turned up at the Caribbean Enjoy restaurant in Streatham, south London. Witnesses said that Noye had changed his appearance drastically, possibly after having plastic surgery. He was with a group of men who seemed to be very cocky and sure of themselves. When they left one of them asked the waiter for a discount because they were police — that was a big joke on Kenny Noye's part. He wanted them to be seen.

The number of Kenny Noye 'sightings' suggested that he was either taunting the police by popping in and out of Britain at his own free will despite his status as a wanted man or he was spreading rumours of his presence just to test the response time of the police.

Noye allegedly returned twice more during the summer and even hid out at one of his mistresses' houses in a Kent village. He'd bought the woman the property shortly after his release from prison two years earlier.

Criminal sources suggested to police that Noye was renting a villa near Lisbon in Portugal. They also insisted he was continually flying in and out of Elstree Airfield just north of London.

It was even claimed that he'd popped into a house in Essex for a relative's birthday celebrations.

In the middle of all the publicity about Noye's alleged involvement in the roadrage killing, came news that detective John Donald, the policeman he paid for information while in prison, had been jailed for 11 years.

Donald, a member of the South East Regional Crime Squad, appeared at the Old Bailey accused of taking bribes and passing on information on drug operations to a number of criminals including Noye. Two other detectives suspected of being involved with Donald were arrested and later cleared, partly because Donald refused to give evidence against them.

The judge at his trial said that Donald had been exploited by south London drug dealer, a close associate of Kenny Noye and his good friend Michael Lawson.

Mrs Justice Heather Steel said: 'He was prepared to pay very large sums for what he wanted. Perhaps your greatest betrayal of all was the offer of information to two international criminals, Kenneth Noye and Michael Lawson, who were running a multimillion pound drug ring.'

John Nutting prosecuting told the court: 'Noye is a

notorious professional criminal. Dishonest and unscrupulous, he has attracted the attention of various law enforcement agencies in this country for two decades. He exercises a malevolent and baleful influence both from inside and outside prison.'

Donald also supplied Noye's associate with information about other operations, including one relating to the largest amphetamine factory ever found in the UK.

Donald showed no emotion as he was sentenced, although the court was told he had been subjected to hostility from other prisoners and faced a harsh time in jail.

Some of the evidence presented at the trial gave an extraordinary insight into the level of corruption that had occurred.

When one south east London 'face' was arrested in Walworth he gave John Donald his cash card to help himself to any money he wanted in exchange for him not opposing bail for the man. John Donald had truly been Kenny Noye's favourite type of policeman.

By the middle of August, Noye's other mistress Sue McNichol-Outch was exposed to the public in various newspapers. She claimed she hadn't seen Kenny Noye for months.

John, her former husband and one-time school friend of Noye, told reporters: 'I am aware of my ex-wife's relationship with Ken because I have been interviewed by police about it. I haven't seen Ken for donkey's years. It's not for me to comment on the activities of my ex-wife.'

It was clear that police were interested in *anyone* with connections to Kenny Noye.

Over in Sevenoaks, Brenda Noye was also fielding journalistic inquiries. She had never forgiven the media for the way they treated her husband following the killing of John Fordham. Asked whether she'd heard of Sue McNichol-Outch, Brenda snapped: 'Who? I don't know that woman, never heard of her.'

She claimed her husband was being persecuted over the roadrage killing.

'Don't talk to me about him wanting to come back to help police. He would be an idiot to come back. What they would do is stick him in a category A prison for two years, pick the jury and get the guilty verdict they want. I have no idea where he is and I don't want to know. As far as I am concerned, he is better off out of it. My husband is an innocent man. You [the media] have crucified him. I think it is absolutely despicable. I don't know how you can live with yourself.'

Ironing clothes in the kitchen of the house in Sevenoaks she continued: 'I live in fear of my life. I moved here after the Brink's-Mat case because I feared for the safety of my family. Now I am living in fear again because of all this publicity. Nobody had heard of my husband before that bloody Brink's-Mat case. OK, he was a gold smuggler, but he was put in a position where he had to defend himself.'

Brenda insisted she would stand by her husband whatever happened and dismissed reports that she wanted a divorce.

'I have been married to him for 26 years,' she said. 'I am not going to end my marriage.'

27. Life Goes On

By September 1996, Kent police frustration was mounting because Kenny Noye really did seem to have disappeared into thin air. All the surveillance reports, alleged sightings and underworld rumours had come to nothing.

The *Daily Mirror* put up a £10,000 reward for the arrest and conviction of the roadrage knifeman. Although they conceded that Kenny Noye had not been officially named as a suspect, the paper made a point of mentioning him in the second paragraph of their story announcing the reward.

Kent detectives even issued an internal wanted poster in the *Police Gazette* in the same week as the *Mirror* reward was announced. It included two photographs of Noye and warned that he was 'violent, carries knives'. The special notice was sent to police forces throughout Britain. It even gave fresh details of the attack that left Stephen Cameron dying by the roadside. The description of Noye omitted a characteristic scar beneath his left eye because police had been told he'd had it removed by plastic surgery.

In December 1996 armed police swooped on a motorway service station after a tip-off that Kenny Noye planned to use it for a Christmas party.

Officers mounted a huge surveillance operation at busy South Mimms, Hertfordshire, on the M25 motorway 25 miles from the motorway slip road where Stephen Cameron was killed.

No one knows whether Noye turned up, but by the time police raided the service station there was no sign of him.

Others suggested that the entire raid had been provoked by a fictitious tip deliberately fed to the police by associates of Kenny Noye who were still testing the police's ability to react swiftly to such information.

* * *

In October 1996 yet another of Noye's associates met an untimely death.

Keith Hedley was a wealthy 57-year-old builder and haulage contractor. He was also a suspected money launderer with a sprawling home near Sevenoaks, which had been searched during the Brink's-Mat inquiry. He was never charged despite the discovery of a sawn-off shotgun. The Hedleys and Noyes had been close for years when they both lived in West Kingsdown. But Keith Hedley and Kenneth Noye had fallen out over some money that Noye reckoned he was owed.

On 26 September 1996, Hedley was woken on his 45ft motor yacht Karenyann in Corfu by the sound of men apparently trying to steal his 250hp dinghy.

According to friends who were guests on board, Hedley ran through the boat to collect a shotgun, which he always kept loaded and fired two shots into the sky to scare the thieves.

The raiders returned fire with three shots, two of which hit Hedley on the shoulder and stomach, fatally wounding him. Corfu police blamed the killing on pirates.

While there is no suggestion that Noye was connected to the murder, Hedley's death was yet another example of just how dangerous it was to be an associate of Kenny Noye.

* * *

In November 1996, seven men accused of taking part in Noye's hole-in-the-wall scam were found guilty.

Noye's friend, John 'Little Legs' Lloyd, was described by the judge as one of the main organisers of the crime. Police had suspected him for ten years of being involved in the Brink's-Mat bullion raid. He and his common-law wife Jean Savage still lived in Kenny Noye's old bungalow in Hever Avenue, West Kingsdown.

The hole-in-the-wall defendants also included Paul Kidd, 36, Graham Moore, 32, Stephen Seton, 65, Stephen Moore, 41, Billy Hayward, 65, and John Maguire, 36, all but one from Kent and south-east London. They entered guilty pleas after failing to have the proceedings stayed as an abuse of process.

Kenny Noye was named in court as playing a part in the organising of the crime, but there had never been enough evidence for police to be certain of a prosecution.

Back in Kent, Brenda Noye was liquidating some of the family's assets. In April 1997 she sold the family squash club, Racquets Sport and Leisure, in Dartford, Kent, for £140,000. By Kenny Noye's standards it was a modest profit considering the £100,000 they'd originally paid for the club twenty years earlier.

New owner Paul Finn, 27, a former barman at the club explained why Brenda Noye had sold up.

'She used to take an active part in running the place, but when her husband disappeared she lost interest. I think she just wanted to retire. She does not appear to be the least bit short of money.'

Despite the so-called cash flow problems, Brenda held on to her N-registered Mercedes. The police were not that surprised. 'Her husband might have disappeared off the face of the earth, but she still seems to have access to money,' said one detective.

Older son Kevin, 24, was earning a high salary in the cut-throat world of City of London stock dealing.

Meanwhile Noye's other son Brett, 22, had quietly launched a career as a property dealer.

The boys remained very protective of their mother and even encouraged her to get out and see her friends more. They also persuaded her to learn to play golf.

One family friend claimed: 'Basically, they have been

trying to get Brenda used to the idea that she might never see Kenny again. They have to get on with their lives.'

For behind the determined looks and rigid loyalty to her husband's cause, Brenda Noye was very worried by Noye's disappearance and all the accusations flying around about him. Frequently she looked like someone with the weight of the world on her shoulders. In a series of exclusive interviews with Brenda Noye at the family home in Sevenoaks in March 1997, she talked in detail about her life since her husband had disappeared. It was an enlightening conversation peppered, at times, with a surprising degree of humility.

'They're all calling him a wicked murderer and he's not. There is no evidence whatsoever. I'm surprised they haven't blamed him for any recent rail crashes. I mean it is absolutely ridiculous and the police are behind it all. They've got a vendetta against him and they are continuing to hound him for the rest of his life. I have tried so hard to make people aware of the injustice that has gone on and nobody wanted to know. No one wants to be involved because they are petrified they are going to be dug up as well. Everyone's told me so many lies. I cannot believe the things they have said about him. They've made him into a monster, he's a really nice guy. I know I'm prejudiced because I'm his wife, but believe me if this wasn't the case I would have divorced him years ago. It's just not fair. You know what I mean. The only conclusion I can come to is that they're doing this because they can't stand the guilt they feel about Fordham dying. Nobody could have felt more for Mrs Fordham and her family than we did. Believe me I couldn't sleep for months over that. You know what with the children and her. But what the hell, I mean when you're bloody standing there and someone jumps on you like that, what do you expect anyone to do?

'It's just not on. When the Brink's-Mat thing happened I cried my heart out through people like you. Talk about kicking you when you're down. There's nothing I would like more than to put the record straight. It's about time someone realised this is not just Ken we're talking about. We're talking about me, the children, his parents, his sister, his whole family and my family. They don't just destroy one person. They destroy everything around them and it is just so unfair. Once I was an idiot, an absolute idiot. But I'm a lot older and a lot wiser now. He spent ten years trying to put the record straight, to come out and just live a normal life, that's all he's done, you know he just wanted to live a normal life.'

Brenda Noye claimed it was the fourth time since Noye's release from prison in the summer of 1994 that he'd been accused by police of a crime. She refused to elaborate on exactly what offences he'd been accused of but she did give a clear indication of the sort of activities he was involved in right up until his disappearance.

'He won't answer their questions. He won't talk to them. They'll lock him up and they'll put him on trial, and the jury will be like it was in the Brink's-Mat trial, they'll be taken out to lunch and wined and dined. And go and get their shopping carried for them and everything. And all the journalists will just turn a blind eye, wicked Kenny Noye goes down again. And about twenty other lives are destroyed once more. He's got no chance of a fair trial even if for some obscure reason he would ever have to stand trial. Can you believe what it's like not having done anything and knowing that you've got this hanging over your head?

'I just can't believe it's happening again. I really cannot. How can there be an end? How can there possibly be an end? There's no way I would want him to come back and get put in prison for something again. All he ever wanted to do was settle down with his family. He's missed ten years of his sons growing up. He just wanted to spend time with them, guide them and be with them. And what's he ended up with having? Two years with them. Can you imagine what it's done to his family?'

In spring 1997 one of Kenny Noye's oldest friends appeared in court accused of handling the stolen Land Rover Discovery linked to the roadrage attack on Stephen

Cameron.

The man who lived in Noye's kingdom of West Kingsdown, was remanded in custody by Dartford magistrates. Police believed that he was the man who sold the Discovery to the man called 'Anthony Francis'. Then another of Kenny Noye's associates came to a nasty end in a classic underworld hit.

'Scarface' Danny Roff was the prime suspect in the 1990 murder of great train robber Charlie Wilson in Spain. He was known by his distinctive scar under his right eye and a penchant for heavy gold jewellery.

Roff, 36 — already paralysed from an earlier attempt on his life — was executed in what was believed to be a contract killing as he arrived home in his Mercedes in Wanstead Road, Bromley, Kent, just a few miles from Noye's manor. Two masked gunmen ambushed Roff and shot him at least five times in the head and chest.

While there is no suggestion that Roff's death is connected to Kenny Noye the link between the two men is indisputable.

In early 1997 some sources began suggesting that Kenny Noye had himself been executed in a gangland contract killing.

The stories were treated with understandable scepticism by police who were more convinced that Noye wanted authorities to believe he was dead.

There was even a rumour that Kenny Noye had already travelled to Brazil to check out potential 'retirement' properties. His contacts from his gold-smuggling days were said to have found him a choice of seven different houses to view in the north of the country. Some believed he intended to get plastic surgery carried out in Rio and then return to Britain within the next two years. But, as usual, there was no concrete evidence to back up these claims.

Meanwhile at the £250,000 house where Noye's mistress Sue McNichol-Outch lived in Bromley the only reminder of Kenny Noye was a teddy bear in the first-floor window. Kenny Noye gave it to her shortly after they had started their affair and she told friends she would treasure it forever. She did not say whether she ever expected to see Kenny Noye again. But others were not so keen on Kenny Noye.

Kathy McAvoy, wife of jailed Brink's-Mat robber Micky McAvoy, remained on very good terms with Noye's old friend Jean Savage, but she described Noye as thus: 'He's a fool and an idiot. Only an idiot would do the things he's done. He was a fool because he allowed himself to be caught in certain situations.'

Kathy McAvoy also insisted that Noye was not liked by the other members of the Brink's-Mat gang. 'He's been portrayed as a hero, but he isn't. He's nothing like that. He was no more than a fence.'

Kathy McAvoy would only agree to meet this author in a crowded shopping mall in Bromley, south London, after certain assurances had been made about my intentions. She re-iterated that among the rest of the Brink's-Mat circle there was little love lost for Kenny Noye.

'He's just a load of trouble. Not even one of us really. A bloke from the suburbs who acted like he was from southeast London when he wasn't,' said Kathy McAvoy. 'I feel sorry for Brenda. He's left her to face all the music and it can't be easy. She's a lovely lady,' she added.

Kathy McAvoy had talked to other underworld figures about Noye's disappearances and there was a collective response that 'we'd like him to just stay away for ever.'

28. Home Sweet Home

Kenny Noye continued slipping quietly in and out of Britain in the nine months following the roadrage attack on Stephen Cameron.

His network of informants and contacts kept him one step ahead of the police. Such was his status in certain parts of Kent that he could meet contacts relatively openly without the fear of arrest. That was a measure of the power wielded by Kenny Noye.

He was taking a leaf out of his old friend John 'Little Legs' Lloyd's book who'd done exactly the same thing when he was a supposed fugitive following the Brink's-Mat raid.

The nearest police ever really got to finding Noye was in early 1997 when they received an anonymous tip that he was holed up in a small terraced house in Catford. Armed officers swooped on the house but Noye had already left the country once again.

One well-known south-east London criminal met Noye in a pub in Dartford, Kent, just a couple of months after his disappearance.

'I wasn't surprised to see Kenny Noye in a pub. I don't think he's hiding,' explained the man. 'I had a drink with him. He seemed on good form. The bloke's not hiding from anyone. Of course I was a bit shocked. There was Kenny at the bar having a drink with a few of his friends. He looked like he was enjoying himself. If he was in hiding I don't think he'd be on his own doorstep. I don't even think he's got anything to hide.'

In fact, as many of Noye's friends, family and associates have pointed out, he deliberately made sure he was seen in some of his old haunts to let people know that he'd done nothing wrong in his own eyes.

As one associate explained: 'In Kenny's world it's important to be seen out and about. By turning up at various places he's telling his cronies that he's not scared of the Old Bill or anyone. He's also saying that if they want to find him they can come and try. But he knows he's got the contacts and the knowledge to always be one step ahead of the game.'

Even Kenny Noye's cousin Michael, who joined him on so many childhood exploits, was the subject of a police surveillance operation as detectives desperately tried to discover where Noye had gone.

'They actually thought he'd get in contact with me, but Kenny's got much more sense than to do that,' says Michael.

In fact, the police were probably absolutely correct in suspecting that Noye had been in touch with his cousin, but there was no way that Michael Noye would admit such a thing. It was more than his life was worth.

However, Michael Noye did admit when interviewed for this book that 'Kenny isn't a million miles away. He's around.'

When asked whether he was coming in and out of Britain, Michael arched his eyebrows and rolled his eyes. He refused to be any more specific because he knew that his loose lips could cost him dearly.

The key to Noye's survival was that all his criminal associates, friends and family believed he had been wrongly accused of the roadrage killing.

Krays' henchman Freddie Foreman summed up the attitude of many when he said: 'Obviously anything that goes wrong, any major crime that happened recently, Kenny Noye is going to have his name put up front. I mean he's going to get the blame for it. If they can pin anything on him they do.'

Foreman insisted that Kenny Noye was 'a very decent person and people are going to help if they can.'

In other words Noye would continue to get help from his underworld contacts to avoid the police hunt following the roadrage killing.

At her house in Bexleyheath, Kenny Noye's mistress at the time of the Brink's-Mat inquiry, Jenny Bishop, steadfastly refused to talk about her ex-lover. With two Rottweilers growling at her ankles the well-built blonde, who bears a remarkable similarity to Brenda Noye, ignored all questions.

Noye associates past and present know that silence is their only guarantee of a peaceful life.

Then there is the question of whether anyone other than his close family and friends would even have recognised Kenny Noye if he visited Britain.

Former West Kingsdown neighbour Pat Bosley has little doubt that it would be very difficult.

'He always kept a bit of a low profile anyway, so his face is difficult to remember. I suppose he was a bit like the invisible man. You know, you can't quite remember him. The police might have a very difficult job trying to find him.'

By the end of 1996, Brink's-Mat insurers believed they had recovered almost the whole of the original value of the stolen gold bullion.

But that didn't allow for the fact that the £27 million had probably been turned into hundreds of millions through successful investments by the criminals.

Kenny Noye had negotiated his way out of trouble, but there is absolutely no doubt that he still retained a small fortune from his involvement in the Brink's-Mat gold bullion distribution and his many other 'interests'.

But all the money in the world might not help him this time.

As Freddie Foreman pointed out: 'Time is a great healer and the longer you can put between an accusation the better. Perhaps they'll come up with the truth and find out it was nothing to do with him at all. The man is doing the only sensible thing that he can do and that's to keep out of the way until the situation resolves itself. Everyone needs friends especially when you're on your toes but lots of people don't want to get involved and they don't want to help you and that's when you find out who your friends are.'

* * *

While Kenny Noye was understandably keeping the lowest of profiles after his disappearance following the death of Stephen Cameron, the same cannot be said of his favourite brief, Henry Milner. Since first representing Noye during the Brink's-Mat investigation, Milner had gained a reputation as the solicitor of choice for high-profile clients, such as three of the suspects in the Stephen Lawrence murder. Yet occasionally, Milner talked openly with frankness and humour about the twilight of gangland criminals. He was proud of how he'd helped turn many cases around even after clients had been subjected to the old police habit of 'verballing up' suspects with false confessions. 'It's a lot of fun defending criminal cases,' he admitted to one journalist in 1996.

Milner's north London upbringing, Jewish boarding school education in Oxfordshire and degree from the London School of Economics couldn't be further removed from the London underworld. At weekends, Milner retreated even further from his day job with three hobbies: Tottenham Hotspur, bridge and traditional American music

Legal eagle Henry Milner's one-man operation offered an exclusive service to ten or twelve rich clients a year. It was entirely a personal service. And he only got his clients through word of mouth.

Milner's office, squeezed between two jewellery shops on London's Hatton Garden, is small. His only employee, secretary Eileen, has worked for him for 23 years. His tiny waiting room has nothing but a handful of glossy mags to peruse. The lawyer's own office is panelled with dark oak and constantly filled with clouds of smoke from his ever-present fat cuban cigars. They sit on his desk in a walnut veneer box crafted in a prison workshop and sent to him by a grateful client.

Milner's first big professional breakthrough as a lawyer came in 1978 when he represented one of London's best known 'faces' who, as Milner later admitted, 'appeared at the Old Bailey as regularly as Frank Sinatra at the Albert Hall.' Milner's 'lovable rogue' was eventually acquitted of criminal charges in six successive court cases. That was when word went round that Henry Milner was a brief to be trusted.

So when Brink's-Mat went down in 1983, Milner was sitting pretty to receive a windfall of clients. First through the door was Mickey McAvoy followed by Tony White. Then came Kenny Noye. Milner was once asked if there were any cases he would not handle. He responded: 'That's a difficult question because I do a lot of cases the public finds distasteful, like drugs. But I have never handled cases involving sexual offences on elderly people or young children.'

Milner happily concedes that a certain degree of optimism is an essential ingredient in his type of work. He admitted: 'You've got to look confident even if you don't feel it. If you show a weakness or fear they will jump on it. Defendants are as shrewd as anything. They know whether you are on the ball.' But even he sometimes got it wrong. On one occasion he was representing an Iranian accused of possessing 100 kilos of heroin. Milner was convinced the case was hopeless and that he'd be doing well if he got 18 years. Milner even begged his client to plead guilty but he refused. By some miracle, the Iranian was aquitted.

Milner insists he does not have a close relationship with any of his clients, including Noye. He says he's never been out socialising with them apart from having the occasional sandwich at lunchtime. He prided himself on always having complete control of a case, helping to decide which witnesses to call, influencing a counsel's closing speech and occasionally putting his foot down. He was also renowned for picking top barristers with a knack of winning.

Over the years, Milner had become well accustomed to the age old question from many of his clients. 'What are my chances?' To his credit, he always tried to give the straightest possible answer. He told one journalist: 'You start with "hopeless", "very, very poor", "under 50 percent", "evens" or "quite good". If you put it above "good", you're in trouble if they're found guilty.'

One of Milner's favourites is: 'You can't guarantee anyone winning a case any more than love comes with a guarantee.'

Which probably left Kenny Noye's chances as not much more than evens in the Stephen Cameron case.

29. Costa del Crimo

Twelve hundred miles from Henry Milner's London office, to the south of the Spanish city of Cadiz, lies a fifty-mile stretch of coastline know as La Janda in the province of Andalusia. Spanish poet A. Machado once described it as an area 'where the land ends and the sea begins'. Kenny Noye had been told by some old criminal associates in Spain that La Janda was the perfect location for a man who wanted to keep a low profile.

The coastline runs between a patchwork of cliffs, dunes, mountains and vast, wide deserted sandy beaches. Local guides claim 3,000 hours of sun a year. Three coastal towns, Barbate, Conil and Vejer, dominate the area, but they are nothing more than sleepy market centres. And just a few miles inland, huge expanses of pine tree forest provided shade and rest from the searing temperatures. The ancient Greeks called this stretch of Spanish coast 'Hercules' Columns'.

But what caught Kenny Noye's attention was that although the area was isolated in one sense, it was still near enough to the excesses of the British crime pack on the Costa del Sol for Noye to see a few familiar faces occasionally. As usual, he wanted the best of both worlds.

The specific stretch of seaside that captivated Noye was 15 miles of wide, bleached white sandy beaches stretching from a tiny village called Zahara de los Atunes in the south to Los Canos de Meca in the north. All the inland scenery was framed by the constant blue of the Atlantic Ocean. Noye also liked the fact that the only sizeable town of Barbate had a yachting harbour tucked alongside the fishing port.

In the early winter months of 1996, Noye turned up at regular intervals in Barbate, calling himself Mick, and claiming to be a builder looking for property investments. He'd spent at least three months criss-crossing the globe and even stayed some time in Russia having expensive plastic surgery at the hands of a notorious Moscow surgeon. The new Kenny Noye had cheeks that seemed to have been stretched back almost like a chipmunk, and that old familiar broken nose from his childhood had taken on a longer, thinner, almost Roman look. Ironically, the overall effect of the plastic surgery was to make Noye look years older.

Now, despite those numerous trips back and forth to Britain virtually unhindered by police, Noye believed he could not continue simply to float around. He needed a proper base from which to start a new life.

The first place that caught his eye was the tiny beachside community of Los Canos de Meca, six miles north of Barbate. According to the electoral roll only fourteen people lived full-time in Los Canos so it was the ideal base for a man who was the most wanted in Britain at that time. Noye recced Los Canos carefully by telling estate agents in Barbate he was looking for cheap property to invest in. He even turned around two tiny Finca's (farmhouses) for a modest profit just to show he was a genuine property developer. Occasionally he popped into a beach-side bar in Los Canos called Las Dunas. The bar could not have been more different from Noye's favorourite taverns back in south east London and Kent. Las Dunas was predominantly frequented by under-25s staying in local hostels and spending up to twelve hours each day riding the nearby Atlantic surf. The walls of the bar were littered with warning signs about not serving alcohol to anyone under 21 and threatening legal proceedings against anyone caught in possession of drugs. Meanwhile, in the courtyard outside, dozens of youngsters puffed openly away on cannabis joints.

But the sign which caught Kenny Noye's eye the most was

one that warned of a closed circuit video camera filming the bar area. The owner of Las Dunas had been forced by insurers to install the camera after a number of incidents in which the police had had to be called. Noye worked out where the camera was located and went out of his way to sit in the opposite corner from where it was permanently pointed.

Not surprisingly, Noye got talking on a number of occasions to one of the few English speaking customers at Las Dunas, a well-spoken Englishwoman who ran a local equestrian centre. Noye told the woman that he'd bought and sold a number of local properties and he was on the lookout for a rental home for himself. Just then Miguel Garrido, the owner of the Las Dunas, chipped in that he knew of a nice three-bedroom beachside villa just a short distance away. Noye agreed a monthly rental with the owner of the property less than an hour later.

The following day Garrido spotted Noye by the beach and walked up to him and tapped him on the shoulder. 'Three big guys who were with him lunged right at me and pulled me to the floor. At that point I knew he was someone not to be messed around with,' Garrida later recalled.

Within weeks of settling in Los Canos, Noye realised that in order to survive in Spain, he needed drastically to improve his network of money men to feed him financial support. In those early days in Spain, Noye travelled once a month by car almost four hundred miles across Spain to a village just south of Alicante to meet an accountant and money launderer he'd known since the Brink's-Mat days. They would then hand over at least £30,000 in pesetas for Noye to use to keep himself on the run. He made sure that none of his traditional sources of money were touched just in case the police were watching them.

* * *

While staying in Los Canos, Noye used a dusty airstrip a few miles off the E4 motorway that ran north to Seville — 60 miles from La Janda — to fly in and out of Britain by private plane whenever there was business to sort out. Often he'd land at a tiny air strip just north of Bristol from where he would head down the M4 to London for those meetings before flying out again as quickly as possible.

Just before Christmas 1996, Noye began making inquiries amongst his contacts back in Britain about the best way of getting involved in a lucrative drug-running operation in Spain. Noye had plenty of spare cash and he wanted to invest it in a familiar kind of 'business'. He also knew that in Spain, hashish smuggling was virtually ignored by the over-stretched local police whose priorities lay with A-class narcotics such as cocaine and heroin.

Initially, Noye arranged a meeting with the head of a large cartel of hashish smugglers based in the nearby bustling port city of Cadiz. But Noye did not trust the Spanish criminals he met and was careful not to reveal his real identity during a series of tense discussions. Then he got in touch with another old contact in Marbella, an ex-armed-robber-turned-drugs baron, who told Noye he would get him an intro to a bigger operation run by a kingpin smuggler in nearby Gibraltar, the British colony that lay just seventy miles to the east of Noye's Los Canos de Meca hideout. Noye had already thought about visiting the Rock to buy some much needed tax-free electrical equipment for his home. But he'd been wary because he presumed if he was arrested on the British colony he'd be flown straight back to London without even an extradition hearing. But Noye's Marbella friend and a couple of other criminal associates assured him that Gibraltar was safe to visit because passport control at the colony was so lapse no one ever asked British citizens even to open their passports to examine photo ID.

In January 1997, Noye got the nod from his man in Marbella that one of Gibraltar's most notorious gangsters was keen to meet him and discuss some 'business opportunities'. That was music to Noye's ears. The Gibraltarian was rumoured to have a fleet of dozens of inflatable power boats that ran backwards and forwards between the Spanish mainland and North Africa carrying shipments of drugs. The drug baron was proud of the fact that he deliberately used inflatables because they were less expensive to replace than traditional boats.

By all accounts, the two men got on very well. 'This guy is a typical Gibraltarian; more English than Spanish and Noye felt he could trust him,' said one police source in Spain. In fact the Gibraltarian was under constant surveillance by British and Spanish police. But Noye was so careful about revealing his identity in public that no one had any idea he was the person meeting him.

Noye told the Gib smuggler he was prepared to risk an initial outlay of £50,000 on the proviso it was only used to buy hashish. Noye remained convinced that hashish was a much less risky investment. As one of his Kent associates told me at the time: 'Noye felt much happier sticking to smuggling puff. It suited him perfectly.'

Noye told the Gib smuggler he wanted to see how things progressed and that he would eventually pump hundreds of thousands of pounds into the operation if decent profits were forthcoming. Noye's role was purely as a financial backer. The Gibraltarian told Noye he used sailing boats for hashish smuggling because they had larger hulls and even if police did uncover any of the drugs they could usually be paid off because pot was not considered the number one priority.

Within weeks of that first investment, Noye upped the stakes with his new Gibraltarian friend by deciding to buy a yacht, therefore cutting out the transport charges, leaving himself with a bigger slice of the profits. He purchased a fifty-foot yacht with cash from a Norwegian in Cadiz. At first he kept it in the small yacht marina at Barbate occasionally sailing it south to the surfing resort of Tarifa. Because the vessel was not registered in his name or connected to him in any way, Noye was able to use it for his own hashish smuggling team. He also made a useful secondary income by leasing it out to some of his drug-smuggling associates, including the Gibraltarian, safe in the knowledge that if anything happened to it they would be obliged to buy him another boat.

But getting involved in such business enterprises also made Kenny Noye more twitchy about his own survival on the run. Eventually he decided he would be better off moving to a quieter spot further inland from Los Canos. He relocated ten miles east to the mountain village of La Muela and rented a detached villa located at the end of a half-mile long drive. At least three times a week he'd drive to the nearby town of Vejer la Frontier to eat at one of its renowned restaurants. The rest of the time he stayed in the house.

Perched on the foothills of the Andalusian Mountains, the town of Vejer la Frontier particular caught the imagination of Kenny Noye. Conquered by the Arabs in the famous battle of La Janda, it remained in the hands of the Muslims for more than 500 years. Noye adored walking the town's narrow cobbled streets and he particularly liked the fact that there were virtually no British tourists anywhere in sight.

Meanwhile, back in the tiny village of La Muela, Noye also discovered a well run little pizzeria called Il Forno, just half a mile from his house. It served superb pasta and he would make a point of returning to it many times.

But within a couple of months, Noye decided he wanted to be on the move again. He realised he much preferred it by the sea. He began looking for a oceanside location where there would always be a few tourists — mainly German — to provide just the right level of cover. He also concluded it was time he bought himself a proper house. Police activity back in Britain had slowed right down but he wanted to find himself a long-term home where he could feel more settled.

30. On the Bloody Trail

'So is it possible to meet him?' I asked Kenny Noye's cousin Michael during our first telephone conversation back in February 1997.

At the other end of the line Michael paused and then took two long breaths.

'It all depends.'

'On what?'

'Things.'

Another beat of silence followed.

'First of all I have to meet you to see what you're all about,' explained Michael Noye.

At exactly midday on Saturday, 1 March, I arrived at a slightly dilapidated pub called The Three Daws, in the Kent Thameside town of Gravesend — a town so-named because tens of thousands of the bodies of victims of the great plague of London were transported down the river to the town for disposal.

There was no sign of a man fitting Michael Noye's description, so I wandered up to the bar and ordered a drink. The only other people in the pub were a couple in one corner talking quietly and two rather bulky men in their mid-forties sitting on opposite sides of the room sipping pints of bitter.

One of them lumbered to his feet and headed for the pay phone at the entrance where he made a brief call before returning to his drink. Fifteen minutes later Michael Noye turned up.

Cousin Michael was very much the ferret-type he had sounded on the phone — long brown crumpled leather jacket and dirty white trainers, he was a gaunt, worried-looking man in his late forties.

He was pencil-thin and his eyes darted around the room the moment we reluctantly shook hands. He accepted an orange juice and we walked to a table in a room off the main bar overlooking a small, rundown pier that ran apologetically out into the River Thames.

Just then the two bulky customers who'd been sipping their pints in separate corners of the bar appeared beside us. Michael Noye made no attempt to introduce them. They simply sat down either side of us with their backs to me. I suppose it was meant to be intimidatory. It worked.

Michael Noye soon made it clear that he might be able to get a message to Kenny, but first of all I would have to pass a few tests.

'We want to see a proposal of what you're trying to do,' said Michael with the emphasis on 'we'. 'Kenny will want to know if it's going to be to his advantage to talk.'

Throughout all this, my two new fat drinking partners did not utter a word. When I volunteered to buy them all another pint, Michael Noye told me what they wanted and I delivered it to them. There wasn't so much as a word of thanks. They didn't budge, sitting with their large, sweaty backs to me throughout. They were close enough to hear my every word and I could hear them slurping their beer.

Michael Noye supplied his mobile phone number and a fax number for the 'proposal' he said Kenny Noye required.

He explained: 'Then I can pass it on to the powers that be and see if it's alright for us to help you out.' Michael continued: 'The general idea is to get the nod from Kenny. I'm going to leave copies of your proposal in the right place, so that they find their way back to him.'

Noye then hesitated and looked me straight in the eye.

'The word is already out about you. You've stirred up a right bloody hornet's nest.'

'How come?'

Noye didn't answer. Instead he turned to look out the window at the grey waters of the Thames. His two companions didn't budge an inch or say a word.

An awkward silence followed. The subject of Kenny Noye was closed.

There was no point in making small talk about the weather or the depressing view. I'd been given my orders and that was that. Then the fatter of the two men got up and went to get Michael Noye and the other man a drink. He didn't offer me one.

I decided it was time to leave.

On Sunday 16 March 1997 cousin Michael agreed to meet me once again. This time he wouldn't say exactly where. I was instructed to get to Gravesend by 10am, then call him on his mobile phone.

Michael Noye decided it was a little early for a drink and told me to meet him at a nearby café.

Ten minutes later he arrived and immediately announced he'd received my 'proposal' on the Kenny Noye project. This time Michael Noye was alone. Perhaps I was now to be trusted.

'They're still thinking about your request. But I think we're heading in the right direction.'

'Good.'

'We've been asking around about you,' added Michael, as he tucked into white toast with lashings of butter.

'Will I be able to meet him?' I asked.

'I dunno for sure, but I think we'll manage something.'

Then he took one of his familiar pauses.

'You've got to understand what you're getting yourself into here,' explained Michael, eyes snapping around the almost empty restaurant to make sure no one was listening.

'What d'you mean?'

'Well for starters, Kenny likes to know all about people before he meets them.'

'Really?' I asked.

'Kenny's already checked out what you've done before, where your children go to school and things like that.'

I stopped in my tracks at the mention of my children.

'Why would he want to know where my kids goto school?'

'Why do you think?'

Michael paused again. 'That's Kenny's way. He likes to be in control.'

'Are you saying he'd threaten my family?'

'Who knows?' Michael Noye smiled and arched his eyebrows for a moment.

'Do I need to be worried about my family?'

'I don't know. That's just the way Kenny does things.'

'He'd go after my kids?'

'He does things his way.'

Michael Noye then completely changed the subject by producing some photographs of his cousin Kenny. One of them showed a baby holding a huge wallet in its tiny hands.

'We always have a laugh about this one. It's the only time Kenny was ever seen getting his wallet out,' chuckled Michael.

He also had a photo of Kenny Noye's father in navy uniform taken during the last war. He was about to give them to me when he changed his mind.

'I don't think Kenny's father would appreciate me giving you that one.'

He did give me a couple of previously unpublished shots, but they showed Noye in the same way he has been pictured in many newspapers over the years.

I tried to bring the subject back to the man himself.

'How do you think I'd get on with him?' I asked Michael.

'Who? Kenny?'

Another customary pause for thought followed.

'You'd get on fine. But he'll want to use you and manipulate you in some way because that's how he operates. He likes to be in control.'

Michael took another deep breath, checked out the restaurant for the last time and got up to leave.

'Tread carefully,' he muttered.

A few days later, I spoke to Michael Noye again on the telephone. He told me that Kenny Noye knew all about my efforts to find him.

'Once I get the nod we can start setting things up.'

'What exactly does that mean?'

'You'll see.'

I never heard from Michael Noye again. He even refused to return my calls.

Not long after this I spoke to Noye's wife Brenda. She'd heard all about my efforts to make contact with her husband.

'You've been talking to all sorts of people. It won't make any difference. No one knows where Kenny is,' she said dryly.

A few weeks later another relative of Noye's told me: 'Kenny told Michael not to go near you again.'

Kenny Noye's bloody trail was clearly going to be full of characters who would do anything in their power to prevent me finding the man himself.

31. Sweat and Fear in La Janda

Even a wily old fox like Kenny Noye began to feel lonely and homesick as he spent longer and longer periods of time in Spain. As the months following the Stephen Cameron killing rolled by, he knew it was dangerous to get too used to hopping on a private plane back home to cut a deal and keep his fingers in a few pies. Eventually he contacted an old criminal associate in the Costa del Sol resort of Fuengirola and asked him if there was somewhere discrete he could stay for a day or two whenever he was in need of a pint of Guinness and some familiar surroundings. Noye was told there was an empty apartment above a bar called The London Pub on the seafront at Fuengirola. His contact told him he would be welcome there any time of the day or night and that no questions would be asked about his identity.

Noye then began making occasional appearances in The London Pub where he called himself 'Mick the builder'. Only one person had any idea of his true identity and he was sworn to secrecy. Many London Pub regulars remember 'Mick the builder' to this day. 'He was always with the same bloke. I knew there was something familiar about his face but none of us ever twigged who it was until a lot later.' When Noye was in Fuengirola, he often booked up a hooker to drop by the apartment above the bar after a night of heavy drinking. He also rediscovered his appetite for cocaine on account of another contact of his in the area who had been one of London's most notorious dealers before retiring to the Costa del Sol.

* * *

Kenny Noye had never been shy about using false names as Kent police discovered when they tried to follow his trail in the aftermath of the Stephen Cameron killing. But in Spain he settled on the name 'Michael Mayne' and he had official paperwork made out in the name in case he ever got stopped by local police. He also kept a passport handy in the name of 'Green', just in case of emergencies.

Noye even grew a goatee beard and started wearing wire-rimmed glasses to ensure that he did not get recognised.

During his first year based on La Janda coast he bought and sold at least three smaller properties while renting those larger houses in Los Canos and La Muela for himself. At one estate agents called Apartamentos Turistos on the Paseo de las Palmeras, in Zahara de los Atunes, a few miles south of Los Canos, Noye even got himself a mail box where his post could be sent. Sometimes he'd spend five or ten minutes chatting to the English-speaking staff about potential property deals in the area. Noye was particularly taken by one very pretty brunette assistant.

All the workers at the office are to this day too scared to talk about 'Michael Mayne' and their true impression of him. But it was only after Noye began regularly popping in to check his mail box that he became fully aware of an especially isolated beachside community in a tiny urbanisation called Atlanterra, one-and-a-half miles south of Zahara. Atlanterra had always been one of La Janda coastline's best kept secrets. Not one signpost on the approaching roads ever named it. It was particularly popular with older German tourists trying to escape the crowded beaches of the Costa del Sol and those younger surfer types in nearby Tarifa and Barbate. It was even rumoured that in the mid-fifties, Atlanterra housed two Nazi war criminals who in turn recommended the area to their relatives back in the Fatherland.

The community had slowly expanded in the early 1980s after almost thirty years with nothing more than half a dozen houses and a modest hotel down by the beach. Then a dozen or so rich, middle-aged Germans bought land on the hillside overlooking the Atlantic. They created an urbanisation — a high-class housing estate — and hoped and prayed that as few people as possible would be encouraged to spend their annual holidays in the vicinity.

Kenny Noye became even more interested in the urbanisation when he heard there were no phone lines connecting the community to the nearby exchange at Barbate. That meant Noye could use local public phones down the main road into Zahara without creating much attention.

While on the lookout for a suitable property in Atlanterra, Kenny Noye was introduced to a twitchy German marketing consultant called Hans Bartom in a Barbate bar. Bartom wanted to sell his large villa on the urbanisation overlooking the Atlantic. Bartom wasn't too popular with other residents on the exclusive estate because he was cold to most neighbours. 'He was drove around the urbanisation in his convertible Mercedes,' recalled one neighbour.

Bartom had failing debts connected to his failing business back home near Hamburg and, although Kenny Noye didn't realise it, he had been trying to sell his house in Atlanterra for at least four years. 'But he was asking a ridiculous price so it was no surprise he couldn't sell it,' explained one resident. Noye was immediately interested in purchasing Bartom's property because of its location up on the hillside overlooking a handful of shops and bars that made up Atlanterra centre. Later that same evening, Noye followed Bartom in his Mercedes along the narrow, winding roads to Atlanterra. He was shown round the house and by the next morning had agreed to purchase it for a price of 50 million pesetas (£200,000) — to be paid in cash naturally.

'Give me your lawyer's number and we will get them to draw up contracts,' Bartom said after shaking on the deal with Noye, who was calling himself 'Michael Mayne'.

'I don't want to declare this so we'll create an offshore company to buy the house,' said Noye, casually. Bartom wasn't bothered. More than half the property deals involving foreigners in Spain involve so-called 'black', undeclared money — and in any case he was just delighted to get the house off his hands. Within weeks, Hans Bartom had sold the house and all its furnishings to Noye and returned to his other home near Hamburg. He told all his neighbours before he left that his wife was seriously ill and needed expensive medical treatment and that was why he had sold the property for much less than he was originally asking. He never returned to Atlanterra, and one neighbour who talks to him by phone once a month admitted Bartom had said Noye could be 'some kind of criminal'. His priority had been to sell the house.

Noye knew from his other, smaller property investments in Spain that it was impossible to carry out a house purchase without the involvement of a lawyer. He'd avoided local lawyers because they tended to have a lot of friends in nearby police stations. But during an earlier trip to meet his Marbella-based armed-robber-turned-drug-baron contact, Noye had been put in touch with a 'reliable' lawyer. He was a brief who, Noye was told, would never let him down. When this author tried to pay a visit to the same lawyer in February 2000, he was physically ejected from the legal offices.

Within weeks of moving into the twitchy Herr Bartom's house in Atlanterra, Noye started using the La Sal restaurant half a mile away, down near a partly-constructed development of beachside apartments. Staff were highly amused by the fact that he brought at least three different women in to dine during the following year. 'The first one was blonde and he introduced her as his wife. Then there was a dark-haired woman slightly younger. Then came another blonde,' recalled attractive brunette owner Charo Alvarez Araujo.

At La Sal, Noye struck up a friendship with the German co-owner of the bar, Miguel 'Mike' Leffler. Leffler was a keen paraglider and local property developer. Noye, it seems, was obsessed with talking about property investments and building work. He met him at least three occasions socially and admitted: 'He never said much about himself on a personal level. But he said he'd bought and sold quite a few local properties.'

Meanwhile Noye's interest in finding new 'businesses' to invest in continued. During 1997, he not only continued occasionally popping in and out of Britain but he also travelled on his 'Alan Edward Green' passport to places as diverse as Jamaica and Tangiers. In Tangiers he visited the home of a notorious London drug lord on a number of occasions. His trips to Jamaica were also linked to a new business partner, a former cell mate from his days in prison in the late 80s. That ex-inmate had close connections with the Yardies and Noye was considering going into business with the notorious gangsters in order to step up his hashish smuggling operation.

During the second half of 1997 Noye disappeared from his home in Atlanterra for at least six weeks. One Austrian neighbour never forgot the day Noye returned. 'I was out in my garden when he drove up. I waved over at him and immediately noticed his hair had become more blonde than the grey it was when I'd last seen him.'

In fact, Noye had decided to bleach his hair blonde after dropping into his favourite London Pub in Fuengirola, following a meeting to discuss a drugs deal in Marbella. 'Noye thought it would make him even more difficult to recognise,' explained one source. 'He also knew it made him look like a lot of the gay guys round in Fuengirola which would further confuse anyone who thought they'd spotted him.' Noye was constantly aware that he had to keep changing his appearance to avoid recognition. Dying his hair blonde seemed a small price to pay for his continuing freedom.

32. Taking Care of Business

In Spain, Kenny Noye soon discovered that prostitution was virtually part of the fabric of society. Outside most large cities there were always 'nightclubs' where men could take their pick of girls who then hired a room connected to the club for sex. Isolated and sometimes spending weeks at a time entirely alone, Kenny Noye's need for sexual relief soon led him to begin exploring a strip of such clubs on a busy main road close to the nearest big city of Cadiz. He soon found what he was looking for.

The club was located on the main road, fifteen miles north of Atlanterra and consisted of a bar where at least a dozen girls would wait to be chosen by male customers whom they would then take into one of the adjoining bedrooms. One girl whom Noye regularly hired during his visits to the club during his stay in Spain, said he often paid her more than £1,000 for four hours of sex — but then spent at least half of that time just talking. 'I remember he called himself Mike and he seemed a decent man. He never made me do anything bad,' said the girl. She also recalled how Noye visited the club at least three times in the company of a much younger man whom he would give money to hire a girl. 'He was almost young enough to be his son,' she said.

After visiting the club a few times, Noye asked one of his Spanish contacts in Marbella whether there were any clubs worth investing in as they seemed a fairly sound bet as far as businesses went in the area. Eventually Noye was introduced to two men who ran a prostitution ring which employed almost 300 women, mainly from Eastern Europe and South America, in eleven clubs stretching along a 200-mile coastline from the Costa del Sol to well north of Cadiz. The two men were bringing the women into Spain illegally and keeping them virtually prisoners before 'distributing' them to the clubs where they were put to work. Once they entered the country their passports were confiscated and they were left with no choice but to work as prostitutes.

Noye was fascinated by the economics of the business when he heard that each woman handed over 6,000 pesetas daily to the club owners and another 1,000 pesetas for each client with the two men getting 50 per cent of all profits. But he didn't like the 'prisoner aspects' of the operation, and in the end decided not to get involved. He also presumed that immigration authorities might eventually start focusing their attention on the brothels.

In many ways Kenny Noye treated his little isolated kingdom in the far western corner of Spain the same as he did south east London and Kent. As 'Mick the Builder' he built up a network of contacts and made sure that his old and trusted cronies kept him informed of any developments in the Kent police investigation into the death of Stephen Cameron. He paid £20,000 cash for a Mitsubishi Shogun car with Belgian plates — P646 TMU — which he had been assured would never land him in trouble if he was ever stopped by the local police. It was just like that Range Rover Discovery he'd been driving at the time of Stephen Cameron's death.

Noye was also seen at a number of hotels in some of the nearby resorts in the company of women. At the Hotel Resedencia Bari on the Playa Los Bateles on the beach front at Conil, staff remember him bringing at least three different women in. 'He always paid cash and would come here about seven in the evening and leave about three or four hours later.'

* * *

Kenny Noye remained obsessed with discovering what, if any evidence police had linking him to the death of Stephen Cameron. If he could be certain the police had no real concrete evidence against him then he'd seriously consider letting detectives track him down and go back to England to face the charges. But Kent police let it be known that new witnesses to the roadrage killing had come forward. The truth was that in the 18 months following the murder of Stephen Cameron they had no other witnesses apart from Danielle Cable. If Noye had come forward and challenged Danielle's identification then the case against him would probably have been thrown out of court in the preliminary stages. But Kent police were determined to bring him to justice.

So Noye sat put in Atlanterra. He had a luxurious villa with a pool, a string of beautiful women to bed, an expensive car and absolutely no money worries. What more could he want?

* * *

The cliffs just below Kenny Noye's house in Atlanterra were a perfect launchpad for hang-gliders and paragliders, and often more than a dozen of them would descend to the beach below like vast insects. But one morning the easterly wind from the Atlantic Ocean brought with it a thick, sea mist that descended upon Kenny Noye's house like something out of a horror movie.

Noye the fitness fanatic wasn't deterred by the fog so he took his mountain bike out of the garage and set off through the nearby roads to work up a sweat. Within 200 yards of his house, he was stopped by three men wearing dark suits and two-way radio earpieces. That was when Noye discovered one of his neighbours on the Atlanterra urbanisation was a senior member of the Spanish government.

From then on, Noye found himself regularly being stopped by Spanish special branch officers protecting the minister whose holiday home happened to be one of the nearby properties. The fact that a team of armed police were staying in a house a few hundred yards from his own home did make Noye a tad twitchy. But he didn't let it stop him getting his daily dose of health and fitness.

* * *

Noye's network of friends and relatives kept Brenda fully informed of his movements, and she visited him in Spain on at least three occasions. But all Noye's associates knew their phones were bugged and that was why Noye always insisted on only communicating by public phone. He was determined never to let his guard drop. His trail might have seemed to have gone cold back in Britain since the initial furore surrounding his alleged link to the Stephen Cameron killing, but in some ways that made Noye even more careful.

Noye's false name — Michael Mayne — did not have to show up on any household bills because he was not obliged to change the name on any of the house utilities after purchasing the property from Herr Bartom. Inside the house, Noye had all the satellite TV stations tuned and would spend hours watching films or Sky News to see what was happening in the rest of the world. He also made a habit of picking up a few English papers every time he went into the nearby town of Barbate. His favourites were the *Sun* and *The Daily Telegraph*.

The property in Atlanterra had a unique vantage point in that Noye could see all his neighbours and any vehicles coming in either direction along the road that ran across the bottom of his fifty-foot driveway. His obsession with buying more property and making inquiries about possible deals brought him into contact with local contractor Lope Albercar, construction manager of a huge complex of flats and hotels being built next to the beach in Atlanterra. 'He came to see me to ask if I knew any good builders,' recalled Lope. 'He also wanted to know if he needed planning permission to move his swimming pool. I found him polite but extremely focused. We never seemed to discuss anything except his building plans.'

Some months after first moving into the house in Atlanterra, Kenny Noye encountered one of his neighbours as he was pulling out of the drive in his beloved blue Shogun four-wheel drive. Mr and Mrs M spoke immaculate English and told Noye they had lived on the Atlanterra urbanisation for many years. Noye, keen to expand his property interests and find out more about his neighbours, accepted their invitation for an early evening cocktail at the couple's house. Noye — who had a reputation back in places like West Kingsdown as a man who hardly ever even talked to his neighbours let alone met them socially — spent more than an hour with Mr and Mrs M. They never forgot how he virtually interrogated them about property prices and building work. 'He was very charming but there was a coldness in his eyes that I found chilling,' said Mrs M, who to this day is too afraid to be identified.

Noye wanted the couple to recommend him a good builder because he intended to do some extensive renovation work to his property. They told him about a local man called Peppin Gomez who was used by many of the urbanisation's residents. At that moment, Noye pulled out a pen and notebook and wrote down all Gomez's details. Then he got up and said: 'Goodbye.'

As Mrs M later recalled: 'He was out the door in seconds and we never had another conversation with him ever again.'

Builder Peppin Gomez was immediately hired by Noye to move the pool and reshape the garden as well as move a number of partition walls inside the house and build a new kitchen. Noye told Gomez to make all his bills out to a company called Truntong, the name of the company the villa was registered in, which turned out to be fictitious.

* * *

Just around the corner from Kenny Noye lived the only

other British person on the entire Atlanterra urbanisation. She was married to a Dutchman but she hadn't forgotten her English roots. This lady frequently saw Noye driving past her house in his Shogun on the way down the hill to the shops and bars below. She was particularly intrigued because Noye's car had Belgian plates and was always so immaculately clean. 'No one here bothers to keep their car that clean because the roads are either muddy or dusty,' she explained. 'I'd spoken to him briefly in the local shops and I knew he was a south Londoner, so I wondered why on earth he drove around in an expensive Belgium-registered car.'

Meanwhile another German neighbour — Herr Tewe Dungholt — from the picturesque Casa Petina opposite Noye's house, had an encounter of an entirely different kind. And it was an encounter he would never forget. Dungholt made the mistake of jumping over Noye's perimeter wall after noticing his gardener on the front lawn. Just as Herr Dunghold began striding across Noye's garden, Noye emerged from the side door to the house holding something shiny in his right hand. Noye shouted out aggressively at Dungholt: 'Who the fuck are you?'

Herr Dungholt later recalled: 'It looked like a knife and I could see he was not happy.'

The moment Dungholt began speaking in heavily accented English, Noye relaxed his guard and put his weapon down. And a plastic smile immediately wiped across his face. Dungholt told Noye he was curious about the extensive nature of the building works Noye had started carrying out. 'He seemed to be turning it into a proper home rather than just a place to spend his holidays,' recalled Dungholt.

But Noye didn't offer Herr Dungholt the hand of friendship so he beat a hasty retreat.

Down the hill in Atlanterra, Noye's distinctive, ever-shining blue Shogun was regularly spotted either parked outside the local supermarket or one of three local bars and restaurants. By the early months of 1998, he even began inviting a select band of friends and relatives over for holidays. But Noye was always very careful to make sure they either rented properties at least three miles from his house or stayed in a hotel some distance away from his property. One of his most regular visitors was a middle-aged, balding London 'face' called Billy, who would stay in the luxurious, but extremely modestly priced, Hotel Antonio out on the main road to Barbate. Billy was so afraid of flying that he drove down through France and Spain in his white Ford Granada rather than face a two-hour flight to nearby Jerez or Seville.

A hard-faced man in his late forties, he is well remembered by hotel staff because he was always on his own and spent virtually no time either in his room or in the hotel restaurant — except for one very bizarre occasion. 'He was actually eating dinner alone in the dining room and then joined up with a group of Danish and German tourists in the bar afterwards,' recalled one member of the hotel staff. He was ordering bottles of champagne and all these tourists didn't know what to make of him. Then he started to get very loud with one man after trying to kiss his wife. In the end we had to escort him to his room. He checked out the next day and we never saw him again. We knew he was a friend of the man Mick from the house on the hill because this man used to be sometimes picked up in his blue truck.'

One of Noye's German neighbours on the urbanisation, Hermann Ritz, remembered 'Mick' as being a strange man: 'I thought he was Belgian and so did many of the other people here. Even the local garage where he serviced his car thought he was Belgium because of the car number plates.' Ritz sensed Noye was unfriendly when they first met. 'When people move to a new house they usually try to make some social contact. But Mick never seemed to be interested in talking to anyone. 'We were all puzzled why he went down into the village to use a public telephone — it was the talk of the urbanisation. Most of us had mobile phones and we couldn't understand why a man of his wealth did not.'

Ritz eventually fell out with Noye during a bizarre conversation about Noye's plans to learn Spanish. 'He asked me if I would teach him Spanish. I said yes but told him I would charge him 2,500 pesetas [£10] an hour. He got very angry and we never spoke again.' Kenny Noye had a problem putting his hand in his pocket — even in Spain.

Back at his house Noye urged builder Peppin Gomez to speed up the construction work so he could start buying some decent furniture to replace the tatty pieces left by previous owner Herr Bartom. Noye's eye for a business deal — either legitimate or illicit — remained untarnished by his virtual incarceration in Atlanterra. He even began asking around about the ownership of the rusting hulk of a hotel building that had never been completed in the early 1970s after a slump in property prices. He inquired at local estate agents and developers about the ownership of the building. Eventually, according to people he talked to in Atlanterra, he made contact with a local Spaniard who owned the site and had been sitting on it for years in the hope that Atlanterra would one day become a thriving tourist resort and he'd be able to make a financial killing. Noye persuaded the man that the hotel could be relatively easily completed and he suggested they become partners in the hotel in exchange for him putting £100,000 (25 million pesetas) into the first stage of renovation work. He promised more funding once work got under way. The man agreed and Noye produced the cash within weeks. The work never materialised but Noye undoubtedly plans to retrieve his investment plus interest penalites if and when he returns to Atlanterra.

In the early 1998, Kenny Noye found having to drive miles to use public phones in Zahara and Barbate such a strain he bought a stolen pay-as-you-go mobile phone during a fleeting visit to the Costa del Sol. He knew it was a risk, but he felt he could afford it.

Over in the nearest big town of Barbate, Noye became a regular at the town's only Chinese restaurant. He was often seen there with a man in his mid-20s — the same man who was also spotted inside a number of local brothels with Noye. He also ate at Sergio's restaurant in the village of

Zahara, just a mile or so north of Atlanterra. Noye even asked if any of the staff knew of a short-let apartment nearby because he had a friend flying in for a week and he wanted somewhere to put her up.

In Atlanterra, Noye's determination to keep in shape seemed to know no boundaries. Often he would drive down the hill to the vast deserted beach below and surf the waves alongside a group of local teenagers. They remembered him as being extremely well dressed and fit looking. A combination of many years keeping in shape in jail and his healthy lifestyle in Spain meant that Kenny Noye was an outstandingly fit, strong man for his age. His wrists were as wide as his ankles. Many who encountered him in Spain said he was literally a bull of a man. Very tanned and very muscular. Inside the villa in Atlanterra, Noye created a makeshift gym in the main reception area as builder Peppin Gomez continued his construction work. In some ways that house in Atlanterra was becoming like another version of prison to Kenny Noye.

One day Noye was sipping a cerveza in the bar of his favourite La Sal restaurant in Atlanterra when he asked his friend co-owner Mike Leffler if he would be prepared to hang-glide over his house and take some aerial photos of the property. 'He wanted to pay me very well. I was delighted.' Leffler was going to Germany for a few weeks so the two men agreed that he would do the aerial photography on his return.

* * *

Back in England, Kent detectives were growing increasingly worried about the safety of Danielle Cable, their only proper witness to the roadrage killing of her fiancé Stephen Cameron. Police informants were claiming that Noye was trying to hire a hit man to kill Danielle to ensure that she could not give evidence against him. One grass even told detectives that Noye planned to give himself up once he had eliminated the 'problem of Danielle'.

A decision was taken to give Danielle round-the-clock protection and move her to a safe house. Detectives warned her that she might have to keep on the move for many years to come.

They were taking Noye's alleged murder threats very seriously and they could not afford to let her out of their sight.

33. The Mina Factor

By the spring of 1998, Kenny Noye had been on his toes for eighteen months. He was still seriously considering the wisdom of continuing to avoid the police investigation into the death of Stephen Cameron.

Brothels with £150-an-hour hookers were not enough for Kenny Noye. He needed real female company. The man whose wife Brenda even once admitted that he 'related better to men than females' wasn't just looking for sexual gratification. He needed someone he could talk and relate to. So when he attended a business meeting in Marbella his attention was caught by a familiar looking, extrovert brunette woman who'd arrived on the arm of one of Noye's oldest criminal associates.

Mina Al Taiba — or Marinella, the name she was using that evening — was occasional escort to some of the Costa del Sol's most respected faces, including one of Britain's most notorious armed-robber-turned-drug barons. The 38-year-old had actually first been introduced to Noye when he visited Amsterdam to discuss a major drugs deal with two German contacts in 1995 — a year before the Stephen Cameron killing. Her Spanish-registered 4-wheel drive Mitsubishi (number plate N9592 MU) was a familiar sight on the Costa del Sol. She claimed she was from Lebanon and that her family now lived in the Spanish North African colony of Ceuta, just a one-hour boat ride from Gibraltar. But many on the Costa del Sol underworld considered Mina's claims to be Lebanese rather far fetched. Said one source in Marbella: 'I heard she was a Columbian from the ghettos of Cali but she didn't like telling anyone.'

Mina had been associated with some of the richest dope smugglers on the Costa del Sol. She was also known as an extremely discreet woman who could be relied upon not to 'shout her mouth off'. She also happened to be a strikingly attractive woman with a penchant for Prada handbags and Gucci shoes. While she undoubtedly equated money with sex, she'd always had a soft spot for Kenny Noye since that first encounter three years earlier in Holland. She knew he was loaded and even Kenny Noye — notoriously reluctant to part with any of his hard-earned cash — would soon find himself swept up by her big spending habits.

Within a short time of that second meeting in Marbella, Mina and Noye were enjoying intimate nights together at his house in Atlanterra. One of Noye's neighbours regularly noticed her car slung up at the bottom of Noye's drive during the early summer weeks of 1998. 'She tended to stay until very late at night. But her car was never actually there in the mornings.' In fact, Noye had even secretly rented Mina an apartment in nearby Zahara de los Atunes, where she was able to stay with her 16-year-old son during her visits to La Janda coastline from Marbella — two-and-a-half hours east of Atlanterra. Noye eventually built up such a close relationship with the boy that they shared a green Yamaha motorbike — CA 8377 BC — which Noye kept in the garage at the front of the house. During the early summer of 1998, Noye even made a point of mainly shopping by motorbike and rarely removing his helmet to avoid recognition, especially when he ventured into the relatively larger town of Barbate.

Meanwhile he was hearing stories from back home about certain villains who were getting sick and tired of being raided by police officers looking for the elusive Kenny Noye. Noye was well aware that his future depended on a handful of characters back in Britain. Once he lost their support he could find himself in very serious trouble.

In the meantime he tried his hardest to keep a low profile

and enjoy the company of Mina Al Taiba, who was like a breath of fresh air after his years of loneliness and casual, clinical sexual gratification.

* * *

Many of Kenny Noye's associates in the drugs world were not having it all their own way, either.

So-called heroin king James Hamill was jailed for 18 years in February 1998 after being found guilty of running one of Britain's fastest-growing heroin supply rings.

Hamill, 38, had aspriations of becoming one of Europe's most feared criminal godfathers and he'd taken a lot of advice from Kenny Noye over the years. Ironically, Noye had encouraged Hamill to steer clear of using any drugs personally — a rule that Noye himself broke with tragic consequences.

Just two weeks before Hamill was jailed in Aberdeen, one of his closest associates, feared Glasgow gangster Stephen Docherty, plunged to his death from a high rise block. In the high-risk, high-profit drugs empires, life often comes cheap.

Hamill and his trusted lieutenant James Gemmill were proud of their links with criminals such as Kenny Noye. One police source explains: 'Hamill and Gemmill had built up connections in south London and Noye met them on a number of occasions shortly before the road-rage murder.'

At one time Noye and his Scottish friends were seriously considering joining forces and supplying virtually every type of recreational drug to 'customers' across Britain and possibly even into Europe. Also in February 1998, a bizarre incident thousands of miles from Noye's home territory had repercussions amongst the many detectives who'd investigated Noye over the previous 20 years.

The murder of Britist tourist Roy Chivers, 51, by robbers at a luxury Kenyan safari lodge brought back many painful memories for dozens of senior officers. Chivers was knifed in the chest by robbers as he walked through a private reserve with his wife Sandra.

Chivers had been a close friend and fellow operative of Detective Constable John Fordham when he was stabbed to death in Kenny Noye's garden during the Brink's Mat investigation.

There was a certain tragic irony to the fact that undercover policeman Chivers was stabbed to death just like his friend John Fordham. The similarity between the two killings did not go unnoticed by some of Britain's most experienced police officers.

As one explained: 'Roy's murder reminded us all that Kenny Noye was still on the run and we had a duty towards him and John Fordham to never give up the search for Noye.'

Any suggestion that Kenny Noye was in any way involved in the death of Roy Chivers is ludicrous... but stranger things have happened...

34. Mucho Dinero

In mid-June 1998, Kent police got a call from a long-time informant who gave them the mobile phone number of another criminal whom he said was in regular contact with Kenny Noye. When the grass demanded a £100,000 tip-off fee if it led detectives to Noye, they began to take him very seriously.

Kent detectives immediately requested assistance from MI5, who sanctioned round-the-clock surveillance of the man's phone from their hi-tech headquarters overlooking Vauxhall Bridge in London. MI5, Britain's domestic security service, had since the mid-90s been regularly involved in tracing criminals through surveillance and records of money transactions. In the previous two years the security services had directly helped bring to justice a number of major villains, including one of Noye's pals involved in the hole-in-the-wall scam.

Ever since Noye's disappearance in May 1996, police had been bugging all his business associates, his wife and family as well as his long-time mistress Sue McNichol-Outch. But it wasn't until they were given that other associate's mobile number that they got their first real break in the hunt for Noye. For the following month every call received and made by the man supposed to be in touch with Noye was monitored. Not one conversation even vaguely suggested the existence of Noye.

By the fourth week, Kent police were starting to get sceptical about the tip and were about to ease off the telephone surveillance operation when MI5 monitored a phone call during which Noye positively identified himself to the criminal during a mobile phone conversation. A series of more than thirty calls then followed between Noye in Spain and his associate in Kent. But because both mobiles were unregistered pay-as-you-go phones, it was impossible even to vaguely narrow down Noye's location. All MI5 could say was that Noye was somewhere in southern Spain. Then Noye told his friend in a call to send him some important documents to a mail box in the tiny beachside community at Zahara, just two miles from Noye's home in Atlanterra. The hunt for Kenny Noye had suddenly turned the corner. Kent police knew they had to act fast.

They immediately sent two senior detectives over to Spain. Meanwhile MI5 officers continued monitoring all the calls in the hope that Noye might incriminate himself over the killing of Stephen Cameron. Kent police decided that rather than instantly arrest their man they would stretch out their investigation in the hope that they might gather more vital evidence against the suspect. Also, although Kent Police had located the postbox in Zahara where Noye was getting his letters, they still had absolutely no idea where Noye was actually living. Then, to make matters worse, he didn't go near the mail box for days.

There was also another, even bigger problem, as one investigator later explained: 'No one other than Danielle Cable had seen Noye for years. He could have been sitting on a chair right next to the rest of us and we wouldn't have had a clue it was him.' Police also suspected that Noye had had facial plastic surgery in a bid to ensure he was even more difficult to recognise. That was when the unprecedented decision was made to fly Danielle Cable out to Spain and get her to positively identify Noye before he was arrested. And since they did not even have his home address, officers knew they would have to spend at least a week simply touring the area around Zahara in the hope that Danielle and the team might bump into Noye and recognise him.

So began one of the most bizarre weeks of investigation in the history of police detection.

* * *

Over in Los Canos de Meca, Kenny Noye tapped up his old local friend, bar owner Ricardo Garrido about the possibility of renting one of Garrido's beachside cottages just behind his Las Dunas bar 'for a lady friend'.

On 15August 1998 Noye handed over 100,000 pesetas (£800) cash to Garrido for a one-month let on a two-bedroom house just fifty yards from the bar. Two days later, Noye was shadowed from his mail box in Zahara to Los Canos where Kent detectives watched him help Mina Al Taiba and her teenage son unload their luggage from her Mitsubishi. But there was still no question of arresting Noye yet. They were not close enough for Danielle Cable to make a positive identification of him. It was decided not to follow Noye to his home yet in case he got wind of the police team's existence.

The following day Kent detectives and Danielle Cable wandered into Noye's favourite Chinese restaurant in Barbate just as Noye was walking out in the company of Mina's young son. They hadn't even realised he was in the restaurant. Danielle Cable was so surprised to see Noye that she did not have enough time to positively identify him.

The two British detectives accompanying Danielle then decided they had to be better prepared. They briefed Danielle that they would all pretend to be tourists so they wouldn't stand out. Two Spanish police officers joined the group from Cadiz and it was agreed they would speak only Spanish whenever they were near to any other people.

It wasn't until 24 August that they finally struck gold.

The group had all grown weary of each other after a non-stop round of lunches and dinners at different restaurants in the hope of bumping into Noye. It had been decided not even to stake out the house in Atlanterra because he might realise what was happening. Detectives also considered it too risky to arrest Noye at the house because it backed on to military land covered in dirt tracks that might enable him to escape into the nearby mountains.

Kent police were very well aware that they couldn't afford to take the sort of risks that had so tragically cost Detective John Fordham his life all those years earlier. So, on a local policeman's recommendation, an entourage of two cars including Danielle headed up into the hills inland from Barbate and Zahara de los Atunes to an Italian pizzeria called Il Forno in the tiny hamlet of La Muela, where, coincidently, Kenny Noye had once stayed in an isolated rented house. The moment the detectives and their female companion walked into the bustling restaurant, Danielle spotted Noye and dark-haired Mina in the corner of the veranda area of the restaurant. 'Danielle was so startled she almost gave the game away,' recalled one of the officers later.

Instead of turning around and heading back to their vehicles, the group decided to front it out and they sat down at two tables as far away as possible from Noye and his new mistress. 'It's him,' whispered Danielle Cable who was visibly shaking.

The Kent officers got her to calm down and one of them, acting like a tourist, got out a small hand-held video camera and began filming Danielle's reaction as well as panning around the restaurant in the hope of snatching a few frames of Britain's most wanted man. At the other side of the restaurant, Kenny Noye and his girlfriend were so engrossed in each other they hardly even noticed the group, who were only speaking in Spanish.

The following day — 20 August — after positively identifiying Noye at the Il Forno pizzeria, Kent detectives called in a specialist team of Spanish officers dedicated to the arrest of terrorists. They knew they had to mount a more sophisticated surveillance operation to ensure that Noye did not now slip out of their hands. The officers came from the Cadiz office of UDYCO, who combated drugs and organised crime, and included experts in money laundering and firearms. But shadowing Noye continued to prove an extremely tricky task. He was in the habit of driving his immaculate four-wheel drive Shogun at speeds of more than 100mph along the narrow, twisting roads near his house.

Moreover, his lifestyle was far from habitual. One morning he waved goodbye to Mina before heading at high speed to the surfing beaches in nearby Tarifa where he chatted up two pretty Dutch girls. That evening he was back with Mina in Los Canos de Meca. But it was still too early to swoop and arrest Noye because detectives had to be doubly certain of his identification.

A glass taken from the Il Forno pizzeria had been transported by air courier to Scotland Yard for forensic examination. Twenty-four hours later the officers in Spain were told that the man they had been following for days was definitely Kenneth Noye. On 28 August the decision was finally taken to detain Noye as soon as he ventured out to a public place. That evening detectives watched as Noye left his house in Atlanterra and headed off at high speed down the hill in his shiny blue Shogun...

35. Last Dance in Barbate

The beige 3-litre Vectra containing two Kent detectives and a Spanish officer headed off slowly behind Noye's car as it began twisting and turning down the hill from his house into Atlanterra. Two other vehicles — a Golf GTI and an Astra — joined the convoy from different positions as Noye hit the straight road out of Atlanterra through Zahara and towards Barbate. As usual Noye was driving at very high speed, but the officers were all confident he had no idea he was being shadowed.

Noye drove through the busy town of Barbate and headed on to a narrow road that ran through a forest towards the familiar beachside hamlet of Los Canos de Meca. Minutes later he picked up mistress Mina from her rented beachside house and the couple were heading once again back towards Barbate at high speed. Behind them, detectives had decided that because the road was so quiet and the area so sparsely populated they would use only the 3-litre Vectra to shadow Noye. The two other cars moved separately back to Barbate to await instructions.

Then disaster struck as Noye sped through the isolated forest road from Los Canos to Barbate. As one officer later explained: 'We lost him at the second curve. He just disappeared. There was a crossroads up ahead and he could have gone in any of three directions.' Instead of panicking, the detectives remained convinced he'd end up in Barbate so they slowed down and called to the other two vehicles to keep an eye out for him in the town. But for the following half an hour none of the investigators caught a glimpse of Noye's now familiar dark blue Shogun. The officers started to wonder if perhaps Noye had been tipped off about their operation. It was 10.30pm on a busy Friday night and the reality was that Kenny Noye could have slipped through their grasp.

As the minutes ticked towards eleven, it was decided that the three cars should float around Barbate in the hope of spotting Noye's distinctive Shogun with Belgian plates parked up in the busy town. They just prayed he was eating dinner somewhere. In fact, Kenny Noye's love of fresh fish had resulted in him heading for El Campero restaurant in Barbate.

At 11.20pm he and new mistress Mina Al Taiba walked hand in hand to the front veranda of the restaurant and were seated on a corner table located immediately next to the pavement. Noye always preferred to chose such tables because if any 'problems' arose he knew he could slip out quickly. Just as he was sitting down, three detectives in the Vectra spotted Noye's Shogun. They did one circle of the square in front of the restaurant and immediately thought they spotted him sitting at a table by the pavement.

The police then radioed to the other cars to meet them in a street adjoining the square where they parked two of the vehicles, the Golf GTI and the Vectra. It was agreed they would have to act like drunks in order to get near enough to the restaurant to be certain Noye was the man they had seen in there. The detectives bought some litre bottles of beer from a nearby bar and three of them got in the Astra and double parked it virtually in front of the restaurant. Then they began playing Prodigy's 'Firestarter' at full blast on the car stereo. As one detective later recalled: 'Basically we were singing and shouting and acting like it was a Friday night out for the lads.'

Three of the officers then tumbled out of the car and manoevered themselves near enough to Noye's table to establish that he was definitely their man. Noye was just ordering a bottle of Rioja and a seafood salad at that moment. More officers then linked up from the other cars and they began weaving their way back up the pavement towards the restaurant. Then four of the 'drunks' surrounded Noye's table. Noye tried to ignore them in the hope they would go away. The last thing he wanted was a bit of aggro with a bunch of drunken British hooligans.

One of the officers later explained: 'I then dropped my bottle of beer on the floor and leapt on him. There was a smash of a glass on the table and I floored him.' The detective got Noye in a painful headlock and fell to the ground with him. Two other detectives then locked on to each of his arms which were yanked up behind his back while a fourth officer handcuffed him. Eighteen-stone Spanish police chief Miguel Fernandez later claimed he was the one who had to sit on Noye in order to get him handcuffed.

In the middle of all this, Mina coolly got up and disappeared off into the night. Witnesses said the detectives look little notice of her. Then the four policemen literally picked Noye up off the floor and carried him to the back of the Astra. As one of the Kent officers later recalled: 'It was a three-door car and we knew he wasn't going anywhere.'

But in some ways their rough and ready treatment was not justified. As one officer later admitted: 'We treated him like a terrorist but he was a complete gentleman throughout.'

As two officers got in the front of the Astra, Noye

shouted, 'Why am I being detained? I want to see a lawyer and I want to see a doctor.' True, Noye's wrists were cut from the handcuffs. But apart from that there was absolutely nothing else wrong with him. Minutes after his arrest Noye was deposited at Barbate's modest police station where the charges were formally read to him.

Noye was then searched. All detectives found was a cheap wrist watch and a wallet carrying 1,400,000 pesetas (more than £6,000) in cash. 'What's the cash for?' detectives naturally inquired.

'Spending money for the weekend,' came Noye's very cool reply.

Noye also had in his possession a cheque book with five cheques signed to a man called Kerry Stuart Mayne, and a cheque for £5,000 made out to a furniture company. There was also a chequebook registered to Mayne, the fake name used by Noye during his stay in Spain at a local bank in Zahara where he had set up an account. It was also happened to be the name used by one of Noye's main money men who paid regular visits to Spain to keep him supplied with cash.

Noye also had the passport in the name of Alan Edward Green and in it were stamps showing he had visited Jamaica and Tangiers on several occasions. Kent police hoped the fake UK passport would ensure that Noye's extradition could be speeded up because it meant Spanish police would not pursue him under his real name.

By approximately 2am — just over two hours after his dramatic capture — it was decided Kenny Noye should immediately be transferred to a high-security jail near Cadiz, 35 miles north. Kent police knew all about Noye's friends and associates and they didn't want to take any risks with their highly-prized prisoner.

36. The Countdown Begins

At 8am the following morning, Saturday, 29 August, *News of the World* crime reporter Ian Edmondson had just walked into his London newsroom when the phone rang. It was the same contact who'd told him about Kenny Noye's alleged involvement in the roadrage death of Stephen Cameron two-and-half years earlier. 'He's been nicked near Cadiz,' said the contact.

Edmondson didn't doubt the accuracy of the tip off. He knew it came right from the horse's mouth, so to speak. Within hours he was on a plane to Spain. On the other side of London, at the Kensington headquarters of Associated Newspapers, the *Mail on Sunday*'s veteran crime reporter Chester Stern had just had a similar tip from a contact and was also en route for Heathrow Airport.

For three hours these two journalists and their respective newspapers were the only ones aware of Noye's arrest the previous night. Then, at 11am, Spanish and Kent police decided to announce officially the arrest on the news agency PA and the world began waking up to the fact that Britain's most wanted man had finally been apprehended. The media were about to swamp Kenny Noye's beloved La Janda coastline and blow apart his secretive life on the run from British justice.

As dozens of journalists frantically tried to book themselves on flights to Spain, Kenny Noye was taken by armed convoy to make his first court appearance in Cadiz. But the scene outside Cadiz's criminal court was far from chaotic. Noye was head down, hair ruffled, expressionless in a blue shirt as just two local photographers and a young Spanish female reporter looked on. That journalist, pretty 22-year-old Cadiz reporter Carmen Torres, watched as Noye, head bowed, was escorted into the court. Minutes later Carmen managed to get permission from a friendly policeman to go down into the hallway next to the holding cells underneath the court house where Noye was incarcerated in the minutes before his appearance. 'How do you feel, Mister Noye,' she asked through the bars of Noye's cell.

'Fine, thank you,' smiled Noye in the only interview he has ever given to a journalist.

'Are you innocent, Mister Noye?'

Noye smiled again and did not react.

Carmen fired more questions at Noye but got no real response. But she did later conclude: 'Noye was most charming and gracious towards me. He didn't say much but I noticed that his hair looked as if it had been tinted blonde.'

A few minutes later Noye was taken up to the court where he insisted to a judge that British police had no evidence linking him to the Cameron killing. The judge listened intently and then remanded him back to the grim high-security Puerto 2 prison in Puerto de Santa.

Back in England there was already growing concern that Danielle Cable might have to face the ordeal of being a witness in a high-profile murder trial since Kenny Noye was already pleading his innocence from Spain. At her home near Swanley, in Kent, Danielle's mother Mandy told one reporter that her daughter still suffered nightmares about the murderous attack. 'All she wants is justice for Steve,' said Mrs Cable. Other relatives said that Danielle had, not surprisingly, never been the same since that fateful day in May, 1996. And Stephen Cameron's parents Toni and Ken also felt the killing had ruined their lives and that of their son's fiance. Mr Cameron even explained: 'She can't pick up the pieces of her life at all. She is terribly lonely.'

The afternoon following Noye's first court appearance,

dozens of reporters appeared outside his house in Atlanterra and began interrogating anyone who'd had any contact with him. His builder Peppin Gomez arrived at the house in Atlanterra totally unaware that Noye had been arrested. He had been hoping to collect 3 million pesetas (£12,000) owed for renovation work he was carrying out on the property. Instead he was surrounded by journalists.

Peppin, 52, told reporters he only knew Noye as 'Mickey'. He had been impressed with 'Mickey's' reliability when it came to money. But Peppin did wonder why Noye refused to give out his mobile phone number. He told the crowd of reporters: 'There was no trouble with the money after the first month's work. He was friendly but always asked for a receipt when he paid me. He said it was for tax reasons and he was going to put it through his company in England, which he said was called Tortorn. He was also trying to buy the land next to his villa so he could build another house.'

Peppin's biggest concern about Noye's arrest was that he wouldn't get paid the remainder of the money for the work he had been contracted to carry out. But even in the days following his dramatic capture, Noye had every intention of making sure Peppin got his money so that the renovation work would be completed. He was certain he'd be back in Atlanterra sooner rather than later.

Meanwhile dozens of other British and Spanish reporters were scouring the area around Barbate for clues as to how Noye managed to stay on the run from justice for so long. And within 24 hours of his capture Fleet Street newspapers were already dubbing him a 'serial womaniser'. The *Sun* even referred to the master criminal 'dating a series of girls in southern Spain while in hiding.' The paper claimed that on the night of his arrest, Noye had been cheating on long-term mistress Sue McNichol-Outch with his brunette friend Mina Al Taiba.

Evidence of Sue's presence in the area was provided to journalists by Barbate optician Rafael Quiros. He remembered 'Mike' well because the first time he called at his shop just off the main shopping street in Barbate, he had kept his motorcycle helmet on until after he was inside the opticians. A week later — on the Tuesday before Noye's arrest — a blonde woman who called herself Sue called back to pick up the glasses Noye had ordered. Quiros presumed she was Noye's wife because she spoke with a similar English accent and was of a similar age. It seemed that Noye enjoyed juggling his love life even when he was trying to keep a low profile from the law.

More background about the police operation to track down Noye began to emerge in the days following his arrest. Kent police confirmed Noye's alleged love triangle by saying they had watched Noye entertain at least two different women, identified as Sue McNichol-Outch and Mina Al Taiba, in a number of local restaurants. This seemed to back up the optician's story about a woman called Sue. Some of the residents on the urbanisation where Noye owned his house, claimed that Noye often only spent weekends at the property and would then head over to Los Canos to stay with a girlfriend in the week. Builder Peppin Gomez recalled at least two women visiting the house, a blonde with a teenage boy and a dark-haired woman also with a son. He said neither of them spoke Spanish.

Meanwhile, Kent Police knew they had just 28 days from the time of Noye's arrest to submit a formal application for Noye's extradition back to England. The Crown Prosecution Service insisted to Kent police there was sufficient evidence to justify the application. But they knew full well that if Noye was accused of committing any offences locally in Spain, such as using a false passport, then he could be kept in Spain to face those charges before any extradition could take place. It was a legal tightrope, even though the days when London villains arrested in Spain could stick two fingers up at British justice were long gone. Nevertheless, as one Kent policeman explained: 'You still have to be very careful. It's very easy to screw up when you're trying to negotiate delicate legal matters in another country.' Not surprisingly, Kent Police feared that the longer Noye remained in Spain the more chance he might have of avoiding extradition. They wanted to get him back to Britain quickly.

In jail in Cadiz, Noye reluctantly agreed to provide blood samples and allowed doctors to conduct a thorough forensic examination. The results of those tests were immediately conveyed to Kent investigators so they could be compared to evidence found at the scene of the killing of Stephen Cameron.

Despite the grim surroundings of the El Puerto de Santa Maria prison, Kenny Noye knew things could have been a lot worse for him. His attitude was that just so long as he remained in Spain there was a chance he could avoid extradition. Prison staff were surprised by Noye's relaxed attitude. He explained it away by insisting he had nothing to hide and that he was entirely innocent of the Stephen Cameron killing.

Shortly after the arrest, Spanish Police stated off-the-record to reporters that Noye's mistress Mina Al Taiba was a police informant who had tipped them off about Noye's movements. That was purely a smokescreen to protect the British grass who helped pinpoint Noye's location by telling them the mobile phone number of Noye's associate. The Spanish police had happily helped throw up the red herring. But in exchange they wanted some public credit for the capture of Kenny Noye. As one Kent police source later explained: 'That's why we were happy to suggest the girl fingered Noye. It made the Spanish police feel better. Draw your own conclusions.'

In fact, Spanish police were embarrassed to discover that master criminal Noye, who had been the photographic subject of an Interpol warrant for more than a year, was in their sights for more than two months when they had Mina under surveillance during her encounters with a certain drug baron. At no time did they realise her new lover was the most wanted man in Britain. But it did mean that officers inside the Malaga office of UDYCO — the Spanish equivalent of the Special Branch — were immediately able to identify her as a high-class hooker with known criminal connections. It also conveniently enabled the police to blame Mina for grassing up Kenny Noye.

Meanwhile Mina Al Taiba herself, not surprisingly, insisted she had no idea her lover was a murder suspect. She maintained she believed he was an eccentric British millionaire who craved privacy like so many foreign tycoons in Spain.

Mina told friends she had been attracted to Noye because 'he was a real English gentleman.' However, rumours persist to this day that Mina did play a part in informing police of Noye's existence. One police contact in Cadiz told me shortly before Noye's trial for the killing of Stephen Cameron: 'This woman was well-known in Marbella and called herself Marinella. She dated many rich criminals on the Costa del Sol. She was also an informant for the police in Marbella and the moment she told them about Noye they informed the British police.'

Whatever the truth of the matter, Mina Al Taiba has remained close to Kenny Noye throughout his incarceration. It seems unlikely that she would have continued standing by him if she had been the grass the Spanish claimed. As one south east London criminal pointed out: 'Kenny Noye knows the score and he clearly does not believe this bird was involved in getting him nicked.'

On Saturday 29 August, less than 12 hours after Noye's arrest in Spain, Brenda Noye heard a familiar knock on the door of their house in Sevenoaks. Kent police had surrounded the property and immediately swamped it with scene-of-the-crime experts. Large black plastic bags of items were taken away.

Twenty miles away in Swanley, Stephen Cameron's father Ken told reporters: 'I am not prepared to comment now, but I will have plenty to say after the trial.' The British Consul in Seville, Carlos Formby visited Noye in Cadiz shortly after his arrest and asked him if he wanted them to contact his wife about his incarceration. Noye refused to communicate with the official. He knew the odds against him staying in Spain were not good. But he reckoned it would take them a lot longer than a few weeks to get him back to England. He was quite happy biding his time but he didn't want to let anything slip to some strange diplomat. Noye intended to work the system for whatever it was worth, whether it be Spain, Britain, or any other country for that matter.

Back in Atlanterra, Noye's double life left other residents on the urbanisation bemused. It even emerged that Noye had finally tried to get Spanish telecom to put a phone line in his house just before his arrest. But they had refused because he failed to produce documents in his name. In fact, many in Atlanterra presumed when they saw police activity in the village that it was part of a massive drugs bust. Such raids were a common occurrence along the deserted coastline all the way down to Noye's favourite shopping centre — Gibraltar.

37. Familiar Surroundings

Forty-eight hours after his arrest, Noye was transferred from the Puerto 2 prison north of Cadiz to Valdemoro jail near Madrid. Within hours of arriving in Madrid, Noye demanded to see a doctor because he claimed he was sick and had been beaten by prison staff in Cadiz. Noye wanted wardens in Madrid to take photos of his supposed injuries. But the Spanish totally denied his request.

Little did those Spanish prison officers know that Noye was doing exactly what he'd done in the hours following his arrest for the killing of DC John Fordham in the grounds of his house fifteen years earlier. It seems that Kenny Noye's criminal mind never stopped turning over.

Just a few weeks after Noye's arrest in Spain, his wife Brenda sold their house in Sevenoaks for £500,000 to a Japanese businessman and moved to Cornwall. She purchased a secluded £250,000 clifftop house called Redsands in the small fishing village of Looe. Two doors along at a house called Bosawna lived a fisheman called David Collings. According to some of the other residents in the street, Brenda and Collings quickly become close friends.

Collings, 49, had first struck up a friendship with Brenda when he asked her if she minded watering his plants and keeping an eye on his house when he was away on fishing trips. The pair soon began appearing together in their local pub, Tom Sawyer's Tavern. Collings' rugged, weather-beaten features and scruffy fishermen's smocks were a stark contrast to Brenda's designer clothes and carefully styled hair. And while she often popped out to nearby Plymouth to go shopping in her £80,000 Mercedes, he settled for a rusty Nissan truck.

Collings' own marriage had collapsed two years previously and the two seemed made for each other in emotional terms. Some cynical observers in Kent concluded that Noye had encouraged his wife to separate from him officially while he fought extradition back to Britain. Brenda insisted the separation was simply the first step in divorce proceedings. But to date there has not been any evidence of a legally binding separation between the couple.

Meanwhile, Kenny Noye awaited news of whether he was to be extradited back to England from his Madrid prison cell. Officials in Spain's Justice Ministry told journalists they expected the matter to be quickly resolved and insisted that Noye would be on a plane back to Britain within five or six weeks — just so long as the Crown Prosecution Service did not delay its request.

Under the terms of the Extradition Treaty the CPS had 40 days to act and the papers were expected to be filed within days. Some weeks after his incarceration in Valdemoro jail, Noye made a huge tactical error. For some reason, only known to himself, he wrote an insulting letter to the Spanish judges examining his case with a view to extradition back to England. The contents of the letter have never been fully revealed but one source claimed that Noye had been so insensed by the way the Madrid judiciary had promised his swift return to Britain that he wrote them a note with 'threatening undertones'.

One lawyer in Madrid explained: 'Noye made a big mistake sending that letter because the judges became infuriated with him. Up until that moment they might have looked at his case with more sympathy, especially since the evidence against him seemed somewhat flimsy.' Instead, Noye was informed that his punishment for writing such an 'insulting' letter was to be put into solitary confinement.

The judges were so upset by that letter that Noye's then

lawyer in Madrid, Manuel Murillo, was summoned to the office of the President of the High Court, Carlos Cezon. Murillo later recalled: 'The President of the court was very angry. I was not shown the letter and I was not told its contents in detail. But the judge described it as very insulting. Now the judges have taken away his privileges and ordered him to be kept separate from other prisoners.' But most ominously of all for Kenny Noye, as his lawyer also conceded: 'They have also ruled that his extradition should be treated as a matter of urgency.'

Murillo, who had represented Noye at all his early Spanish hearings, decided that he could no longer act for Noye. 'The man has no respect for the judges. You cannot write this way to them. It is wrong.' In solitary confinement, Noye was only allowed out for 40 minutes every Saturday at 12.30pm to talk to mistress Mina, his only visitor. Some observers at the prison noted that Mina always turned up exactly on time to avoid having to queue up with the wives and girlfriends of other inmates. But most significantly she was always accompanied by a burly minder. Whether this bodyguard was paid for by Noye or the Spanish police fearful of an attempt on her life will never be known.

Noye's 'insulting' letter to the judge had another detrimental effect on his situation inside prison in Madrid. In Spain, prisoners awaiting trial are allowed conjugal visits twice a month from their girlfriends or wives. But Noye had lost this due to his behaviour. For Kenny Noye the eternal romantic this must have been a double blow.

In the months following Noye's arrest a number of his south east London associates turned up at the house in Atlanterra. One of the most regular visitors was a blonde, ruddy-faced man. Noye asked him to supervise the building work and ensure the house was kept in pristine condition for his eventual return. 'Noye was still convinced he'd get back to Atlanterra,' said one police source. Another regular visitor was a young man in his early twenties believed to be the son of one of Noye's mistresses. He was the male Noye often took with him to the local brothels when in need of sexual gratification.

In early November 1998, Kenny Noye had his first ever opportunity to read the 32-page dossier compiled by Kent police outlining their extradition case against him. Noye and his new Spanish lawyer, Senor Pelayo Hornillos, met at the Madrid prison where Noye had been incarcerated since two days after his arrest. Afterwards, Noye issued a statement through his lawyer that poured scorn on the Kent police case against him. 'I want to look at every point raised in this document. This is the first time I have seen the full allegations against me. I am going to make up my mind this weekend. I need to check out a lot of dates to work out exactly where I was.'

Minutes after leaving his meeting with Noye, his lawyer insisted: 'Noye's immediate reaction was that the allegations are completely false. He told me, "It was not my vehicle and I was not there. I had nothing to do with this." '

Meanwhile, back in his jail cell, Noye continued avidly studying every word of the English version of the extradition case against him. His lawyer even claimed: 'It may well be that he wasn't even in Britain at the time.'

On 16 November 1998, Noye appeared before Baltasar Garzon, Spain's top investigative judge, who was also the same legal official handling the extradition request against former Chilean dictator General Augusto Pinochet who had been detained in Britain some months previously. Noye's lawyer said afterwards: 'The only evidence in the dossier against him is from this young woman who was the fiancé of the victim. But she has got so used to seeing Noye's photograph in the press, in magazines and on television in connection with the murder. Also, when police asked her to point him out in Barbate, where he was later arrested, it was in a bar where he was the only person who was not Spanish. The photofit picture of the killer does not look like my client. It is also an obvious concern of the defence that, because of the publicity, Mr Noye will not get a fair trial.' Clearly Kenny Noye was going to fight his extradition and that could well mean adopting stalling tactics such as going through the lengthy appeals process in Spain.

Meanwhile the Home Office had appointed one of Madrid's most prominent law firms to act on its behalf. It was the first time such a move had been ever taken by the British Government in an extradition case in Spain.

On 1 February 1999, Noye's defence lawyers insisted that the high-security Audencia Nacional court in Madrid was cleared of photographers and TV cameras before Noye was escorted to his extradition hearing. Still suntanned, Noye wore jeans, a jersey and a jacket as he was led into the dock. His handcuffs were removed and he constantly nodded and gestured to Mina Al Taiba, who sat at the front of the public gallery so as to be as close as possible to him.

Noye immediately claimed at the extradition hearing that he was not even at the scene of Stephen Cameron's murder. He told three judges at the Audencia Nacional that he had been picked out by a woman in a restaurant where he was the only Briton. He also insisted he could not get a fair hearing in Britain because he had already been 'tried in the media'.

He explained his position to the court from behind a bullet-proof glass screen. And he was denied permission to question the Kent police officers present at the hearing, as well as a representative of the Crown Prosecution Service. At one stage, Noye was asked why he was opposed to being extradited. He told the court: 'Because I am innocent and I have had a trial by media. It is impossible for me to get a fair trial.' Noye wore spectacles and read from notepapers in front of him. He told the court he had been in Spain throughout the two years before his arrest but that no warrant had been issued for his arrest until the police located him.

Noye then spoke in great detail about the police surveillance operation. He said that Kent police had sent the woman on 21 August, but did not use her to identify him until a week later. He even questioned what they had been doing in that intervening period. 'They fly the girl out on August 21, I believe, and on August 28 they come to a restaurant with the girl and I am sitting there and they identified me. So the girl is here for one week with the police officers. Una semana [one week]. What are they doing with this woman?' he asked.

Noye then went on to claim the identification was illegal under Spanish and British law, insisting he was merely asking the court to be fair and reasonable. He even asked the judges to put themselves in his position as 'an English person sitting in a restaurant full of Spanish people' and, pointing to his grey hair, claimed the original suspect identified had been a 'man with dark hair and much younger'.

The chief state prosecutor, Eduardo Fungairino, said the court's job was not to determine innocence or guilt, but to allow the extradition because all the papers had been correctly submitted by Britain. Fungairino argued that, because Britain had signed the European convention on extradition, it did not need to establish that there was a prima facie case to answer, and the court had no alternative but to accept the decision by the Kent magistrate to issue a warrant. He claimed it was up to the British courts to determine if the identification was valid and argued that British law matched Spanish law in relation to the alleged offence and sentence.

Noye's Spanish lawyer said the prosecution had put forward insufficient grounds. He said the killer originally described by police was in his twenties, whereas Noye was in his fifties, and pointed out that his client's picture had appeared throughout the British press, showing cuttings to the judges. Indirectly referring to the Pinochet extradition being sought by Spain at the time, Murillo said the British authorities were demanding a 'huge quantity' of evidence and documents. He said the Spanish judges in Noye's case had the powers to request similar details, and should do so, he said.

The judges promised a written judgement within a few days. Noye was warned by his lawyer that if lost he would only have three days in which to appeal. After the hearing,

Noye's friend Mina lashed out angrily at British press photographers waiting to snap Noye as he was escorted back to his Madrid prison cell.

On 25 March 1999 Kenny Noye officially lost his legal battle not to be extradicted back to Britain. The three judges at Spain's National Criminal Court who'd heard his final appeal the previous Thursday had ruled that he should be sent home. The judges were so concerned about security and intimidation that they met behind closed doors before rejecting Noye's defence that he was identified and arrested illegally under both Spanish and British law.

The judges' decision had then to be passed formally in writing to the lawyer representing the British government, the British consul and the Spanish Justice Ministry. Noye's lawyer warned him this process would take at least another month but, in effect, there was now no chance of him staying in Spain. He was on his way home.

It was without doubt a bitter pill for Kenny Noye to swallow.

38. One-way Ticket

On May 20 1999, Kenny Noye was handcuffed and ordered out of his cell at Madrid's Valdemoro jail. Then he was bundled into an anonyous white van which was escorted by two plain Seat saloons out towards the city suburbs. Less than thirty minutes later Noye was handed over to three Kent police officers at Madrid Airport and secretly flown to London's Gatwick Airport. Even the Civil Guard who policed Madrid's airport round the clock were not informed of Noye's extradition back to Britain.

It can now be revealed for the first time that Kent police were so concerned about security for Noye they got permission to use a BAe 146 plane from the Queen's collection of aircraft. Officials from Buckingham Palace and the British Embassy in Madrid gave their approval to the top-secret operation. During its three-hour flight back to Britain, air traffic controllers across Europe even imposed a 'blue corridor', an exclusion zone which prevented other planes from coming within 200 miles of its surrounding airspace.

The plane then landed at the desolate RAF Manston airfield near Broadstairs, in Kent, from where Noye was whisked away by a convoy of police in armed saloon cars.

That night Kenny Noye found himself back in the familiar surroundings of Dartford Police Station. Once inside the holding area, Noye's handcuffs were unlocked. He grimaced and stretched his fingers and massaged his aching wrists. Then he looked up and a huge grin came across his face. Then Noye spotted the closed circuit video camera that was pointing directly at him. His brilliant smile changed in a split second and he resumed the grim expression of a truly evil man.

The next day Noye appeared before magistrates in Dartford to hear those murder charges connected to the death of Stephen Cameron. He was immediately taken to the most secure jail in London — HMP Belmarsh — and placed in solitary confinement at his own request. From his cell, Noye's main views were the familiar Thames Marshes and the infamous Thames Barrier which he'd help supply the equipment to build all those years earlier. Noye really was back on his home territory.

His request for solitary confinement was agreed by staff at Belmarsh because police wanted to ensure he had as little contact with other inmates as possible. Noye had already proved in the past that incarceration did not always cut off his ability to continue wheeler dealing.

There was also another reason why Noye was kept out of the prison limelight. Explained one Kent police source: 'We didn't want anyone getting to Noye. He'd caused a lot of villains problems over the previous couple of years and his reputation as someone not averse to offering info to police was well known in the London underworld. There was a genuine fear that someone might get to Noye and do him personal harm before we could get his trial underway.'

Noye had already been made aware that his trial would not start for at least six months. So it was that he found himself given the complete freedom of Belmarsh's entire Level One, top-security wing. 'A lot of us thought it was a bloody outrage that Noye got given the whole of level one,' one prisoner told me in a taped phone interview shortly after Noye's incarceration. Level One, which houses 30 cells, is so secure that even staff from other parts of the prison are searched individually on entry. It couldn't have been more different from the good old days when Noye ruled Swaleside Prison during his incarceration for the Brink's-Mat VAT fiddle. My source inside Belmarsh continued:

'Noye doesn't communicate with people when he is out and about, which isn't often. But he has his mates and of course he knows a lot of the staff because some of them were with him in Swaleside when he was banged up for Brink's-Mat.'

Another inmate who caught a glance of Noye concluded that his plastic surgery, as my source explained, 'made him look like fuckin' Kenny Dalglish.'

Noye gave the impression of being subdued and unhappy about his incarceration. He even refused to go into the prison's hospital medical wing to undergo tests as was normal procedure for most new inmates. But my source pointed out, 'Noye knows the territory well. He is not easily intimidated. But we were surprised he rejected the medical wing. I reckon he's got something up his sleeve which might come out at his trial. The man's as slippery as an eel.'

Inside Belmarsh, Noye let it be known for the first time that he had drastically altered his defence against the murder charge. 'Noye's making sure his boys let it be known that he's planning to claim self defence on the basis that the other geezer was giving him a pasting and he had no choice but to take him out,' explained my Belmarsh source. But as my contact also pointed out. 'You have to take that sort of rumour with a pinch of salt because Noye is behind everything and he probably had some kind of ulterior motive in spreading this sort of gossip.'

Meanwhile Noye's life on Belmarsh's Level One was mundane, to say the least. He had three meals served in his cell each day. The rest of the time he slept, read or took exercise. He was keen to keep up the weight training he had maintained since those far off days inside jail following his Brink's-Mat conviction. He was allowed to train in the exercise yard every morning for one hour when all the other inmates were still locked in their cells. The entire area was even covered by a net to prevent helicopter break-outs. As my source added: 'Noye looks like a complete kingpin when he's out in the yard all on his tod in his brand new tracksuit with six screws shadowing his every move.'

In September 1999, Brenda Noye claimed in a rare

newspaper interview that she was planning to write a book about her life with Noye. She even optimistically announced that she expected an advance of £1 million for her efforts. The reality was that Kenny Noye was the only one likely to pay her that sort of money, and that would be for NOT exposing any of his innermost secrets.

Interestingly, Brenda had reverted to using her maiden name of Tremain after her arrival in Cornwall despite the fact that their alleged divorce had yet to be legally ratified. When one young local journalist went knocking at the door of her cottage asking her about her new life away from Kent and south east London, Brenda told him adamantly: 'You will have to wait until I have published my own book and then you can read all about it.'

One of her friends even added fuel to Brenda's publishing aspirations by revealing: 'Brenda is keen to set the record straight. She says much of what has been said about her is wrong.' Brenda once again made a point of insisting that she and Kenny had led separate lives since his disappearance following the death of Stephen Cameron. She conveniently omitted to mention the three visits she paid to him in Spain. At the time of writing there was no sign of her alleged 'publishing deal' materialising.

Two hundred miles away in Belmarsh Prison, Noye's most regular visitor was his trusted brief Henry Milner. Noye wanted to be kept informed of every detail of the prosecution's allegations against him, and he expected Milner to tell him of any developments from the smallest newspaper article to any rumours that might have materialised from other sources.

He continued to make a point of telling his prison guards he would be found not guilty and that he planned to retire to the house in Atlanterra as soon as he was acquitted. My inmate source inside Belmarsh told me that in the weeks before the trial, Noye was making a point of ensuring certain news leaked out about the case, and that there were also other interested parties at work on the prison rumour mill. My contact wrote to me: 'I've been hearing a few things that are going to have a bearing on his case. There are a few young bods in here who come from the victim's [Cameron's] circle and they are all preaching as gospel that the victim was a nasty bit of work and so was some of his family. Apparently the kid was some sort of martial arts practitioner, and was not averse to giving it large in pubs and clubs. They are saying he was "a right proper flash bastard and a would-be bully". Some of them are also saying "We're not surprised he got it, he thought he was Charlie Big Spuds because one of his relatives was a bit of a face." Another one said this young fella was 'not shy about having a tear up (fight).'

My source continued: 'I don't know whether it is just rabbit, but I wouldn't be surprised if the defence put the kid up as the aggressor. It ties in with self-defence. Nice bit of character assassination.' More privately, Noye was still seething about how he'd been tracked down to his Spanish hideaway and he started making discrete 'enquiries' amongst his prison contacts. The six-inch-thick walls of Britain's most secure criminal unit did nothing to dilute the power and influence of Kenny Noye. My source told me: 'He's got respect as a top face inside here, and he's fuckin' steamin' about who grassed him up.'

Noye had no doubt that claims published in British newspapers that his brunette mistress Mina was responsible for informing on him were completely untrue. He knew all about her criminal background and work as a hooker in Marbella but if she had played a role in alerting police to his presence it was entirely by accident. 'Noye let it be known that he would pay well for info about who got him banged up. He had his own list of suspects, but he wasn't going to do anything until after the trial,' added my Belmarsh source.

39. Back on Home Ground

Just before dawn on Tuesday 6 July 1999, two police patrol cars and a white Range Rover escorted a white transit van as it swept out of Belmarsh High Security prison at high speed. Inside the van was a manacled Kenny Noye surrounded by armed policemen. Overhead a police helicopter watched the convoy below in case any unwelcome visitors tried to intefere with the wheels of justice. Almost one hour and 23 miles later, Noye and his highly-trained police escort turned into the back entrance of the specialist ID unit at Kilburn Police Station, in north west London.

Police in body armour sealed off the surrounding streets and marksmen lined the roof of every building within sight. Motorists trying to park near the police station were immediately challenged by uniformed officers who then insisted on searching every inch of their vehicles.

Once inside the perimeter of the police station, the handcuffed Noye was escorted from the van by four burly officers. He was taken across the small yard as the police helicopter hovered a few hundred feet above. From the police station windows dozens of on-duty police strained to get a glimpse of the most infamous remand prisoner in Britain. Five minutes later, Noye joined seven other men, each being paid £10 an hour to take part in an ID parade inside the custom-built £1.6 million unit. The eight were asked by a team of officers to sit in front of a one-way mirror in the ID suite as 13 possible witnesses connected to the Stephen Cameron case were led one at a time into an adjoining room. The identities of those 'unlucky thirteen' witnesses were so secret that only three senior Kent detectives knew precisely who they were. Such was the fear that they might be intimidated in the months leading up to Kenny Noye's trial.

The entire ID parade was monitored by officers from the Met and Kent forces on a closed-circuit TV monitor. And as each witness was sat down, a video camera filmed their reaction as they picked out Noye from the line-up on the other side of the one-way mirror. As one Kent investigator later explained: 'The reaction of a witness when they identify a suspect is almost as important because it can show us if they are telling the truth.'

The other problem was that Noye had significantly changed his appearance since the death of Cameron so the ID parade was carried out very slowly. It is not clear to this day how many of the thirteen witnesses positively identified Noye. Noye, remand prisoner CB9123, remained completely expressionless throughout the ID parade. Less than two hours later he was on his way out of Kilburn in a police convoy that swept through red traffic lights in the mid-morning London rush-hour and headed back to Belmarsh Prison and those familiar Thameside surroundings.

A couple of weeks later one of Noye's oldest associates came out of his anti-media protective shell to try and distance himself from Kenny Noye. Bizarrely, the man granted a newspaper a full-length interview in order to 'put the record straight' about a number of rumours, including his alleged close relationship with Noye. 'Kenneth bloody Noye! A drink or two at a boxing match. I've met him once or twice. I never knew him. I don't want to know him. If I'd been harbouring him, why didn't they come and get him?' ranted the associate.

Referring to Noye's alleged travels while on the run following Stephen Cameron's death, the man added: 'Would you hide out in Tenerife? It's a tourist resort, there are easier places to hide.' Then he added coldly: 'I don't know Kenneth Noye.'

It was obvious that many others in the criminal underworld were also trying to distance themselves from Noye in the run-up to his trial. As one south east London source told me: 'We just don't need the sort of aggro that Noye brings with him. The sooner the man's off the streets the better.'

In January 2000, news came that a case involving some of his associates was to be re-opened by police. The murder riddle of tycoon Donald Urquhart's death by a hitman in a crowded street in 1993 resulted in the gunman and getaway driver being jailed. But detectives never established who paid the hitman to kill Urquhart. Then a special police squad looking at a number of unsolved so-called professional killings announced they had fresh evidence which pointed to the man who wanted Urquhart dead. A few weeks later another 'face' known to Noye and rumoured by some to once have been a 'close friend' was hitting the headlines in a case that must have amused the incarcerated Noye.

Mother-of-two Evelyn Fleckney, who lived just near Noye's old home in Sevenoaks, was dubbed Britain first female drugs baron by newspapers. But it was her relationship with her secret lover, a detective in the South East Regional Crime Squad, which would have caught Noye's attention.

Fleckney, already in prison for 15 years for dealing in cocaine, cannabis and ecstacy, decided to grass up her lover Detective Constable Robert Clark, and in the process helped disband the entire SERCS squad based in Dulwich, right in the middle of Kenny Noye's old stamping ground. Some of south east London's best known faces toasted Evelyn Fleckney's health when news of the squad's demise became common knowledge.

On 6 February, two days after news of Evelyn Fleckney's activities hit the front pages, another of Noye's old cronies was grabbed by police as he walked into a luxury hotel in Barcelona, Spain. Ex-bank robber turned suspected drug baron Mickey Greene had criss-crossed the world as he kept one step ahead of justice for more than 15 years. One police source said that Green had been grassed up by one of the most famous 'faces' in Britain who was angry about a drugs deal in which Green greedily skimmed all the profits off for himself. It was rumoured that Greene had buried at least £10 million in cash in the hills above the Costa del Sol, but whether he would ever see that again remained to be seen. At the time of writing he was in a prison in Barcelona awaiting an extradition hearing.

Back in England, the London underworld was abuzz with the alleged identity of the man who ultimately brought about Kenny Noye's arrest. Stories were circulating that he was to be paid at least £100,000 for the information. But that payout was dependent on Noye being found guilty at his trial for the murder of Stephen Cameron. As one criminal source said: 'If Kenny walks that grass will lose £100,000 and I can tell you there'll be an even bigger price on his head for turning in Noye.'

Meanwhile police were saying: 'Noye's friends believed for a long time that he was going to return to England and speak to the police but it never happened and Noye continued to live his life like business as usual. Noye became too cocky and this was his downfall.'

Back in Belmarsh, Noye was finally given a projected date for his trial on murder charges connected to the death of Stephen Cameron. The hearing would begin at the end of March 2000, and would be conducted in Noye's old stamping ground, the Old Bailey, London's premier criminal court and the place were he made his two most famous public utterances after juries had previously delivered their verdicts.

In November 1999, I was approached by a Noye contact and asked if I wanted to meet one of the money men who had known all about Noye's movements while he'd been wanted for questioning about the death of Stephen Cameron. The meeting was to take place in a hotel bar to the west of London and, my contact warned me, 'this geezer will get up and walk away if you try and ask him anything directly about Kenny Noye.'

The man who showed up spent the following three hours telling me in great detail about most of Noye's movements during his two and half years on the run. And he even dropped into the conversation that he and 'two or three others' had tipped the police off about Noye being 'somewhere in Spain'.

Much of the information told to me by this character has been indirectly referred to throughout the last section of this book. When it came to explaining why many other criminals wanted to bring Noye's flight from justice to an end, this fellow said: 'It was time for the old bill to haul Kenny in. He knew they'd catch up with him in the end.'

Then this man implied that Noye somehow orchestrated his own capture. 'I got the nod from someone I know was encouraged by Noye himself because he was so confident Kent police did not have enough evidence against him to win the murder case.'

In March 2000, Kenny Noye would find out if all his manipulative efforts would get him off the hook.

40. Epilogue –
The Final Chapter?

All the countless theories, rumours and innuendo about the circumstances behind the so-called roadrage killing of Stephen Cameron were finally put to rest when Kenny Noye walked into the number two court of the Old Bailey on Thursday 30 March 2000, nearly four years after that fatal incident on the M25.

Gone was the confident swagger that had accompanied his last appearance in the very same dock of the very same building 14 years earlier. This time, now grey-haired and dressed in a grey cardigan, he sat hunched almost like an old man in the dock between three prison officers. His eyes constantly panned the jury of eight women and four men from the moment he was led in.

Before the case could proceed, judge Lord Justice Latham ordered round-the-clock protection for each juror. He even told them: 'There are many people who have an interest in this case and its outcome. I have arranged for you to be provided with escorts that will, I am afraid, affect your daily life to some extent.' However, he said the jurors should not consider this safeguard 'to be in any way prejudicial' to Kenneth Noye.

The judge also instructed jurors not to talk to anybody about the case, including their families. 'It is absolutely vital... that Mr Noye is given a fair trial. The defendant is entitled to be tried on evidence you hear in this court. It's absolutely critical you put out of your mind anything that might be triggered by part of the evidence you may hear.'

A hushed court then heard how Noye admitted stabbing the unarmed Cameron through the heart and liver and leaving him to die at the Swanley interchange. Noye pleaded not guilty to the murder charge and insisted the killing had been an act of self-defence.

The prosecution alleged that Cameron had been murdered by Noye after a violent exchange which 'was essentially born out of anger and maybe pride.' Prosecuting QC Julian Bevan told the court: 'The driver of that vehicle was Kenneth Noye, as he now admits.'

Mr Bevan continued: 'Stephen was unarmed, he was empty-handed when he was stabbed to death by the driver of another vehicle following a violent exchange. Kenneth Noye got out of that vehicle to remonstrate with the driver of the vehicle behind him, which was a little red van in which Stephen had been the passenger.'

Mr Bevan told the jury that Noye, fearing he was losing the fight, got a knife from his vehicle and returned to stab Cameron. 'The answer to this crime is a simple one,' Bevan informed the court. 'He was angry by the way that van was being driven. Immediately after the stabbing Kenneth Noye got back in his vehicle, a Land Rover Discovery, and sped off along the M25 leaving a dying Stephen by the road. The Crown's case is that the stabbing to death was not merely unlawful. It was murder. Stephen Cameron's decision to get out of that red van to deal with a potentially ugly situation cost him his life.'

Mr Bevan even referred to how the driver of a passing Rolls Royce had seen Noye smile after he'd stabbed Stephen Cameron to death. The court was also told how Noye had claimed throughout those earlier extradition proceedings in Spain that he was not the killer. But, Mr Bevan told the court, 'he now admits he was the person who held the knife and stabbed Stephen Cameron.'

Stephen Cameron's fiancée Danielle Cable wept as she gave evidence on the first full day of Noye's trial. She told the jury: 'The man was holding the knife out, the blade towards Steve... it was so quick. The next thing I saw was

Steve coming towards me. He was clutching his chest. I could see blood on his chest. He stumbled to the driver's side of our van and collapsed to the ground. I felt dreadful and ran crying and screaming for help.'

Clutching a handkerchief in her right hand Danielle, now 21, battled to control her emotions as she relived the attack. Throughout her testimony, Noye fixed his eyes directly on her, occasionally turning his steely gaze towards the jury. She gave her evidence standing side-on from Noye and her face was hidden much of the time by a curtain of hair which she nervously fiddled with. She did not once look across at Noye as he stroked his chin nervously. Danielle insisted that her fiancé delivered only a couple of kicks and 'did not do a great deal more' to Noye. 'Stephen was telling me to stay back and I was shouting and screaming at him to get back in the van. He seemed determined to stay out there.'

Noye's counsel, Stephen Batten QC, then cross-examined Danielle and said to her: 'The man [Noye] was on the ground being severely kicked, I suggest.'

Danielle replied, 'He was never on the floor.' She agreed, however, that she never saw the man lunge at Stephen Cameron with a knife.

Then Mr Batten asked Danielle, 'Miss Cable, is it a fact that you told the police far less than you really saw because you find it difficult, totally naturally, to believe that any of this was Stephen's fault?'

'No. I don't believe it was his fault at all. That's not what I have told you.' Batten continued to try and suggest it was Stephen Cameron who had started the fight. She denied that, but did admit Cameron once lost his temper and got in a fight with a neighbour when they held their engagement party. Danielle agreed that the neighbour remonstrated with Stephen for urinating in his back garden.

Mr Batten then asked, 'Would you think that Stephen was a young man who thought he could take care of himself without too much difficulty?'

'Yes, I suppose he thought that he could take care of himself.'

Danielle denied that after the killing she told relatives Stephen had made a rude gesture at Noye, and was responsible for the dispute. She said, 'I haven't told anybody about the incident. That's not true.'

Noye continued sitting stony-faced in the dock throughout that first full day at the Old Bailey. He barely even moved a muscle when prosecutor Mr Bevan pointed to photos of huge splashes of red on Stephen Cameron's van.

Media and observers at the trial were struck by how different Noye looked, even compared to when he'd been finally apprehended in Spain less than two years earlier. He'd lost a lot of weight and appeared almost frail. His cheekbones jutted out sharply and his legs looked skinny. Even his once squared-off shoulders seemed to have shrunk so that his woolly cardigan virtually hung off him.

On the third day of the trial, witnesses gave conflicting accounts of who threw the first punch during that fatal incident on the M25. One of those closest the scene of the fight, motorist Mr Stephen Darling, told the jury that he'd seen Noye climb out of his car and slam his door 'as if he was uptight'. He said, 'I saw the older man throw a punch. He punched the younger fellow in the face. The younger man was getting the better of the older man. I saw him throwing punches and kicking and the other man was backing off.' But Mr Darling then drove away before the end of the fight.

Another witness, Helen Merrall, who also drove off before the end of the fight, said she believed that Stephen Cameron had landed the first punch. Then a trucker called Jonathan Saunders told the jury he had swerved to avoid the pair as the fight spilled on to the road in front of him. Saunders said he saw Noye raining numerous blows on Cameron. 'He was kicking more than anything.' Then he watched as Noye fled the scene.

The court was also told how Noye had been carrying a knife in his car for weeks before the stabbing. The admission came from Noye's own barrister after evidence from a car valet called Carl Simcox. The valet told the jury he had seen two separate flick knives in a Mercedes and a Land Rover

Discovery used by Noye. One was black and one brown, he said. Noye's QC Mr Batten suggested there had only been one knife, a lock version with a corkscrew.

Then another witness, Julie Hyatt, told the jury how she saw a vehicle similar to Noye's L-reg Discovery being driven into a scrap yard the day after the killing. The court was also told about the flurry of phone calls he made that day. Prosecutor Mark Ellison gave the hushed court room details of all the calls, which he said were accepted by the defence. Those calls started with the 2.04pm phone call made by Noye just 49 minutes after Cameron's stabbing.

The Old Bailey was also told how Noye's link to the crime was first established when an AA card in Noye's name was found at a friend's scrap yard three days after the killing. The jury heard how Noye flew by helicopter from Bristol on May 20 to a golf course in Caen, in Normandy, France, and then flew to Spain the following day.

Friday April 7 was the day Noye took centre stage in the trial. Looking calm and collected but wiping his nose with a spotless white handkerchief, he strolled confidently to the witness box. Noye looked like a librarian in his buttoned-up grey cardigan over an open-necked blue shirt complete with grey pudding-bowl haircut. His testimony was delivered to an atmosphere of hushed expectation. Noye spoke in a dull, expressionless monotone. Just a couple of feet away, Stephen Cameron's parents never once took their eyes off the man who'd killed their beloved son.

Under cross-examination by his defence QC Stephen Batten, Noye claimed he mistook Stephen Cameron and his girlfriend for a couple he knew and that was why he stopped his car. He also insisted that when he'd apologised to Cameron for the mistake, the younger man had said: 'You will be you cunt, I'll kill you.' Noye said that Cameron then kicked him in the waist and he tried to punch him back. He said Cameron also pushed him. Then Cameron punched him on the cheek, Noye told the court, and he fell to the ground where the younger man began kicking him and saying he was going to kill him.

Shortly after that Noye got his knife out.

Noye insisted Cameron had been 'in a complete wild rage'.

Then he carried out his own dramatic re-enactment in the witness box in front of Stephen Cameron's visibly distraught parents. Noye demonstrated an underarm jabbing motion with which he killed the unarmed man. He claimed he had pulled his knife out from his trouser pocket and told Cameron, 'Don't come near me, nutcase.'

Noye then told the jury, 'His girlfriend was shouting "Get off", I am saying, "Hold up" and he is saying, "I will kill you". I cannot fight, I'm a fit man but I was exhausted. I thought I can't take much more, nobody is trying to stop the fight, not that they could stop him. Then I thought, if he catches me again he will take the knife out of my hand and definitely use it on me so I struck out with the knife. I had my head down. I just went like that [demonstrating with a round-arm jab]. I can't remember exactly how I done it, we were close together and I just struck out. I can only remember striking out once but I accept it was twice. He definitely knew I had the knife.'

Noye told the jury he kept a knife by his side every day because he feared being attacked by criminals in league with the police or being kidnapped to reveal the whereabouts of the missing Brink's-Mat gold. 'I was in fear of my life from two sources,' he told the court. 'First the police definitely detested me and I bore in mind they might put in a villain who has done something really serious and done a deal to have something done to me. Secondly, I could be kidnapped. They have never recovered three tons of the gold that went missing and they thought I had it.'

Noye then admitted his connections with Nick Whiting, one of numerous Noye associates who died in violent circumstances. 'When I was in prison, my friend Nicky Whiting got killed. He had a car showroom and they went down and took him away one evening and he was killed, stabbed and shot, and that's what the police said. They thought he was my right-hand man. I don't know who kidnapped him but Nicky had no connection with the gold. He was a businessman. That's why I carried a knife.'

Noye claimed he was frequently stopped by police following his release from prison in 1994 and then he smiled for about the only time in court when describing how they regularly kept him under surveillance. 'They used to follow me around quite a lot.' He even told the jury that police had tried to fit him up while he was in prison for the Brink's-Mat offences by trying to tempt him into that £50,000 cocaine deal monitored by the FBI so that he would 'get 25 or 30 years'. He claimed police deliberately barred him from getting parole and he said that on his release from prison he took major security steps to protect his then new house in Sevenoaks, installing four security cameras, locks and bolts and floodlights.

But Noye continued to insist he never really intended to use the knife on Stephen Cameron. 'I took it out to keep him away from me, that is all,' said Noye. 'A normal person would not have continued to come forward with that knife pointed at him. I never intended to use that knife on him.'

Immediately after talking about how he'd killed Stephen Cameron in self-defence, Noye then shocked the court by revealing to the jury how he had stood trial for the murder of undercover policeman John Fordham. He even said he had killed Fordham for the same reasons. But Noye denied that at the time of the Cameron killing he knew full well that a thrust from the four-inch blade could easily kill another human being. Prosecuting QC Mr Bevan said to Noye: 'Ten years earlier you witnessed the Fordham experience. You were acquitted by a jury but a knife was used against a police officer. You knew from that experience the lethal effects a knife can have if stuck into somebody's body.'

Noye disagreed.

He was then asked, 'Are you saying that after that ghastly experience you didn't realise it could kill?'

Noye said, 'I appreciated it could kill, but I didn't know where I had to thrust the blade.'

Noye also admitted using the name of Anthony Francis and

using a false address for registering ownership of the Land Rover Discovery. 'I didn't want no one to know where I lived,' he told the jury. 'I didn't want no one to know what cars I owned.'

Noye's composure cracked only once, when prosecutor Mr Bevan probed him on his reasons for stabbing Stephen Cameron.

'You believed he would take the knife off you?' asked Mr Bevan.

'Yes,' replied Noye.

'And slit your throat?'

Noye was rattled by the melodramatic response and said, 'No, no.'

'Let's just leave it there, shall we?' said Mr Bevan.

Then Noye snapped, 'No. We won't leave it, we will get that sorted out right now.' He then talked in detail about fleeing the country after the M25 incident because he was certain he would not get a fair trial. He even admitted: 'If I had not been found in Spain by the police I would not have come back.'

Prosecutor Mr Bevan pointed out, 'And not faced such responsibility as leaving the parents of this dead boy totally ignorant?'

Noye responded: 'They would have been.'

'Mr Noye, did you not consider the human side?'

'Yes I did,' insisted Noye.

'And dismissed it?'

'I have said to my sons since they were little, "if you ever get in a fight just walk away." '

The court was then dumbstruck when Noye broke down close to tears as he described the moment he learned from his wife that Stephen Cameron had died. Noye also insisted he had 'never hurt anybody, I have never even hurt an animal.'

But under cross-examination he admitted he had 'deliberately' stabbed Cameron and, explaining why he carried a knife, added: 'I would have preferred a stun gun or a CS gas canister but they would be illegal.'

Noye even angrily described press reports following the

Fordham death as 'absolutely scandalous. There is no other word for it.' Then, listing the reasons why he believed he'd never get a fair trial for the Cameron killing, Noye said, 'The police, the press and the way I am brought here to the Old Bailey like a monkey in a box. I personally cannot ever see me getting a fair trial.'

Noye also admitted that after the Cameron killing, 'I was shaking. I had a bloody face, I was just devastated. I was walking around in a daze.'

He admitted leaving the car and his knife with a friend knowing full well they would be disposed of. He also confessed to lying at his extradition hearing in Spain about not being at the scene of the Cameron killing and then completely changing tack to put forward a defence of self-defence. Prosecutor Mr Bevan added: 'You thought nothing of telling the Spanish court a complete lie to help your position?'

Noye replied solemnly: 'Yes.'

Noye claimed that he took just £10,000 in cash with him to Spain and supplemented that with income from some 'property deals' in Spain.

Concluding his cross-examination, Mr Bevan told Noye: 'You ran away in fear, not fear of not having a fair trial, you ran away in fear of the truth emerging from all the people at that junction?'

Noye replied, 'Well, the truth has emerged.'

On Monday, April 10 it was the turn of the loyal Brenda Noye to take the witness box. Looking considerably less stressed than in the months following her husband's escape to Spain, she insisted to the jury that her husband had acted 'honourably' by fleeing the country following Cameron's killing. 'It was the only thing he could do,' she said. 'He had my blessing.'

Brenda described her husband as an 'honest' and 'very honourable' man, but that he had feared he would never get a fair trial in Britain. She claimed she had no idea that her husband had been involved in the roadrage incident when he came home with a cut on his nose and swollen eyes in the hours following the killing. She even admitted that Noye had wanted her to follow him to Spain but she had declined the offer although it was said in court she had visited Noye at least three times while he was on the run.

Brenda claimed she'd been told by the police that 'they would not rest until they saw him spend the rest of his life in prison and that they would destroy my family.' She also told the court that when she visited Noye in Spain she had told him about the excessive media coverage. 'I told him about the press coverage and how our lives and the children's lives were intolerable because of it,' she said.

She even admitted taking steps to prevent the police following her abroad, but denied using false papers. As Brenda Noye left the witness box, she looked up at her husband in the dock, smiled, and whispered: 'All right?'

After Brenda Noye came Sean Johnson, a boyfriend of Danielle Cable's aunt, Michelle Cable. He claimed to the court he had witnessed Stephen Cameron 'go mental' with Danielle after she bumped his car on a kerb and knocked off the exhaust. Johnson also told the jury that Stephen Cameron had exploded at another woman driver, screaming and punching her car window.

Cross-examined by prosecutor Mr Bevan, Johnson then admitted he had been jailed for three-and-a-half years for attempting to rob a post office with a sawn-off shotgun. He also conceded involvement with a cannabis smuggling ring linked to one of the great train robbers, Gordon Goody. Johnson then admitted becoming close friends with Noye's son Kevin since the roadrage attack. He even confessed that the Noye family had paid for his stay at a hotel during the trial.

When Mr Bevan asked Johnson when he last saw Kevin Noye, he replied, 'Last night.'

'And did you discuss with Kevin the case?'

'Yes,' responded Johnson.

Sniggers were then heard from the public gallery.

The following day, Noye was actually seen to weep in court as he heard the read testimony of David Williams of Milton Keynes who had broken his back in a 1973 accident and was convalescing in Cyprus when he became friendly with Kenny and Brenda. He wrote: 'He was extra kind and considerate. He made my holiday... He never treated me as disabled or patronised me.'

Then another witness emerged through the defence who claimed that he had faced the full wrath of Stephen Cameron during an earlier roadrage incident.

Meanwhile Noye, the charming Casanova, reared his head when a beautiful blonde journalist he had tried to flirt with 16 years earlier during the Fordham trial walked into court. Noye immediately recognised the reporter and his first words to her were: 'Are you married yet?'

When the journalist replied, 'No, but you are,' Noye laughed.

'So what? I was when I first met you.' It seemed that even in the austere surroundings of the Old Bailey Kenny Noye couldn't resist trying to win over a pretty girl.

On the afternoon of Tuesday April 11 prosecuting counsel Julian Bevan QC gave his closing speech to the court and accused Noye of invention and exaggeration in his version of what had happened during the killing of Stephen Cameron. Mr Bevan insisted to the jury that Noye had made up his claim that he was in fear of his life to provide legal justification for the death of Cameron. 'In truth, when he got out of his Discovery car, he was spoiling for trouble and when he realised or believed he could no longer win the punch-up with Cameron, he resorted to using a knife. Even if the unarmed Mr Cameron was punching and kicking Noye, for him to take out a knife and thrust it twice in Mr Cameron's chest was force way beyond such force as was reasonable in the circumstances.'

Defence counsel Stephen Batten QC used somewhat different tactics when addressing the jury on behalf of his client. He told them to ignore the 'cavalcade' bringing Noye to court every day and the fact that they (the jury) were protected on their way to and from the Old Bailey. Mr Batten also reminded the jury that both Noye and wife Brenda had spoken in the witness box about their concerns that he might not get a fair trial. 'The jury should approach this case as if they are trying Mr Smith, of whom the public has never heard,' Mr Batten said in his closing speech. 'Keep the hype as low as possible because it is the fairest way to try this case.' And referring to the evidence that Stephen Cameron had kicked Noye, Mr Batten said: 'He seems to have been practising kicking skills. There is no harm in practising martial arts in itself. Perhaps it is monstrous to suggest that he was trying out his skills on the older man while his fiancé was watching. Perhaps it is not so monstrous.'

Then judge Lord Justice Latham informed the court Noye knew how lethal a knife could be. He told the jury they would retire to decide on one of four verdicts: Guilty of murder; not guilty of murder but guilty of manslaughter; not guilty of murder but guilty of manslaughter by reasons of provocation; or not guilty. He informed the jury that a person was entitled to defend himself and use such force as was reasonable in the circumstances. The person had honestly to believe that he was under attack. The key point was the moment when the knife was used. The judge said: 'If you are satisfied he was not acting in the honest belief it was necessary, but it was in retaliation or to carry on a fight, the use of the knife was unlawful.'

The judge then pointed out that the jury might conclude that the use of the knife was instinctive and that Noye did not intend to cause serious injury but risked causing Stephen Cameron some harm. If that were so, they could return a verdict of manslaughter.

By the time the jury were finally sent out on the morning of April 13 the scene was set for a dramatic climax to the latest chapter in the life and crimes of Kenny Noye. Accompanied by armed police bodyguards, the eight women and four men were sent to a hotel overnight following almost a day of deliberation. The following morning the judge advised the jury that he would accept a majority verdict and asked them to come back into court at midday for an update on their progress.

Sitting at the back of the court that morning was Noye's mistress Sue McNichol-Outch. There was a look of fascination on her face as she glimpsed down at the man she had encountered on many occasions. Noye even looked up and smiled at her.

Then the jury appeared. Their verdict was, by 11-1, guilty of murder.

Noye let out a deep gasp and held his head in his hands.

Stephen Cameron's father leapt from his seat just feet away, hands aloft in celebration and shouted, 'Yes!'

Then Lord Chief Justice Latham told Noye: 'The jury having found you guilty of murder, there is only one sentence I can impose and that is one of life imprisonment.' Noye looked unsteady on his feet as three burly prison officers led him down the 21 steps from the dock of number two court to the cells below. A few minutes later a van, its siren blaring, took him back to Belmarsh prison.

Outside the court Detective Superintendent Dennis McGookin, the Kent detective who led the last two years of the roadrage investigation, said: 'He's an evil man. He's been jailed for life and that's where he should remain.'

After the verdict, the son of DC John Fordham broke his family's 15-year silence on Noye. 'You make your own tomorrows and I think he has made his. You can't go on committing crimes,' said John Fordham. 'I am very pleased for the Cameron family, very pleased with the verdict. But it doesn't bring my dad back.'

John Fordham's heartbroken surveillance partner Neil Murphy who was with him on the day Noye stabbed Fordham to death in his garden, said, 'I'm trembling with happiness. It's taken a long time but he has finally got his comeuppance.'

In the hours following the verdict, it emerged that Noye's defence, estimated to have cost between £500,000 and £1 million, was funded by the taxpayer. He had been granted legal aid because on paper he was not worth a penny.

* * *

In early 2002, letters written by Noye from his cell at the top security Whitemoor Prison, in Cambridgeshire, to an attractive brunette pen-pal called Lisa Donovan were disclosed to the world. They revealed an interesting insight into the current state of Noye's mind and his attitude towards the murder of Stephen Cameron.

Noye also boasted to the pretty housewife that he enjoyed watching TV's The Sopranos – the Channel 4 series about American Mafia bosses – because it 'brings back memories.' But more significantly, in one of the notes Noye accused his victim Stephen Cameron of being a bully. Noye wrote: 'I was on my way to the pub, minding my own business, when the other chap decided to show off to his girlfriend. He'd obviously done it quite a few times before... he was just a fucking bully.' Noye concluded:

'I had a lot of plans for the future, but they're all fucked up now I'm in this pisshole.'

Before his appeal was rejected, Noye had confidently predicted he'd get his sentence reduced to manslaughter because 'we had a right tear-up.' Noye went on: 'He's 21, a kick boxer and bouncer and I'm 52... respect your elders, that's what I was taught when I was younger. I'd never bash up an old man.'

Then, following the rejection of the appeal, Noye went off on a rant about how the judges at his trial were crooked and claimed that a media witch-hunt cost him his liberty.

Meanwhile back in Whitemoor Prison, Noye continues to languish. He seems to be growing more bitter by the day. By early 2002, his daily duties involved cleaning the corridors and the showers. He was also taking Spanish lessons to relieve the monotony of prison life. He still harbours a dream that he might one day return to Spain.

Noye also continues to keep supremely fit. He went weight training every day and could run the equivalent of 2,000 metres in under nine minutes on a machine. 'Keeping fit is his way of telling the Cozzers that he'll beat them in the end.'

Meanwhile, Noye's status as Public Enemy Number One ensures he receives the utmost respect from staff and inmates at Whitemoor. As one policeman pointed out: 'This isn't the last we shall hear of Kenny Noye...'

Afterword

Kenny Noye is expected to serve at least 20 years of his life sentence. But friends and associates predict that he will continue to amass a fortune from his numerous criminal activities. And he is already alleged to have offered £5 million to any villain who can help spring him from jail.

Noye's appeal against his convictions was turned down in October 2001. His lawyers then announced they were intending to appeal to the European Court of Human Rights.

Brenda Noye now lives quietly and comfortably in the fishing village of Looe, in Cornwall. Her biggest luxury is a virtually brand new £50,000 Mercedes sports car. Her marriage split with Kenny Noye has yet to be ratified. She has been a regular visitor to Noye in prison. No one is quite sure where her income originates from but sons Kevin and Brett are regular visitors to the cottage along with some of Noye's most notorious associates.

Mina Al Taiba continues to keep in close contact with Kenny Noye through phone calls and letters. She lives in a £150,000 Madrid apartment paid for by Noye and has described herself as Noye's 'number one girlfriend'. But after his sentencing for the Cameron murder she declared that she would not visit him in Britain because he 'has his own family there.'

Mrs Anne Fordham was asked whether she would like to contribute towards this book, but she told a mutual acquaintance that she had no wish to remind herself of the awful events that led to her husband John's death as he worked undercover outside Noye's mansion in West Kingsdown.

Brian Boyce retired after 30 years, distinguished service at Scotland Yard and currently works for one of Britain's most respected security companies.

Brian Reader, whose visit to Hollywood Cottage came just before the death of DC John Fordham, keeps a low profile these days at a modest house ten miles from West Kingsdown. His wife Lynn refused to allow this author to see her husband.

Danielle Cable has been given a new identity, a new home and a new life by police. She is planning to marry the new man in her life but faces a lifetime of always looking over her shoulder in fear of Kenny Noye's associates.

Micky McAvoy was recently released from prison where he served a 25-year sentence for taking part in the Brink's-Mat robbery. He has told friends he just wants to forget about the past and start afresh. No one knows whether McAvoy is still expecting to get his share of the Brink's-Mat cash.

Kathy McAvoy loyally awaited her husband's imminent release from prison. Originally charged with dishonestly handling £300,000 of Brink's-Mat cash, she was given a suspended 18-month sentence. Once the owner of a large farm in Bickley, Kent, she now lives modestly near Bromley in Kent.

Brian Robinson, known as 'The Colonel', also served 25 years after being convicted for his role in the Brink's-Mat robbery. No one knows if he stands any chance of ever seeing the proceeds of his crime. But he was released from jail at the end of 2001.

John 'Little Legs' Lloyd is currently serving time in prison for his part in trying to set up the hole-in-the-wall scam. His common-law wife **Jean Savage** continues to live in the house they bought from Kenny Noye almost twenty years ago. Lloyd even paid the Brink's-Mat insurers a five-figure sum, despite the fact he was never criminally prosecuted for his part in the raid.

Tony White was undoubtedly very proud of his role in the Brink's-Mat robbery, even though he was never found guilty of involvement in a court of law. However, his luck finally ran out at Bristol Crown Court in July 1997 when he was sentenced to eleven-and-a-half years for his part in masterminding one of the biggest cocaine-smuggling rings ever seen in this country.

Michael Lawson was acquitted in 1986 of handling the Brink's-Mat gold. Once the holder of a franchise to sell luxury Mercedes, he then moved on to run a used-car business in Dartford. He made an out-of-court settlement with loss adjusters acting for Brink's-Mat, but remained very friendly with Kenny Noye until his disappearance in 1996. He now lives near Brenda Noye's home in Cornwall.

Michael Noye is still in touch with most members of his cousin Kenny's immediate family. He refuses to say how he earns a living, and he has moved to rented accommodation close to Brenda Noye and Lawson in Cornwall.

Graham Noye has left the Bank of England and works as a plumber in the same area of Kent that his cousin Kenny comes from. He was interviewed by detectives during the hunt for Noye but says he hasn't seen his cousin in years.

Neil Murphy has retired from the police and currently lives with his wife, a doctor, and two children in Wales. He is seriously considering emigrating to New Zealand. Murphy says he will never forget what happened to his partner John Fordham who, ironically, spent much of his working life in New Zealand.

John Childs has long since retired from the Metropolitan Police.

He lives in Surrey and works as a freelance surveillance specialist. His lasting memory of Kenny Noye is seeing him standing over John Fordham, brandishing a shotgun as he burst into the grounds of Noye's mansion.

The two men — **Michael Steele and Jack Whomes** — who murdered drug dealers Pat Tate, Craig Rolfe and Tony Tucker, were each given three life sentences at the Old Bailey in January 1998.

There is absolutely no suggestion that Kenny Noye was anything other than an associate of the following dead or maimed people:

1/. JOHN MARSHALL, 34, found shot dead in his black Range Rover in Sydenham, South London, just after Noye's disappearance in May, 1996. He also knew Ecstasy dealer Pat Tate.

2/. DANNY ROFF shot dead outside his home in Bromley, Kent, in March, 1997.

3/. KEITH HEDLEY killed by alleged bandits on his yacht in Corfu in November, 1996.

4/. PAT TATE, CRAIG ROLFE, TONY TUCKER shot dead in their Range Rover in an Essex field in December, 1995.

5/. SIDNEY WINK — gunsmith and dealer — put a pistol to his head and pulled the trigger in August, 1994.

6/. DONALD URQUART shot in a London street in 1992.

7/. NICK WHITING stabbed nine times and then shot twice with a 9mm pistol in 1990.

8/. STEPHEN DALLIGAN shot six times in the Old Kent Road in 1990.

9/. DANIEL MORGAN found with an axe embedded in his skull in a South London car park in 1987.

10/. GEORGE FRANCIS shot by a hooded gunman in May, 1985 but survived.

11/. BARBARA HARROLD blown up in bizarre parcel bomb attack on her Kent home in 1979.

12/. ALAN DELABRAL shot dead by a hitman in the car

park of a store in Dartford, Kent, October 2000.
13/.BRIAN PERRY shot dead in broad daylight as he got out of his car in Bermondsey, in November 2001.

Every January Scotland Yard pays for two of DC John Fordham's colleagues to visit his memorial stone in West Kingsdown and place flowers there on the anniversary of his death.

Other Blake Publishing titles by Wensley Clarkson

DOCTORS WHO KILL
THE MOTHER FROM HELL
THE FEMALE OF THE SPECIES
DEADLIER THAN THE MALE
A YEAR IN LA LA LAND
MEL: THE INSIDE STORY
TOM CRUISE UNAUTHORISED
STING: THE BIOGRAPHY
CAGED HEAT
KILLER WOMEN
SISTERS IN BLOOD
THE GANGSTERS
HITMAN (a novel)